International
Library of the
Philosophy of
Education

Illusions of equality

International
Library of the
Philosophy of
Education

General Editor
R. S. Peters
Professor of Philosophy of Education
Institute of Education
University of London

Illusions of equality

David E. Cooper

Department of Philosophy
University of Surrey

Routledge & Kegan Paul

London, Boston and Henley

First published in 1980
by Routledge & Kegan Paul Ltd
39 Store Street, London WC1E 7DD,
9 Park Street, Boston, Mass. 02108, USA and
Broadway House, Newtown Road,
Henley-on-Thames, Oxon RG9 1EN
Set in Baskerville 10 on 11pt
and printed in Great Britain by
Lowe & Brydone Printers Ltd, Thetford, Norfolk

British Library Cataloguing in Publication Data

Cooper, David Edward
Illusions of equality. – (International library
of the philosophy of education).
1. Educational equalization
2. Education – Philosophy
I. Title II. Series
370.1   LC213   79-42801

ISBN 0 7100 0360 9

Contents

Contents

General editor's note

There is a growing interest in philosophy of education amongst students of philosophy as well as amongst those who are more specifically and practically concerned with educational problems. Philosophers, of course, from the time of Plato onwards, have taken an interest in education and have dealt with education in the context of wider concerns about knowledge and the good life. But it is only quite recently in this country that philosophy of education has come to be conceived of as a specific branch of philosophy like the philosophy of science or political philosophy.

To call philosophy of education a specific branch of philosophy is not, however, to suggest that it is a distinct branch in the sense that it could exist apart from established branches of philosophy such as epistemology, ethics, and philosophy of mind. It would be more appropriate to conceive of it as drawing on established branches of philosophy and bringing them together in ways which are relevant to educational issues. In this respect the analogy with political philosophy would be a good one. Thus use can often be made of work that already exists in philosophy. In tackling, for instance, issues such as the rights of parents and children, punishment in schools, and the authority of the teacher, it is possible to draw on and develop work already done by philosophers on 'rights', 'punishment', and 'authority'. In other cases, however, no systematic work exists in the relevant branches of philosophy – e.g. on concepts such as 'education', 'teaching', 'learning', 'indoctrination'. So philosophers of education have had to break new ground – in these cases in the philosophy of mind. Work on educational issues can also bring to life and throw new light on long-standing problems in philosophy. Concentration, for instance, on the particular predicament of children can throw new light on problems of punishment and responsibility. G. E. Moore's old worries about what sorts of things are good in themselves can be brought to life by urgent questions about the justification of the curriculum in schools.

There is a danger in philosophy of education, as in any other applied field, of polarization to one of two extremes. The work could be practically relevant but philosophically feeble; or it could be philosophically sophisticated but remote from practical problems. The aim of the new International Library of Philosophy of Education is to build up a body of fundamental work in this area which is both practically relevant and philosophically competent. For unless it achieves both types of objective it will fail to satisfy those for whom it is intended and fall short of the conception of philosophy of education which the International Library is meant to embody.

David Cooper's *Illusions of Equality* is a splendid example of the sort of book which the International Library strives to encourage. Nowadays almost everyone is in favour of equality in a general sort of way, but Mr Cooper maintains, in his first chapter, that they are not really equalitarians. To make explicit what is distinctive of equalitarianism he turns, with a critical eye, to John Rawls's massive work on justice and, with Rawls's help, formulates what he takes to be typical of equalitarianism.

Armed with this apparatus, he deals with equality, and education, especially the clash between equality and quality. He then turns to the relationship between various social factors such as social class and equality in education. He deals also with the new proponents of the sociology of knowledge, who claim that inequalities are due to the traditional ways in which we organize and legitimate knowledge. Finally he turns his attention to questions concerning culture and the desirability of a common curriculum.

He ends by hesitantly avowing himself an inegalitarian – not because he is strongly opposed to equality but because, believing fervently in the importance of quality in education, he cannot see how this can be maintained or improved under current conditions by pursuing equalitarian policies.

This is a highly controversial book, which is both readable and argued with ingenuity and rigour. It should commend itself to all who are interested in this very topical issue.

R. S. P.

Preface

Tom Wolfe begins his delightful indictment of abstract painting, *The Painted Word*, by recalling the moment when it came to him why, despite years of effort, he had been unable to see what there was in 'abstract expressionism', 'flat art', 'op art', and the whole caboodle. Standing before yet another chaotic canvas, he suddenly realized there was nothing to it: that was why he had failed to grasp what, as Henry James would have put it, 'the thing' was about. I went through a similar, if less Pauline, experience in 1973 when I was preparing a paper, 'Quality and equality', for a Royal Institute of Philosophy Conference on Philosophy and Education. Ploughing through yet another egalitarian tract, I realized that the reason why, as a student and after, I had never identified the exact charm of the doctrine was that it has got none. That – and neither obtuseness nor moral blindness – had been the cause of the difficulty. I have since become increasingly convinced that where a policy or principle is right it is never, save *per accidens*, one that egalitarians advocate; and that where it is one which it is of the essence of egalitarianism to pursue, it is never right.

Wolfe proceeds to speculate just how many people, scattered about the Guggenheim or even the Tate, actually like abstract art. A few hundred, he guesses – but a few hundred who have, with great skill, deluded several millions into believing there is something to 'the thing'. It would be interesting to speculate how many egalitarians, scattered about the LSE or the DES, there really are. A small number, I suspect – but like Wolfe's few hundred, this sturdy group has performed the remarkable feat of convincing legions of people that they all are, or should be, egalitarians too. You are entitled to be suspicious of my claim that only a fraction of those who invoke the name 'Equality' are real egalitarians – but I hope to make the claim good in what follows.

Had this book been written five years ago, my mood would have been more optimistic; for the signs were that the egalitarian tide in education had turned. At least, this was so in the world of ideas. Faced with the growing results of egalitarian policies in education, several teachers, philosophers, politicians and a few sociologists took pen in hand to warn us, if belatedly, against the ideology of equality. Most notably, we had the series of Black Papers. But there is less call for optimism now – and this, in the world of ideas, for two reasons. First, the ideology found a sophisticated champion – albeit a champion with reservations about the cause – in the political philosopher John Rawls. Although his *A Theory of Justice* appeared in 1972, it took a while for its impact to be generally felt, for its massive bulk had to be reduced, in a number of commentaries, to dimensions more suitable for mass digestion. Second, a whole new style of egalitarianism, inspired by the publication of a book entitled *Knowledge and Control* in 1971, has since grown up. A heady concoction of extreme radicalism and quasi-philosophizing, the doctrines of that book have permeated through generations of students of education. There are new battles, then, to be fought.

I should like to thank Richard Peters for encouraging me to write this book, my colleague Antony O'Hear for commenting on chunks of the original draft, and Ruth Harrison for typing chunks of the final draft. I owe special thanks to Antony Flew for his full and remarkably prompt comments on each chapter. I also apologize to him for having introduced him to yet more of those egalitarian tracts which he, as much as anyone, has warned us against.

David E. Cooper

1   Egalitarianism

1   Reality and rhetoric

One question of equality is this: why has it become the dominant motif in educational debate and policy? Equality, in some shape, is a stated educational goal of countless writers and politicians; it often serves automatically as a yardstick for judging sundry educational practices; and it provides the initial and sustaining thrust behind *avant-garde* ideas which have captured the fashionable imagination in recent years. Illustrations are scarcely required to secure these remarks – but here are some. For A. H. Halsey, 'the role of education must largely be to maintain such a society [a society of equals] once it has been attained',[1] while, for another sociologist, Brian Simon, education's 'objective should be equality'.[2] Politicians favour the terminology as much as sociologists; both Crosland and Boyle were happy to agree – or seem to agree – on the goal of ensuring 'equal opportunity of acquiring intelligence'.[3] Teachers, of course, are not to be outdone. A spokeswoman for the 'Rank and File' group of teachers urges, *inter alia*, that 'the education budget . . . be multiplied many times to achieve equality', that 'public and direct grant schools be abolished, that 'all teachers . . . be paid a single salary scale', that 'higher education be free for all who wish it', and that selection and competition be replaced by 'collective endeavour in fully comprehensive schools in which the contributions of all are equally valued'.[4]

As for the automatic use of equality as a yardstick, consider a recent article in *The Times Educational Supplement* (21 June 1978), 'Dismal catalogue'. The 'catalogue' is a list of the respects in which immigrant children at a Redbridge school are not doing as well as their white classmates. Nothing is said about how well the children are doing; for all we are told, they may be doing very well indeed. It is simply taken for granted that not doing as well as others is sufficient cause for being dismal.

That it is the whiff of egalitarianism which gives life to some favourite *avant-garde* ideas is clear from a quick reading of Ivan Illich. He has clinched his case against schools by the end of chapter 1 of

1

Deschooling Society on the grounds, solely, that schools benefit some so much more than others.[5] Only in later chapters does he produce pedagogical arguments to the effect that even those who benefit most would have done better elsewhere. We shall see in chapter 4, also, how the educational critique by the 'new sociologists of knowledge' is galvanized by what they see as the failure, measured in egalitarian terms, of post-war, 'liberal' reforms in education.

Much said about equality and education has been reflected in what has been done in educational policy. Several of the most striking innovations, at home and abroad, have been explicitly backed in terms of equality: comprehensives, EPAs, 'positive discrimination' in favour of minority groups, CSE, non-streaming, 'Head Start', 'free universities', bussing, student representation on Senate and so on. Nor should it be forgotten that the reforms of an earlier era – so much castigated by latterday egalitarians – were once defended in terms of equality. This is clear from the reports leading to the 1944 Act. For the Spens report of 1938, the 'fundamental requirement' was to replace the existing system's bias in favour of 'academic' children by 'the establishment of parity between all types of secondary school'; while for the Norwood report of 1943, the job of the new schools will be 'to do justice to all their pupils', based on the realization that 'a curriculum on the whole suited to some is condemned because it is unsuited to others'.[6]

It is difficult, indeed, to think of any recent innovation which somebody has not defended in the name of equality. This fact – or simply a glance at the innovations I mentioned and at the quotations given earlier – must cause the suspicion, or certainty perhaps, that there is no real unity among the demands and policies proclaimed in the name of equality. When Sir Edward Boyle and 'Rank and File' can both invoke it; when those who set up the Tripartite system and those who dismantle it can make the same sounds; when the CSE and non-streaming are given a similar-sounding defence – then surely it becomes a certainty that there is only a spurious unity in the ranks of those who proclaim equality.

Unfortunately, it is only too easy for such a spurious unity to arise. The reason is one of logic. Any policy will have the effect of making some people more similar to one another in some respect. Non-streaming makes children more similar in respect of the teaching they receive; while the CSE makes them more similar in respect of their chances of passing some examination. By focusing on such a respect, any policy can then be defended by referring to an equality achieved by it. Policy X achieves greater similarity in respect Y. The trick is to concentrate on this respect, then omit specific mention of it, so as to finally announce, 'Policy X leads to greater equality.'

2

These remarks suggest part of the answer to our original question. It is not so much equality, but the jargon and terminology of equality, which dominates educational debate and policy. It is 'equality', rather than equality, which is ubiquitous. More prosaically, the various demands for equality form a motley group some of which, on reflection and analysis, are not to be seen as egalitarian in nature at all. Which of the demands couched in this terminology are genuinely egalitarian is, of course, something we must look into shortly.

The question, then, is really two. Why so much egalitarianism, and why so much of its terminology? Substance and shadow, reality and rhetoric, both require explanation. The first question can be treated at different levels. It could be taken, for example, as a request to identify the reasons which reflective egalitarians give for being egalitarians – for, presumably, some egalitarians are such for the reasons they give. As befits a philosopher, I shall be considerably concerned with looking at the reasons which might be offered in support of egalitarian demands. But it might also be treated as a request to fathom the social and historical factors which have encouraged egalitarianism and sustained its blossom. One can easily guess at some of these factors: the century's grim record of vicious kinds of discrimination; fashion; the influence of marxism (whose originator, however, was in many respects no egalitarian); the vested interest of myriad administrators and writers kept in permanent business by and for the sake of egalitarian measures.[7]

One of the main factors, though, relates to the other question; for there are many people, I imagine, who graduate to genuine egalitarianism via acceptance of principles and policies which, without being egalitarian at all, are typically couched in the terminology and rhetoric of equality. There is nothing characteristically egalitarian about wanting to alleviate hardship and poverty, though it has become characteristic to express such concerns in the·terminology of equality. Mistaking such respectable concerns for egalitarian ones can easily encourage acceptance of goals which really are egalitarian. The process perhaps goes like this: 'Since I am for equality of rights, of freedom from hardship, and so on, I must be an egalitarian. Since egalitarians demand various other things, like reduction or abolition of income differentials, I suppose I must be committed to these as well.' It is not so different, perhaps, from the following, currently prevalent, process: 'Since I'm against things like paying women less for doing the same job as men, I must be for women's liberation. Since women's lib involves saying things like "spokesperson" and rejecting cigarette lights from men, I suppose I must be committed to this sort of thing too.' But just as objecting

3

to unfair payment to women does not mean being a women's libber, in the current connotation, nor does a concern with human rights and the alleviation of poverty mean being an egalitarian.

There are those who, impatiently, would wish to short-circuit any attempt to explain why men are so concerned, really or apparently, with promoting equality. For, they would say, it is self-evident to all but the morally blind that equality should be a major goal of social policy. The explanation of why some are egalitarians (or want to seem to be) and others are not is of the same variety as the explanation of why some men can see colours and others cannot. R. H. Tawney remarked in connection with the non-egalitarian, 'if a man likes that sort of dog that is the sort of dog a man likes'.[8] But it cannot do to treat as self-evident a principle, or set of principles, which until recently found little serious acceptance. In fact it is difficult to find any examples, until fairly recently, of social thinkers who considered equality as any kind of ultimate end. Even those earlier thinkers who are sometimes dubbed 'egalitarian' – the Levellers or Sir Thomas More, for example – seemed to have favoured certain sorts of equality for, at most, instrumental reasons. The Levellers' leader, Winstanley, for example, offers two purely pragmatic defences of 'levelling' incomes: firstly, 'riches give men power to oppress their fellow-men and stir up wars. Secondly, riches are impossible to obtain by honest means'.[9] And the author of *Utopia*, in so far as he flirted with the idea of equal, communal division of property, did so on the ground that otherwise wealth would fall into the hands of evil men who would condemn the 'residue [to] live miserably, wretchedly, and beggarly'.[10] The idea that equality is valuable as an end, or is logically embedded in something – justice, perhaps – which is valuable as an end, is a thoroughly recent notion.

The claim that various historical 'egalitarians' are nothing of the sort, together with the related claim that there is nothing egalitarian about many of the demands today made in the name of equality, will cause some suspicion. It is of the first importance that I justify such claims – not only to allay this suspicion, and not only because it is a first step towards clarity concerning egalitarianism, but also because, by revealing how the egalitarian nature of some demands is illusory, we shall be well on the way to explaining the prevalence of the terminology and rhetoric of equality. For it is to be presumed that many people couch their demands in this terminology because they believe, however mistakenly, that it really is egalitarianism which generates them.

A man cannot be identified as an egalitarian simply because he goes about propounding principles in the form 'There should be equality of X'. Whether this is an egalitarian demand will depend partly on what X is, and partly on the ground offered for the proposal. If X is 'protection of existing property holdings', then the proposal is not egalitarian; nor, whatever X may be, is it an egalitarian proposal if defended on the ground that it will help secure a rigid caste system. What the values of X must be for demands of the above form to count as egalitarian is a matter to which I shall return later in the chapter. For the moment, I concentrate on the kind of ground on which they must be based.

A necessary condition for 'There should be equality of X' counting as egalitarian is that the ground given for increasing or decreasing some people's amount of X makes essential reference to the amounts of X which other people have. The demand that certain people should have more money is only egalitarian if supported, primarily, on the ground that others already have more. It immediately follows that many demands often couched in the above form are not, as usually defended, in the least egalitarian (by which I do not mean they are inegalitarian – rather that the issue of equality does not figure relevantly in the usual defences). Consider, for instance, the principle implemented by the 1870 Elementary Education Act – that there should be equality in the right and means to receive elementary education. The standard justification is, simply, that elementary education is a good and important thing for a child – good and important irrespective of whether some children are or are not receiving it.[11] Or consider some non-educational examples. Men should be protected under the law, whether or not in practice there are some who are not. A person's basic needs should be satisfied, irrespective of whether there are other people whose basic needs are being satisfied. Hence, on their usual and most obvious justifications, there is nothing egalitarian about 'There should be equality of legal protection' or 'There should be equality of satisfaction of basic needs'.

There are, to be sure, demands which are egalitarian in some mouths, but not others. Consider the principle of equal educational opportunity. This is often invoked by those whose concern, simply, is to remove various unfortunate obstacles – geographical ones, say – which prevent some children from getting a decent education. When so invoked, no egalitarianism is involved. Such obstacles should be removed where they can be, irrespective of whether others face them or not. But it is also invoked by those who desire unrestricted admission to universities, not on the ground that a university education is good in itself for each person, but on the ground that if some can go there, everyone else should be able to as well. That is an egalitarian consideration.

5

It is more interesting to explain how various demands gain their illusory egalitarian appearance than merely to point out that they do. Such an explanation, moreover, will parry the predictable objection that in restricting the application of the label 'egalitarian', I am flying in the face of (some people's) ordinary usage of the term. I doubt that I am flying in the face of many people's usage, but I would not be too worried if I were. Ordinary usage is never sacrosanct; and there is not even a presumption in its favour when there is an explanation at hand of how it has come to be perverted.

In fact it is not too difficult to see how the word 'equality' slips into demands which are not egalitarian, so lending an illusory appearance to them. Jack should receive elementary education; and so should Mary, Richard, Charles, etc. Jack, Mary, Richard, etc., are all the children there are; so all children should receive elementary education. That is, children are alike, equal, in their right to this education; so there is equality in the right to elementary education. But, of course, it is the rights – Jack's one, Mary's one, etc. – which are important, not the equality of them. The latter is the trivial consequence of the facts that each of the children mentioned has the right, and that these are all the children there are. It is, I believe, positively dangerous to express what is essentially a demand for rights in terms of one for equality of rights, since it can encourage the idea that if some people do not get their rights, no one else should either. It is to risk encouraging the strange idea that it is people's relative positions, *vis-à-vis* rights, rather than their absolute positions, which is the major concern. (There are, of course, cases – to be contrasted with the above – where, given the insignificance of some right, it is not the securing of the right which is important, but the giving of it to each if it is given to any; where, in other words, it is arbitrariness which is the main butt of criticism, rather than the failure to give each person something there is good reason for him to have, irrespective of whether others are actually getting it. The 'right' to have a couple of days off work after New Year's Eve, for example.)

We have already noted another way in which 'equality' can slip into a principle, without adding to its substance. Any principle, if acted upon, will make some people more similar in some respect. Hence there will always be some rephrasing of a principle 'Do X', taking the form 'Make people more equal in respect Y'. Since the equality in question is a trivial consequence of acting on the principle, it can be no part of its ground. Certainly it can confer no egalitarian status on the principle – unless we want to say, which surely we do not, that any principle whatever is egalitarian.

A more important reason, perhaps, for the illusory egalitarian air of some demands is the following: often in the past, the effect of securing to people various things which they should have (elementary education, legal rights, income sufficient for 'basics') has been to reduce differentials. This is an empirical, not a logical, matter. It could be, and in some circumstances is likely to be, that by subsidizing the very poor (to help them satisfy basic needs), one would so boost the economy that the very rich become much richer, thus increasing the gap between them and the very poor. Still, a common effect has been to reduce differentials. As a result, objecting to policies which happen to reduce differentials is often, *ipso facto*, to be objecting to policies which secure to people things they should have. Because of this empirical coincidence, it becomes easy to think that it was equality which was the aim, when of course it was the securing of various rights and benefits which was the true aim. It is, needless to say, a logical howler to suppose that because one's aim is X (e.g. securing of certain rights), and that X empirically co-incides with Y (e.g. reducing differentials in rights possessed), then one's aim is therefore Y. Frankenstein's monster aimed to cuddle the little girl; cuddling her turned out to be crushing her; which does not mean the well-intentioned monster aimed to crush the little girl.

Someone might say, 'Granted that many demands couched in the terminology of equality are only rhetorically egalitarian, still isn't your necessary condition for being an egalitarian rather too narrow? What about someone who proposes such characteristically egalitarian measures as abolition of public schools, not on the ground that they benefit some more than others, but that, for example, they encourage social dissension. Isn't he being egalitarian?' I concede that one reason for labelling someone 'egalitarian' who wants to abolish public schools (or private property) is that these are just the sorts of things which people who clearly are egalitarian often want. (In chapter 3, so as not to debar myself from discussing a number of proposals and arguments, I do not in fact stay completely faithful to what I have laid down as a necessary condition of egalitarianism.) Still, I think this reason is more than outweighed by others; for consider some of the consequences of dropping my condition, and concentrating exclusively on the substance of demands, ignoring the grounds on which they are made. For one thing, we should have to consider the following speaker as exhibiting an egalitarian attitude: 'Frankly, I find the idea of our public schools chaps having to rub shoulders with the riff-raff abhorrent. Men form a natural hierarchy, and the typical public school man just is of a better breed than the labourer's son. It's one thing to have miners and dockers next to you in the trenches; quite another to have their

7

sons next to yours in the quadrangle. But what choice do we have? Perhaps if we sacrifice the public schools, we can still avoid the violent revolution which otherwise, frankly, is inevitable.' But this man is obviously not an egalitarian.

A second consequence of labelling a purely instrumental defence of certain equalizing steps 'egalitarian' is that assessment of egalitarianism will be equivalent to assessment of the means by which any moral or social goal is to be achieved. For one could ask of any such goal whether certain types of equalizing steps would help secure it. Suppose it were discovered that the murder rate falls when income differentials are reduced – could that be counted as any argument in favour of the egalitarian attitude towards income distribution? An egalitarian, to be sure, is entitled to, and wise to, point out the beneficial side-effects of the policies he advocates; but surely it is not his appeal to these effects which makes him an egalitarian. To extend the label 'egalitarian' in the way mentioned would be like extending the label 'Kantian' to someone who, without thinking that duty should be done for its own sake, thinks that it would be socially useful to encourage people to be conscientious about their duties.

A fairly minor question might be raised at this stage: given that many principles and demands formulated in terms of equality are not egalitarian, does it follow that 'equality' and its cognates are totally superfluous in formulations of these principles and demands? Is anything added to 'Children have a right to elementary education' by the insertion of 'equal' before 'right'? Some people think that at least the following is added: while having an equal right to X does not entail having a right to an equal amount of X, it does entail that differences in the amount of X received need to be justified, whereas not even this latter entailment is carried by the mere right to X.[12] I do not see this. If I invite people to a party, each of them has a right, an equal one, to expect a drink; but I do not think each of them has a right to an equal sized drink, and nor do I think that I must justify having poured one person a rather larger drink than another. I would not feel obliged to defend myself when one of the guests approaches me with the surly challenge, 'Why did John get one-fifteenth of a gill more than me?' No doubt there are some things people have an equal right to, an unequal division of which would require justification – but I cannot see this as a general implication automatically carried by the word 'equal'.

There is one thing that insertion of 'equal' typically does, which is to strongly suggest that the right or benefit in question is one that some people already have or receive. 'Your children should have an equal chance to go abroad this summer' sounds inappropriate if no child has the least chance of going. Sometimes, when we are criticizing a shortage of rights or benefits, it is useful to bring out the fact that some people are not short of them. Such, I think, is the sole role of 'equal' in the formulation of principles and demands that are only rhetorically 'egalitarian'.[13]

I have argued that much which passes for egalitarianism is nothing of the sort; and have concentrated on the failure of various principles and demands to meet a certain necessary condition. In section 3 I pick up the question of the content, as distinct from the grounds, of characteristically egalitarian demands; and in section 4 search around for some underlying principle which might generate such demands. In the immediately following section 2, I want to draw an important distinction between two ways in which egalitarianism figures in educational policy and debate.

2 Equality in education versus education for equality

Jencks says something peculiar and disturbing when he writes that since, according to his research team, schooling has little to do with subsequent income and status, he is 'much less concerned than most egalitarians with making sure that people end up alike [in schooling]'.[14] What is peculiar is the idea that someone, especially a self-confessed egalitarian, should be concerned with equality within education only to the extent that it may be causally related to equality of income, status, and the like. Peculiar and disturbing such an attitude may be; but it also seems to be remarkably prevalent. A writer, typically, will announce that he is about to reveal the iniquitous inequalities in our education system; but what he then produces is a set of tired figures showing a correlation between subsequent income or job and the type of school attended. Most bishops went to public schools – and so on. Such figures tell one absolutely nothing about educational inequalities, if that expression refers – as one might reasonably expect it to refer – to differences in quality of teaching, educational resources, suitability of curriculum, and the like. It may, of course, be that subsequent socio-economic inequalities are somehow related to such educational differences – but this is rarely argued for. That it is rarely argued for is a sign of a remarkably exclusive obsession with what happens after schooling rather than within it.

More of such an obsession later. The immediate point is simply to insist on the distinction the above remarks imply – the distinction between the socio-economic inequalities which may be reflected in, encouraged or produced by, our educational system, and the genuine educational inequalities found in that system. I shall not,

9

until the next chapter, try to sharpen the difficult notion of a genuine educational inequality; but we might expect discussion of it to involve discussion of differences in at least the following: quality of teaching, teacher/pupil ratios, expenditure on children's education, library and other educational resources, examination and selection criteria, length of schooling, and 'cultural provision' in the home. As the last item, in particular, suggests, there are probably important connections between socio-economic inequalities and genuine educational ones. But the presumed correlation between economic poverty and lack of cultural provision at home should not allow us to fudge the distinction between economic differences – which, *per se*, tell us nothing about inequalities in the education received by children – and differences in 'cultural provision', which presumably do tell us something. It is one thing to object to there being differences in educational provision; quite another to make the further objection that these differences are related to differences in income or social class. There would be nothing inconsistent in wanting to retain educational inequalities whilst trying to break the connection between these and socio-economic ones.

As with many distinctions – for example, the earlier one between real and rhetorical calls for equality – it is more interesting to explain why they get ignored than simply to make them. One reason why the present distinction gets fudged is a generalization of the example from the previous paragraph. It is not an unreasonable prima facie assumption that the very features of the educational system which reflect, produce, or emphasize socio-economic inequalities are those which embody genuine educational inequalities. Public schools are educationally favoured; and presumably they do reflect and emphasize, perhaps help perpetuate, socio-economic inequalities. The assumption is not a matter of logic. There is no reason, in principle, why it should not be educational equality, in various respects, which helps produce greater social inequality. Suppose it were true both that non-streaming helps the brightest pupils most of all, and that the brightest are the richest: in that event, the equalizing step of non-streaming will presumably help reinforce an economic inequality. (When, in the nineteenth century, the career of army officer was thrown more open to talent, the result, apparently, was to increase the percentage of aristocratic officers – for, by the requirements then in force, they were the ones who really had the talent.) Still, to the extent that the assumption is made, the effect will be to obviate, to some degree, the practical need to heed my distinction – for objection to the socio-economic inequalities fostered by the educational system will be seen as, *ipso facto*, objecting to the system's internal inequalities.

A related, but somewhat more subtle, reason why people have glossed over the distinction is that they have been convinced by certain arguments to the effect that social inequalities related to education are a sure criterion of (perhaps hitherto undetected) educational inequalities. Such arguments, ironically, are to be found both in the various reports (Hadow, Spens, etc.) which led to the 11-plus, and in subsequent criticisms of that test. The pre-1944 reasoning went something as follows: if the monolithic secondary system results in middle-class children doing so much better than working-class children, this must be because of an important inequality of educational treatment; only the middle-class child can be getting the education suited to him; what must be done is to set up a system in which each child gets the education suited to him. Critics of 11-plus have argued that, since middle-class children do so much better in the test, this is a sure sign that it is unfair; that equally intelligent children do not have an equal chance. Since the test, despite its pretensions, is not of intelligence, but of the acquired knowledge which, of course, the middle-class child will have more of. A test that was fair, in educational terms, would *ipso facto* not statistically discriminate in favour of a particular social class. Acceptance of such arguments would, again, obviate the need, for practical purposes, of heeding my distinction.

A final factor is a little harder to spell out. If education were a very brief affair, and not divided into stages, there would be a clear temporal distinction between the inequalities found in education and those subsequent socio-economic ones, which may or may not result from education. But education takes a long time, and is divided into stages; and what happens at one stage (e.g. the primary) can have obvious effects on what happens at a later stage. These effects, equalizing or otherwise, can be of both an educational and a social nature. If, as a rich boy, I go to a good preparatory school, my chances of going to a better secondary school than others are enhanced – as are my chances of going to a school which emphasizes and perhaps promotes my economic distance from others. So among the inequalities between two boys which are causally related to one of them having been to a preparatory school are educational and social ones. This correlation makes it easier than it would otherwise be, presumably, to gloss over my distinction when discussing the inequalities of the preparatory school system. (Looking over this last sentence, and a number of earlier ones, prompts me to emphasize that I do not use 'inequality' at all pejoratively. If a sociology lecturer, or trade unionist, referred to the 'inequalities of prep. schools', or of anything else, he would automatically be taken as criticizing. Let me stress as strongly as I can that no critical intent lurks in my use of the term.)

11

Even if it is hard to make precise, there clearly is the distinction I am drawing attention to. However close the empirical connections between genuine educational inequalities and other, socio-economic ones, the conceptual distinction remains. In recent years, of course, considerable doubt has been cast on the closeness of these connections – and this makes it of the first importance, for practical reasons, to heed the distinction.[15] At any rate, I am going to heed it. To the extent that the questions can be kept well apart, I shall devote the following chapter to the question of genuine educational inequality, and chapter 3 to the question of the wider inequalities which may be reflected in, emphasized, promoted, or produced by the education system.

What does one say to those egalitarians who, judging from their remarks, would seem, like Jencks, to lose interest in educational inequality unless it is significantly connected with socio-economic inequality? I find it hard to understand such a loss of interest. Many egalitarians seem to begin with a concern for human goods. Their doctrines are about the distribution of human goods. Unless it were taken that some things are good, desirable, beneficial, and valuable, the question of distribution would not arise. No one would be very worried about the distribution of something everyone was indifferent to. Now surely one would indeed have to be one of Arnold's 'Barbarians' or 'Philistines' to suppose that the only desiderata, whose distribution is of significance, are money, what it can buy, social status, and the like. Schools, I shall assume, provide, or try to provide, things which are of value for reasons that have nothing to do with wealth, status, and so on. Knowledge, imagination, and moral sense would, I take it, be included in this provision. It is unclear to me how an egalitarian, or any one else, can be indifferent to the distribution of these goods, while admitting that this is what they are. And how can anyone, egalitarian or otherwise, fail to admit that?

It bears repeating, moreover, that education takes a long time. Many people spend up to 25 per cent of their lives in receipt of formal education. It would be hard, indeed, to understand the idea that what is received during this long period is, in itself, insufficiently important for the issue of its distribution to take on an independent interest.

I am not sure that an egalitarian is entitled even to be less interested in the distribution of education, should it turn out that there is little or no connection between it and wider inequalities. Indeed, one could guess that some characteristically egalitarian proposals in education might actually be strengthened thereby. As Tyrrell Burgess puts it, if there is this lack of connection, then wide disparities between schools are seen to be insupportable, not because of their pupils' futures but because of their present experience. If the internal and external organization of schools has little long-term consequence, there is no excuse for arrangements which cause present deprivation or unhappiness.[16]

(The passage, of course, is heavily loaded – assuming as it does that it is the educational stratagems which egalitarians condemn, rather than those they urge, which have an adverse effect on 'present experience' and 'happiness'. Still, the idea that educational stratagem, egalitarian or not, requires to be assessed, irrespective of its long-term consequences or lack of them, is dead right.)

3 Levelling

Earlier I identified a necessary condition of egalitarianism: its demands must be based on the ground that some should receive more (less) because others receive more (less). Obviously this is not a sufficient condition: it is satisfied, for example, by the demand that millionaires should be given tax relief because others are on the breadline. Would we have a sufficient condition if we conjoined to our necessary condition the further one that the demand must be for greater equality? No, for suppose someone argued as follows in favour of public schools: if some children, poor ones, go to schools their parents can afford (i.e. state ones) then other children, rich ones, should go to schools their parents can afford (i.e. public schools) – thereby making children more equal, since now each, equally, will go to the kind of school his financial resources make possible. Or consider the following demand, which also satisfies the two conditions mentioned: because some people are not taxed at all, no one should be taxed at all, thereby making men equal in their freedom from taxation. Neither of the above demands, clearly, would be regarded as egalitarian ones. Quite the contrary.

Though it may at first sound paradoxical, it is actually a matter of logic that an egalitarian cannot be distinguished by the fact that his demands would produce equalities whereas those of his opponent would not. The reason is that any new equality produced is necessarily accompanied by a new inequality. Tax people progressively, so that you make them more equal with respect to the amount they have left, and you thereby make them less equal with respect to the percentage they have left. Construct very expensive schools for millionaires' children, and you thereby, at one and the same time, create greater disparity in school fees but less disparity in the ratio of fees to parental income. Quite generally, and as a

13

matter of necessity, whenever you make people more equal with respect to X, there is some characteristic Y with respect to which you have made them less equal.

The examples, I hope, make the point clear, but for those who feel the need for a formal proof, here is one. (Those who do not feel the need can proceed to the next paragraph.) The relation of F-identity (sameness with respect to F-ness) is a reflexive, symmetrical, and transitive one which defines one or more equivalence classes of objects. Within each class, the objects are F-identical to one another; and no two objects from different classes are F-identical to one another (e.g. 'sameness of height' defines all those equivalence classes, the members of any one of which are things of the same height). Suppose F-identity defines three classes, $\{a, b\}, \{c, d\}$, $\{e, f\}$; and suppose we equalize with respect to F-ness. We do this by so treating some or all of the six objects that each becomes F-identical with every other. The result is to produce a single equivalence class, $\{a, b, c, d, e, f\}$, defined by F-identity. We may have achieved this, for example, by treating a and b in one way, e and f in another way, so that they become F-identical to the untreated c and d. Now it is easy to construct a relation of G-identity such that before the F-equalization our six objects were G-identical, while after the F-equalization this relation defines three different classes $\{a, b\}, \{c, d\}, \{e, f\}$. That is, by making the objects alike in F-ness, we automatically make them unalike in G-ness. What might G-identity be? Well, for example, the relation of *identical with respect to the treatment received in order to be made F-identical with* c *and* d. Before the F-equalization, all the objects were equal in this respect – since none of them had been given any treatment. After the F-equalization, a and b differ from c and d, which in turn differ from e and f, in the way they have been treated. G-identity might sound an artificial notion; but examples of it can be of the first moral importance. A person who has had nine-tenths of his income confiscated in order to make his income more like that of others might well, and with good reason, think that this confiscation marks a significant difference in the treatment that he and they have received.

The point being made is neither trivial nor merely 'slick', for at least two reasons. First, many of the interesting debates are not about the bare question 'Should we have equality?', but about which of various competing equalities we should have. Indeed, all debates must, *au fond*, be of this sort, given that each equality demanded carries an inequality with it, and vice versa.[17] Thus, those who urge non-streaming on egalitarian grounds are often met with the counter that this will produce inequality in the suitability

14

of the teaching received by different children. Second, the point plays havoc with a favourite thesis embraced even (or especially) by non-egalitarians. This is the thesis that inequalities always need to be justified in a way that equalities do not need to be. Although an inequality often can be justified, says the non-egalitarian proponent of this thesis, that is what it requires – justification. But this cannot be right: if there is a presumption in favour of equalizing X, then there is a presumption in favour of unequalizing Y (the respect in which, necessarily, people are made less equal when they are made more equal in respect of X). And if inequality of Y requires justification, so does equality of X. (For X and Y substitute 'income after tax' and 'percentage of income after tax', or 'content of the curriculum' and 'suitability of the curriculum to individual children'.)

The plain upshot of the point is this: one cannot identify an egalitarian by the fact that his demands would yield equalities (for so would his opponent's), but only by the nature of the equalities. Let us refer to the equalities which egalitarian demands would yield as 'levelling' ones. An egalitarian is one who buys the whole, or most, of a package of levelling equalities.

What are these levelling equalities? I am not at all confident that one can do much better than produce a list of them; not at all sure, in other words, whether there is some important feature common to those equalities we characteristically associate with egalitarianism. It may be that for purely historical reasons, or no reasons at all, this demand has come to be included in the package labelled 'egalitarian' while that demand has not. Nor should one overlook the point, made by several writers,[18] that what gets regarded as egalitarian is partly a function of the age in which it is proposed. Many of the demands made in the name of *égalité* by the bourgeois revolutionaries of 1789 would be conspicuously absent from the list subscribed to by the revolutionaries of October 1917. In a moment, to be sure, I shall search for something which may unite the egalitarian's levelling demands, but I shall not be too upset if the quest fails. Provided, after all, we can agree on what some of these demands are, and that they are worth discussing, we shall have plenty to talk about – even if we are unclear what it is that distinguishes these demands and places them in the package labelled 'egalitarian'.

I take it that, in the latter part of this century at least, no one would deserve to be, or wish to be, labelled 'egalitarian', unless he subscribed to at least the following equalities (or moves towards greater degrees of equality): equality of income; equality of professional and social status; equality of racial status; equality of sexual status; equality of suffrage; equality of 'say' in industrial decision-

15

making. For pressing practical reasons, or because of conflicts between items on the list, an egalitarian may, of course, be willing to postpone, or soft-pedal on, one or more of the demands. In the strict Leninist tradition, for instance, universal suffrage of a real kind has to await the levelling of property. But these are the kinds of demands he must make, in lieu of special reasons to the contrary. Perhaps it is worth, for the sake of contrast, mentioning a few equalities of a non-levelling kind, which do not belong in the egalitarian package. Here are some: equal freedom to pursue profit; equal criteria for moving from one caste to another; equal protection of current property holdings.

In the field of education, I shall assume that at least the following demands belong in the egalitarian package: equality of educational opportunity; greater equality in the educational resources devoted to children; greater use of the educational system to promote the equalities of the previous paragraph; greater equality in the quality of education received. At any rate, I should be disappointed if a man I met, reputed to be an egalitarian educationalist, did not subscribe to these demands. Again, it is worth contrasting these demands with some equalities, in the field of education, which we would not expect an egalitarian to urge in 1980: equality in the right to spend as much as one wishes on one's child's education; equal opportunity to set up uni-racial schools; parity in the ratio of teachers' quality to cleverness of pupils.

Before proceeding to the quest for some unity among the levelling equalities, a few sundry, and cautionary remarks. First, the mere fact that a man subscribes to the demands in the egalitarian package does not make him an egalitarian. He has to ground the demands in the right way; in other words, he must meet with the necessary condition of section 1. Second, it is not at all clear what some of the demands mean. Is equality in educational resources equality in what schools provide, or equality in that as well as in the educationally relevant provisions found in the home, the street, and the 'university of hard knocks'? And what on earth is equality of educational opportunity (a question I try to grapple with in chapter 3)? Third, there is a temptation – worth resisting, I believe – to add to the list of educational demands some rather particular ones which, to be sure, one often associates with egalitarianism in education; for example, non-streaming. My own preference, here, is to regard a particular demand such as this as one which, in conjunction with various empirical assumptions, flows from the levelling demands without, so to speak, belonging to the core constituted by the items on the list. For suppose the usual assumption made about non-streaming is hopelessly wrong; that it massively benefits

16

the children of the rich. In that case, I am sure, it would be dropped by egalitarians as an aim. It is much more difficult to identify the empirical assumptions which would have to go wrong in order for the demands in my list to be dropped by anyone calling himself an egalitarian. (This is not to pretend any sharp or final distinction between demands that should figure on the list and those which are best thought of as flowing from such demands in conjunction with empirical assumptions.)

There are, I think, two basic ways one might search for unity among the various levelling equalities which figure in the egalitarian's package. One way is to try to see them as generated by some underlying principle. It might be argued, for instance, that the levelling equalities are those which are required by the principle that benefits and burdens must be distributed on *relevant* grounds. In the following section, I consider this, and a number of other candidates. A second way is this: pick on one egalitarian demand as central or paradigmatic, and consider any other demands as egalitarian to the extent that they are entailed by a conjunction of the paradigmatic one and certain fairly uncontentious empirical assumptions. The obvious demand to pick on is the demand for equality in income, wealth, and property. Surely that is the demand one most readily associates with egalitarianism, and the one self-confessed egalitarians nurture most fondly. Such a view would, perhaps, explain why equality of sexual status, but not equality of percentage of income after tax, should figure on the egalitarian's list of levelling equalities. But whatever the merits of this view as an historical account of why various demands have come to be added to the egalitarian list, one would not want to use derivability from the paradigmatic egalitarian demand as a criterion for a demand's being an egalitarian one. For one thing, as already mentioned, it would be at best Philistine, at worst plain irrational, to be concerned solely with the distribution of goods of a material kind. Second, even if, historically, various demands appealed to egalitarians only through their connection with the paradigmatic one, it is obvious that many of these have now taken on a life of their own; and are thought to be independently important by many of those who press them.

4 Egalitarian principles

Why would anyone be an egalitarian – a genuine one as distinct from the merely rhetorical type referred to earlier? Is there some underlying principle which moves men to make the demands on my lists? What, if there is one, is the principle which requires that goods be redistributed on grounds that make essential reference to differentials in the receipt or possession of the goods? I shall glance at a few other popular candidates, before reaching the one which shall mainly concern us in what follows.

Some see the famous Principle of Utility as generating and unifying the egalitarian demands – or rather, this principle in conjunction with two crucial premises. The premises are (a) people are alike in their capacity for extracting utility (happiness, pleasure, or whatever) from utility-yielding goods (income, status, or whatever), and (b) such goods are subject to diminishing marginal utility. That is, the utility of the nth good is the same for everyone, and it has more utility than the $n+1$st good. Given this, it will follow that maximum total utility – which the principle takes as the goal – requires equality in the distribution of goods. Since A and B are alike in the value to them of the nth good, then if A has $n+1$ while B has $n-1$, A's extra good should be transferred from him to B – since B's gain in getting his nth good is greater than A's loss in losing his $n+1$st.[19]

This principle (plus premises) does meet with my necessary condition; for the question of whether somebody should be given a good cannot be decided except by reference to what others are getting. The ground for giving more to the badly-off is not the non-egalitarian one that otherwise basic needs, which it is morally imperative to satisfy, will remain unsatisfied; but that, given what others are getting, maximum total utility cannot otherwise be achieved. In one respect, however, the utilitarian can never go as far as many egalitarians want to go. He cannot tolerate, for the sake of equality, the waste involved in confiscating from the better-off goods which, for some reason, cannot be transferred to the badly-off. For that would reduce attainable maximum utility. He is not able to say anything like: 'Better that no one should have X than that people should have different amounts of it.'

For at least two reasons, an egalitarian would be most rash to base his demands on such grounds. (In fact, as far as I can tell, not many egalitarians do.) The first reason, simply, is the implausibility of the conjoined premises. Consider just the premise of diminishing marginal utility. This is totally implausible even in connection with what it might seem most applicable to – money and material goods. Do people earning £10,000 gain less from the next £10 than people earning £8,000 – or even, perhaps especially, people earning £0? Did my ninth pipe, long-playing record, or sauna bath give me less pleasure than my eighth? To make the premise faintly plausible, one would have to make a huge number of counter-factual assumptions. If everyone had similarly expensive tastes, if they had similar

18

expectations, if they were equally able to utilize the extra goods, if they were equally capable of appreciating the utility derived from extra goods – if all of this, and much more, then the law might apply. But it is clear that in the real world such assumptions are too wide of the mark to form the basis for a policy of distribution. (This is not to deny that some people have more than they know what to do with, while others have so little that they do not know what to do.) The second reason why the principle (plus premises) cannot suit the egalitarian is this: it tells us only that people's total bundles of goods should be equal, not that they should necessarily be composed in the same way. It allows, for instance, that two bundles may be equal, in the relevant sense, through one of them containing twice as much X but only half as much Y as the other. This means that the principle could be satisfied in a situation where, say, some people had a great deal of money but very little status or respect, while others had things in reverse. After all, we know from many people's indifference curves that they are willing to trade money off against respect and vice versa. The call-girl becomes a 'sexual object' for diamonds and furs, while the retired colonel goes broke in order to 'keep up appearances'. The upshot is that we cannot, from the principle (plus premises), conclude that there should be equality of sexual status, or equality of income, in particular – only that inequalities in one of these areas be compensated for by inequalities in others. A racist society in which the 'untouchables' were at least rich, or a male 'chauvinist' society in which only the females were allowed to eat good food, might fill the bill. Such a conclusion, I take it, would be anathema to the egalitarian, who is committed to all or most of the demands on my list.[20]

The premise of diminishing marginal utility is even wider of the mark when it is educational 'goods' in question – by which I mean the pleasures and nourishment to be got through learning, enlightened teaching, intelligent reading, and the like.[21] The next good book yields more for the well-read child than for the literary beginner; higher maths has value only for those who have done elementary maths; learning breeds a taste for itself; the 'intensity of imaginative adventure', which Anthony Powell refers to, grows as the child ventures more. Indeed, given this increasing marginal utility, one would attain maximum total utility in educational 'goods' by distributing extra ones to those who have already had most. This means that a utilitarian egalitarian must defend equalities in the field of education on purely instrumental grounds, if at all. Equalizing the educational resources devoted to each child would have to be defended on the ground that this would somehow help to produce that distribution of non-educational 'goods' – income, or

19

whatever – which is required for maximum total utility. How on earth such calculations could be made, I have no idea. Anyway, as I have said before, I do not wish our interest to be restricted to egalitarians with a purely instrumental concern for the distribution of education.

Many writers have seen demands for equality as generated by a principle of pure reason or, as R. S. Peters puts it, a 'presupposition of practical discourse'.[22] A mark of practical rationality, they say, is this: one does not treat A differently from B unless one can point to a relevant difference between them. This can be expressed as: it is rational to treat A and B equally unless one can point to a relevant difference. If A and B are people, and the treatment in question is morally significant, we seem to arrive at something like the following, underlying principle of equality: one ought not to give (allow) A more than B unless one can point to a relevant difference between them which warrants the discrepancy.

Whether that is what it really is, this principle is often treated as an injunction against arbitrary and prejudiced discrimination in our treatment of others. If that is what it is, there is overwhelming reason not to take it as the underlying principle of egalitarianism. That we were *not* all socialists then revealed a defect in George V's understanding of socialism. Similarly, it reveals a defect in one's understanding of egalitarianism to identify it with a principle all of us accept – all of us, that is, who can lay claim to a moral sense. For to be sure, we are all against arbitrary, prejudiced discrimination. That we are all against it, of course, does not mean there must be much substantive agreement among us – since we are likely to differ over what counts as arbitrariness, prejudice, and discrimination. Some people think all examinations are prejudiced in certain directions; others find such a charge silly. The principle, in fact, is a formal one which yields no substantive results unless conjoined with criteria for prejudice, arbitrariness, and so on. Such, indeed, is admitted by Peters when he says that 'very little of a substantive sort is implied', by such a principle, for education.[23] Now one way of making the point that acceptance of such a principle is not tantamount to being an egalitarian is to stress that egalitarians, by making the demands on my lists, are *ipso facto* committed to certain substantive demands – whereas those who accept the principle in question, that is all of us, are not *ipso facto* committed to anything in particular.

If we were armed with acceptable accounts of what counted as arbitrariness or prejudice, there is no reason to suppose that these, together with the principle which enjoins us to avoid such behaviour, would yield all and only the levelling demands of the

20

egalitarian. Certainly one would not have to be any kind of egalitarian to accept several such demands – the demand, for instance, that one should try to ascertain a person's guilt before putting him in prison. Nor is it reasonable to suppose that all of the distributions condemned by the egalitarian result from arbitrariness and prejudice. Perhaps university entrance procedures do intolerably benefit the middle-class youth; but this is not because universities are prejudiced in favour of the middle class, or because the procedures are arbitrary – unless these terms are sapped of normal meaning. It is worth stressing, indeed, that many demands generated by an injunction against arbitrariness and prejudice would not even meet my necessary condition for counting as egalitarian. Suppose someone is nasty to his friends because it is Tuesday; that is arbitrary, and does not cease to be if it is to all his friends that he is nasty. In that case, our criticism of his behaviour could not be grounded on its differing from his behaviour towards other people. As much, in fact, is shown by the example of ascertaining guilt before punishment. The best reasons for not punishing an innocent man have nothing to do with what is happening to other people, innocent or guilty.

Although we are often invited to read the original principle – that one should only treat people differently if one can cite a relevant difference among them – as an injunction against arbitrariness and prejudice; and although that is how we have so far taken it, I think we have to stretch our understanding of the original principle to read it in that way. Am I discriminating, or being arbitrary – in any pejorative sense – when I behave affectionately towards one girl and not another, even though I am not able to cite what it is about them which warrants the difference in my affections? Such an example, moreover, suggests that the original principle is not, taken generally, especially plausible. Whether there is a presumption in favour of treating people similarly unless one can cite a relevant difference among them would depend, it seems to me, on what the treatment is. Certainly one would criticize an examiner who gives different marks without being able to explain wherein the quality of the papers differs. But would one criticize the lover of the previous example, or the shopkeeper who, out of some affection for certain customers, is willing to stay open after hours for them, but not for other customers? If it is suggested that the shopkeeper's (or lover's) affection itself constitutes a relevant difference among the customers (or girl-friends), it is hard to see how the principle can be saved from either being totally permissive or circular. If any old subjective feeling – such as dislike of Jews – can make a relevant difference, it is hard to see that any discriminatory treatment gets ruled out.

21

Whereas matters become circular if the subjective feelings which are allowed to make a relevant difference are those, merely, which it is thought 'proper' or 'reasonable' to take into consideration in one's differential treatment of people.[24]

Sometimes, of course, it is morally imperative to base treatment on relevant differences or similarities among people. Perhaps this is always so when the treatment is being meted out by institutions – since these do not have the personal affections which I exemplified earlier, and which seemed to cause trouble for the unadulterated claim that one should always base differential treatment on relevant differences. Perhaps, moreover, it is especially clear, when it is institutions that are in question, what the criteria for relevant differences will be – so the hope emerges that the principle, applied to treatment by institutions, will yield substantive results, perhaps of an egalitarian kind. It has been argued, in particular, that since institutions have specific purposes, then differences between people will count as relevant or not according to whether they relate to these purposes.[25] Since it is not the purpose of schools to prime children for beauty competitions, differences in looks should be deemed irrelevant to how children get treated in schools.

This idea sounds attractive enough when we are considering institutions whose purposes are clearly defined and agreed upon. Hospitals, presumably, have as their primary aims the curing of illness and saving of lives; so it becomes fairly easy to judge if a difference between two people is relevant to what should happen to them in hospital. A gallstone is, a famous name is not. To the extent, however, that there is little agreement on purposes – as with prisons and schools – the idea is less useful, remaining formal rather than substantive. Is it any part of a university's purpose to provide a centre for 'social mixing', or to cater to the needs of industry? Disagreement on the answers to such questions must inevitably produce disagreement as to what differences among individuals are relevant to admission to a university.

The crucial consideration here is that it is only if one has already decided that education's purposes include that of reflecting or fostering levelling equalities that one could expect the idea in question to yield egalitarian conclusions. Unless, for example, one is already wedded to the idea that there should not be schools which specially benefit bright children, one is not going to think that brightness is an irrelevant feature when deciding on the kind of education to be given. Unless one is already committed to 'social mixing' as a university objective, one is not going to think that lowly social background is a relevant characteristic to be considered by admissions officers. If so, the idea that relevant differences are

22

those which relate to institutional purposes cannot yield egalitarian demands – or rather, it can do so only when these demands are written into the purposes imagined. We can find in this idea, then, no non-circular basis for egalitarianism.

The underlying principle egalitarians are most fond of appealing to is some alleged principle of justice. It was 'above all the outcome of a sense of the injustice of things as they were', writes Harold Laski reminiscing on how he came to embrace egalitarian socialism.[26]

The connections between the notions of justice and equality are multiple; but it is quite plain that some, at least, of the equalities to which justice commits one are not characteristically egalitarian. Their ground is not egalitarian; nor does one become any kind of egalitarian by accepting them. One form of injustice occurs, for example, when a rule is applied improperly, or just not applied. The rule tells us that the prize should go to the first past the tape, but is actually given to the local magnate's son, who came in third. The failure to apply the rule properly creates an inequality: all the runners, except the magnate's son, are such that they would not have got the prize unless first past the tape. But one's objection, of course, is to the flouting of the rule. The criticism is not that only one person got the prize, but that a specific person who ought to have got it did not. Another kind of injustice occurs when a policy specifies unpleasant treatment for people who cannot possibly deserve it; hence the injustice of a system in which the innocent can be punished. The principle of justice, 'punish only the innocent', can, like any principle, be expressed in the terminology of equality – 'There should be equality, for the innocent, of immunity from punishment'. But, of course, there is nothing egalitarian about such a principle. One objects to punishing certain people because they are innocent, not because other people, innocent or otherwise, are being or not being punished. (This is not to deny that, in special circumstances, an extra and subsidiary objection to the punishment of some innocents will relate to what is happening to others. For example, one might object to the way scapegoats are selected, perhaps by insisting 'Never use a person as a scapegoat more than once', in addition to the very use of scapegoats at all.)

Sometimes, to be sure, justice does require that we look to what some are getting to determine the justice of what others are getting. This occurs when justice, by itself, does not determine what each person, taken independently, should be getting (in the way that it does determine that each innocent should receive immunity from punishment). Justice does not demand that a professor should receive £10,000 p.a. rather than £9,000 p.a. – but perhaps it does tell us that if one professor is getting £10,000 then another equally

23

qualified, equally talented, equally experienced, etc., professor should get that too.

In my view, principles of justice can do little or nothing to warrant egalitarian demands. If they can provide such a warrant, it is a non-obvious one which needs to be argued for, and not assumed. For it is totally wrong to equate the demands of justice with egalitarian ones. That some people get more than, or are better off than, others does not even suggest that there is injustice going on. True, we sometimes say things like, 'Isn't it unjust that he's so handsome while his brother is so ugly', but we do not mean such talk seriously (unless, of course, the difference in looks is due to some real injustice, such as a face-transfer performed without permission). We mean, I imagine, little more than 'isn't it sad'. No doubt it is possible, in the same non-serious tone, to bemoan the 'injustice' of any differences among people which, for some reason, one finds unfortunate or undesirable.

The reason why differences – in income or anything else – do not even suggest injustice is the one brilliantly expounded by Robert Nozick.[27] The justice or otherwise of a distribution has to do with how the distribution came about. Before an income differential can be condemned as unjust, we must know something about how it arose. Suppose a number of pioneers hack out equally valuable chunks of property from previously unowned, virgin territory; and suppose that two of them die, both leaving their property to another of the pioneers, under no duress and without violating any claim anyone else might have had to their land. The lucky pioneer will now have three times as much property as any other; but there can be no injustice in this. There was nothing unjust in the original appropriation; and nothing unjust in the bequest. Before one can complain of an unjust distribution, one has to be able to answer Nozick's question of when, exactly, an act of injustice was performed. Of course, the lucky pioneer, or anyone with relatively large holdings, may put his wealth to unjust uses (in the ways Winstanley and Sir Thomas More pointed to) – but that is a different matter.

It follows that to complain, as the egalitarian does, against some differential is never, in itself, to make a complaint about injustice; for to urge that some people ought to have X because others do is not, *per se*, to say anything about how the possession, or lack of possession, of X came about. By far the best, and most honest, policy for the egalitarian is for him to stand up and admit that, often, he is against justice; to urge that justice is but one value which, in his book at any rate, is often to be overridden.[28] However, an overwhelming bashfulness seems to prevent people from making such an admission. (Compare the contortions which utilitarians – whose principle is plainly incompatible with justice in many instances – go through to show that they can accommodate the value of justice. In fact, the egalitarian goes through more contortions; for it is unclear what, other than justice, he can cite in his defence. At least the utilitarian has utility going for him.)

There are egalitarians who, without being bashful, will not concede that the inequalities they condemn are often permissible from the standpoint of justice. They are the ones who argue – as it is indeed incumbent on them to do – that these inequalities are, appearances notwithstanding, the products of many unjust policies and procedures in the past. Since I shall want to consider some arguments to this effect in chapter 3, one example of the kind of argument will suffice for the moment. Much favoured by egalitarians, especially in the USA, have been the various 'affirmative action' or 'reverse discrimination' policies, designed for example to increase the proportion of blacks in responsible jobs and among university students. Many defences are offered; but a favourite one, made explicit in much legislation and in court decisions, is that such policies are required to redress the injustices suffered by blacks in the past. Thus an Executive Order requiring 'affirmative action' policies by federal contractors defends these as 'a starting point in the process of shaping a remedy [for] past discriminatory hiring practices' by employers to whom the order applies.[29] Arguments such as this fail, I believe, to warrant more than a fraction of the egalitarian's levelling equalities – but more of that later.

My denial of a logical connection between egalitarian demands and justice trespasses against the ideas, or at least the words, of the most influential recent writer on these matters – John Rawls. A strong egalitarian grain runs through *A Theory of Justice*[30] in a way that apparently makes egalitarianism integral to that theory. This trespass does not, frankly, embarrass me; for the fact is that Rawls's title is a misnomer. Whatever his famous 'difference principle' is a principle of, it is not one of justice. It does not, even remotely, succeed in the intended aim of corresponding to, or 'explicating' our intuitions as to the justice and injustice of treatment. The reason is the one mentioned before: his principle has no concern with how a given distribution has been reached. It is surely unjust to confiscate from a man goods which he has earned honestly and without any impropriety; yet such confiscation might easily be warranted by Rawls's principle.

The 'difference principle' states (with a proviso to be mentioned later) that 'social and economic inequalities are to be arranged so that they are . . . to the greatest benefit of the least advantaged'.[31]

That is: differentials in income, status, etc., are unjust unless attempts to reduce or remove them would make the worst-off people even worse-off. Such a principle, Rawls thinks, is one which creatures, acting in accordance with a certain rational strategy, would adopt in circumstances of fair choice. The circumstances of choice are fair if, very roughly, none of the choosers is in a position to tell how the principles of distribution he is asked to select among would affect him as an individual. Hence Rawls places his choosers behind a 'veil of ignorance' which shields them, *inter alia*, from knowing their individual strengths, weaknesses, talents, and shortcomings. Were individuals to possess such knowledge, their selection of a principle to govern the distribution of goods would be influenced by it. The physically strong, for example, would opt for a distributional set-up favouring muscle. The rational strategy which these ignoramuses are presumed to follow is the so-called 'maximin' strategy. According to this, the rational choice in certain conditions of uncertainty is to opt for that set-up in which one's worst possible fate is none the less better than in any other set-up. 'We are to adopt the alternative the worst outcome of which is superior to the worst outcomes of the others.'[32] A' Rawlsian ignoramus, following 'maximin', will then, it seems, opt for the 'difference principle' of distribution; for he knows that being among the worst-off in a society governed by it will not be as bad as being among the worst-off in any other.

I shall return, in the next chapter, to these considerations in support of the 'difference principle'. It is clear, I think, that such a principle deserves consideration even though it is not, to repeat, a principle of justice. One might be convinced by Rawls's arguments that a society should be governed by it. For the moment, I want to consider the question of the extent to which the 'difference principle' is egalitarian. Can it serve as the underlying principle which generates demands for levelling equalities?

Certainly demands which are based on it meet with my necessary condition for counting as egalitarian ones. Whether certain people should have a greater share of 'primary social goods' depends, essentially, on other people's shares. Their share should be increased if, without adversely affecting the share of the worst-off, inequalities are reduced.[33] It is surely clear, moreover, that given some well-known empirical facts, the actual effect of operating Rawls's principle would be to produce more equality in the distribution of various goods, income say. For it could scarcely be argued that it would be impossible to reduce present income differentials without making the poorest even poorer – though it is a matter of considerable argument where the point lies, beyond which further

26

attempts to reduce differentials would produce such a result.

In several ways, however, the egalitarian flavour of Rawls's principle is tempered. First, and most obviously, there surely is a point beyond which further equalizing steps would adversely affect the worst-off. So one would not expect the principle to warrant total equality of income and the like. Moreover, this point may be reached when the inequalities are still very considerable – greater, certainly, than those we could expect some radical egalitarian to tolerate. Second, Rawls thinks his principle should only become operative in a society of relative plenty. In a cripplingly poor society, it would be rational for the members to put a premium on material progress at the expense, if need be, of fair distribution. Better to concentrate on making a bigger cake, which may be later distributed fairly, than on fairly distributing the meagre crumbs at present available. Finally, the 'difference principle' is only to operate (in certain circumstances, anyway) when equality of opportunity is already in operation. That is, the inequalities which (for the sake of the worst-off) the principle may permit must satisfy the further condition that opportunity to attain the better-off positions is equal. Many egalitarians, I imagine, would demur here, preferring to postpone the attempt to guarantee equal access until greater equality has been established among the positions to which there is access.

Although the second and third caveats concerning the egalitarian extent of the 'difference principle' make a theoretical difference between Rawls and many egalitarians, it is not clear that they make much difference in practice, when it is a society like our own which is under discussion. After all, ours is a society of relative plenty; so there could be no excuse, on Rawls's account, for postponing the distributional question until greater material progress has been made. Nor, it seems, could one defend present inequalities on the ground that reduction of them would destroy an existing equality of opportunity to come out top.

What of the first caveat – of the fact that in theory certainly and in practice probably, Rawls's principle permits, for the sake of the worst-off, considerable inequalities in 'primary social goods'? I once assumed that no one could be so wedded to levelling equalities as to press for them beyond a point where there are adverse effects on the worst-off. Such pressure, after all, is scarcely compatible with the sense of compassion which, one might hope, is an original ingredient in egalitarianism. That assumption, perhaps, was rash; there do seem to be people, especially educationalists, willing to press their demands beyond this point. Tony Flew goes further than 'seem to be' – telling me that he has actually met lots of people who do press their demands beyond this point. Certainly the *Daily Telegraph*

(19 January 1979) quotes a Mr Astbury, a striking lorry-driver, as countenancing equality of eating to the point of universal starvation: 'If lorrydrivers are unable to afford the food to eat, why should anyone else?' However, now it is my optimistic belief that all except lunatic egalitarians think, however mistakenly, that some of the adverse effects on the worst-off (resulting from levelling equalities) are more than off-set by, perhaps rather hidden, benefits to them. Consider, for example, the suggestion that there would be no envy in the egalitarian society – a benefit which might compensate for reductions in other goods. Silly such a suggestion might be; but one might think it incumbent on someone to make it, or something similar, in order to avoid the appearance of a willingness to swallow an undiluted worsening of the position of the worst-off.

Whether or not they think there are hidden benefits for the worst-off, there are certainly egalitarians who would press for equality of income, power, and the like beyond the point that Rawls's principle warrants. So they must be employing a principle stronger than his. Any such principle, I think, is best represented as containing Rawls's one together with some further condition(s) making an extra restriction on the extent of permissible inequality. One such principle would be the following: inequalities are justifiable if and only if (a) they benefit the worst-off and (b) the benefit to the worst-off is greater than the amount of inequality required to produce it.[34] Clearly this is stronger than the 'difference principle' by itself. Consider two set-ups, A and B: in A the best-off get 100 and the worst-off 50, while in B the best-off get 70 and the worst-off 40. Rawls must opt for A, since the worst-off are better-off in it than in B. The harder egalitarian, who insists on clause (b), must opt for B – since the benefit to the worst-off of system A, 10, is less than the inequality ($(100-70) - (50-40) = 20$) required to produce it.

My strategy will be as follows: in the following two chapters I shall, when referring to 'egalitarianism', generally have in mind Rawls's 'difference principle'. Sometimes though, it will be clear that something stronger is at issue; and where this is so, the nature of the extra strength will be duly noted. There are a number of reasons why I put Rawls's principle at the centre, so to speak, of the egalitarian sphere. First, it is nice and simple. Second, it has been, in its short career, extremely influential. Third, as I noted, it serves as a basic ingredient in other, stronger egalitarian principles. Those other principles can always be represented through adding some further condition(s) to Rawls's. Fourth, it is my intention to reject Rawls's principle as a guide for distribution (particularly when it is education whose distribution concerns us). To do this is *ipso facto* to reject any stronger principle, since each of these contains Rawls's condition as a necessary component. What I shall be saying, if you like, is: 'Perhaps you egalitarians have something stronger in mind than Rawls; but since what he has in mind is already too strong, then your demands must be too strong as well.'

In this section I have looked for an underlying principle which at once meets with my necessary condition for counting as egalitarian, and which might reasonably be expected to yield those equalizing, levelling demands which are characteristic of those we call 'egalitarians'. A number of candidates failed on one or both counts. The most likely candidate is a somewhat strengthened version of Rawls's 'difference principle' – though it is often, for reasons given in the previous paragraph, that principle itself which will be considered. The 'difference principle' is not, *pace* Rawls, a principle of justice – but to say this is not to dismiss it, for it is not obviously absurd, or morally repugnant, to suppose that justice should sometimes be overridden. As yet I have not done very much to explain why the principle recommends itself to some people, including Rawls; and I have said nothing at all about how one might expect it to work out in the field of education. To such matters we now turn.

2 Equality in education

1 'Scholesia' – a model

Someone looking at my library says, 'You have more than the average number of books, which is too many, since it doesn't benefit those having very few books.' Why is this person misusing the 'difference principle'? Rawls's answer would be that the principle only governs the distribution of primary goods – 'rights, liberties, opportunities, powers, income, and wealth'. Books are not primary goods, but things which I put primary goods – my money or freedom to read – towards. But the example shows that we must take some care in seeing what Rawls's principles imply for the distribution of education. Some writers have not taken this care. Coleman imagines that Rawls's principles require 'erasing all the "accidents of birth" . . . [which] necessitates removing the child from all influences of his family . . . and raising him as a ward of state, subject to precisely the same conditions as any other child'.[1] Coleman cannot have noticed Rawls's first – and logically prior – principle, which insists on various fundamental liberties and rights that would obviously be violated by the Platonic policy described (which is not to say that it is at all easy, when reading Rawls, to know exactly when what appears to be demanded by the 'difference principle' is to be objected to on the basis of the 'fundamental liberties' principle).

Rawls himself gives us some, but not total, help with the implications for education. We must, he says, 'allocate resources in education . . . so as to improve the long-term expectations of the least favoured. If this end is attained by giving more attention to the better endowed, it is permissible: otherwise not'.[2] And he adds that the value of education should not be assessed 'only in terms of economic efficiency and social welfare', since it consists in part in 'enabling a person to enjoy the culture of his society and take part in its affairs'.[3] These latter are not themselves primary goods, but prerequisites for an important primary good (not mentioned in Rawls's original list), 'a secure sense of one's own worth'.[4]

The 'least favoured', then, are those with the lowest expectations

30

not only of economic goods, but of the opportunities to enjoy culture and participate in social affairs (of, therefore, securing a 'sense of worth'). Inequalities in the distribution of educational resources are justified only if they maximally raise the expectations of these least favoured persons.

It is clear that Rawls's use of the 'difference principle' in this way is too broad for the purpose of this chapter. For him, a relevant criticism of an educational system is that it contains schools which unjustifiably enhance the economic prospects of their students; whereas that is precisely the kind of criticism whose consideration I wish to postpone. The purpose of this chapter, remember, is to consider genuine educational inequality – the distribution of educational goods in maximally possible isolation from the socio-economic inequalities which may be related to it. Presumably, though, Rawls is interested in genuine educational inequality as well, for one assumes that it is educational goods (knowledge, etc.) which are relevant to cultural enjoyment, participation in social affairs, and hence to 'a sense of one's worth'. (It would be a real educational criticism if the schools turned out egophobic, hermitic Philistines.)

In another respect, however, Rawls's use is too narrow. He talks of the distribution of educational resources, but unless that word is lent a peculiarly wide sense, our concern goes beyond this distribution. The quality of teaching, for example, is not a resource – yet it is something that can vary, and this variation is something whose justifiability we may properly inquire into in this chapter.

If we are to see what the 'difference principle' implies for genuine educational inequality, it will help if we provide ourselves with a simplified model. Follow me, if you will, to a little country called 'Scholesia'. This country is, with the possible exception of its education system, a Rawlsian paradise. Fundamental liberties are maximally secured to each citizen; and income, status, political power, etc., are distributed in accordance with the 'difference principle'. While some have more of these goods than others, this is always justified by the benefits accruing to the worst-off. That education is, or might be, the serpent in this paradise is due to the high degree of isolation of the education system from the wider socio-economic setting. At any rate, a number of correlations between the educational and the socio-economic, which are familiar to us, do not obtain in Scholesia. There is, to begin with, no significant correlation between attendance at one rather than another of Scholesia's two schools and future income or status. Nor is there a significant correlation between attendance at a particular school and the socio-economic position of the parents.

Naturally there are some important connections between educational factors and wider, social ones. Attendance at one rather than the other school is significantly related to the job or profession later entered into. This is not because the schools are vocational; but, with the differences between them, they tend to equip their students for rather different sorts of work. Second, there is a significant correlation between a child's educationally relevant abilities and his parentage and home environment. Brighter children tend to have the brighter parents – though, to repeat what is implied in the previous paragraph, the brighter parents have no tendency to be the better-off in terms of income, power, etc. Finally, education – or educational 'goods' – are valued in the society. Scholesians agree that it is better to be well-educated than ill-educated. This may seem hard to reconcile with the fact that there is no significant correlation between education and status – but this does not appear as a problem for Scholesians who make a distinction, foreign to many of our sociologists, between those characteristics of a person which carry social status and those which are to be valued for their own sake. Physical beauty, for instance, is admired but carries with it no special prerogatives; whereas a Scholesian medal of honour, conferred by the king on his cronies, provides many an *entrée* into otherwise closed doors, commands displays of deference, and enhances one's chances of a lucrative post in Scholesian industry.

Scholesia, which is only about the size of Andorra, has a very simple school system. There are just two schools, North and South. Children go to one or other school at the age of 10, having been educated until then by their parents. The minimum leaving age is 16, but suitably qualified Northerners (i.e. students at North school) may stay on, if suitably qualified, to as late as 21. Schooling is paid for out of public funds – though those Northerners who stay beyond 16 must, in later life, repay the extra expenditure on their education (or that proportion of it which is not thought to rebound to the public benefit).

The following facts about the system are crucial:

1 The Northerners receive a better education than the Southerners.
2 Had any Southerner gone to North he would have ended up better educated than he is; similarly, had any Northerner gone to South, he would have ended up less educated than he is.
3 Had any Southerner gone to North, he would not have ended up as well-educated as any actual Northerner; similarly, any Northerner, had he gone to South, would have ended up better-educated than any actual Southerner.
4 The Scholesian economy is static, so that educational resources cannot be increased, only redistributed.

Two important corollaries of the description so far are:

5 Children, when they enter school, differ in their educationally relevant abilities (including the ability to acquire further abilities, known as 'potential'). This is because they have been educated by parents, some of whom are more educated than others. (Incidentally, Scholesians generally neither know nor care whether differences in the abilities of 10-year-olds are entirely due to parental education or whether they are due in part to genetic transmission.)

6 Allocation of children to the two schools is entirely rational – in the sense that all those who are most able to benefit from the better education at North actually go there. This is implied by (3). (It does not matter for our present purposes what the decision-procedure for allocating children actually is – an infallible 10+ exam, brain-scanning, consultation of the runes, or whatever.)

When it is said that North is a better school than South, it is not – or not simply – meant that its alumni are better educated; for, after all, North enjoyed a more able intake than South. Presumably it is perfectly possible for one school to be better than the other even though, because of the very poor quality of its intake, it turns out less well-educated products. Let us say, then, that the superiority of North consists in the fact that its students are more educationally 'transformed' during their schooldays than are the Southerners. That is: the difference in degree of educatedness of the 10-year-olds is actually increased by subsequent attendance at the schools.

This, of course, is a purely formal criterion of North's superiority. What are the substantive criteria for judging that some children are more educationally transformed than others? Among Scholesians there is some – though not too much – disagreement about these criteria. But there is virtually no disagreement as to the various features of North which equip it to be the better school, to be the more educationally transforming. *Inter alia*, North enjoys the following advantages: a high teacher–pupil ratio; well-qualified teachers; favourable climatic and geographical conditions; a large budget; well-equipped libraries, laboratories, music-rooms, etc. Nor are the following to be ignored: each Northern student is surrounded by fellow-students of a higher educational calibre than found in South, and in vacations he is in a home environment which helps consolidate the education he is receiving at school. Such advantages, unless perversely misused, must reasonably be thought to equip North to be the superior school whatever it may be, exactly, that is meant by 'superior'.

Although there is no complete consensus on what it is to be educationally transformed, the mass of Scholesians agree that some

33

or all of the following features characterize the well-educated person: the versatility to take on whatever work, out of a wide range, that one chooses; the ability to engage in or critically assess Scholesian and other culture; knowledge and information about a fairly wide range of matters – including history, science, and mathematics; imaginativeness; creativity; appreciation of men's great achievements; a developed moral sense. To be sure, there is no precise agreement on what each of these educational goods consists in – on, for example, the extent to which creativity is an essentially aesthetic matter. Nor is there general agreement on the weighting to be given the various goods. Still, there is agreement that North does more than South in enabling its students to become versatile, cultured, knowledgeable, imaginative, creative, appreciative, moral agents.[5]

The North/South system is not short of its egalitarian critics in Scholesia. Inequalities there certainly are: children at the age of 10 are not equal in endowment or potential; the Northerners get a better education; as a result of both factors Northern alumni are better educated. The critics come in various shapes and sizes, the least extreme being those who put the system to the test of the 'difference principle' and nothing stronger. Even among these critics, however, there is divergence resulting from concentration on different aspects of the system's inequality. Some of them employ the following, educational version of the 'difference principle':

(A)   Inequality in the educational transformation wrought by North and South is justified only if the Southerners are, as a result, as educationally transformed by their schooling as they could be in any alternative system.

It is generally agreed that the system does not satisfy this principle. Resources could be diverted from North to South, for example, without adversely affecting the quality of education in South. Other critics who wield the 'difference principle' arrive at the following subtly, but importantly different, educational version:

(B)   Inequality between North and South is justified only if the Southerners are, from birth onwards, as educationally transformed, whether by schooling or other influences, as they could be in any alternative system.

The crucial point to bear in mind – and in virtue of which (B) is stronger than (A) – is that equalizing the quality of North and South would be insufficient to produce equally well-educated persons. This is because of the domestic advantages which the Northerners enjoy before and during their schooling. To achieve equality in educational transformation, the quality of South would have to be

34

higher than that of North, in order to 'compensate' for the Northerners' domestic advantages. The strongest complaint the proponent
of (A) can make is that North is favoured over South; whereas the
proponent of (B) could make the stronger complaint that South is
not more favoured than North.

There are two ways, however, in which proponents of (B) could
be persuaded to press for nothing stronger than the proponents of
(A). Suppose, first, that there is a point, prior to equality between
North and South, beyond which further steps towards equalization
would adversely affect the position of the Southerners. This is quite
conceivable: for example, the effect of lowering standards in North
might be to lessen the quality of teachers (who come from North) –
with bad results for South as well as North. At any rate, if there is
such a point, proponents of (B) will be no more willing to go beyond
it than those of (A). Second, suppose that ways are found of ensuring
that no children enjoy domestic advantages over others, before or
during schooling (by making all children wards of state, perhaps).
In that event, there could be no case for going beyond parity
between North and South in order to 'compensate' for any other
advantages enjoyed by the Northerners.

We know from chapter 1 that there are egalitarian principles
stronger than the 'difference principle' (see p. 28) – and to be sure,
we find some Scholesian egalitarians deploying educational versions
of these. For example there is (A'), which is like (A) but with the
additional demand that any inequality between North and South
be less than the extra benefit to South which the inequality yields.

Debate in Scholesia has tended to focus on principle (A). (B) is
not taken particularly seriously, since it is reasonably assumed that
the engineering required to fully 'compensate' the Southerners for
their domestic disadvantages would conflict with the fundamental
liberties which Scholesians enjoy. After all, these disadvantages
are not of a financial kind which relatively simple fiscal policies
might serve to erase. But the main reason discussion has centred on
(A) is that defenders of the North/South system – that is, the critics
of the egalitarians – realize that if this principle is too strong, so are
the others. If they find themselves unable to resist (A), they face the
threat of having to argue with proponents of stronger principles. But
that is a big 'if'.

More exactly, debate has surrounded the question of whether
North and South schools should be abolished in favour of a single
school, Centre. The quality of education in Centre might not be the
same for all students. Some (the ex-Northerners) might be advantaged if that is found to benefit the education of the others (the ex-
Southerners). Such a difference, though, would certainly be less

than the old difference between North and South for, as we know, some of the advantage enjoyed by North did nothing to benefit South.

The reasons Scholesian egalitarians tend to prefer the single school, Centre, over a system in which two new schools, East and West – which educate equally well (and badly) – replace North and South, are primarily practical. Economies of scale, for example. Still, the issue of which of the two systems to move to is not as burning as the issue of whether there should be any move at all – whether, that is, there is anything wrong with the present, North/South system.

The advantages of thinking in terms of models are simplicity, precision, and method. One starts by asking rather vague questions about complicated systems that face one with innumerable, amorphous, unordered facts. The idea is to ignore many of these facts, to abstract away from them and to replace the original questions by ones about the resulting, simpler system. Not only will fewer complications present themselves, but the new questions will have a precision that the originals did not have. Consider such a familiar model as the classical economist's perfectly competitive economy, in which one has abstracted away from such obvious realities as the ability of some producers to control prices. Not only is the model much simpler than the real economy, but it allows one to replace a vague question like 'When should our business stop expanding?' by a precise one, 'At what point will marginal cost equal marginal revenue?' Concomitant with the advantages of simplicity and precision is the danger that the answers one gives will have no relevance to the real world. But if the model is well constructed, it should display the third virtue of providing us with a methodical way of reintroducing real factors, thereby testing in an orderly way their impact on the answers we gave to the questions about the simple model. Thus the classical economist can, step by step, examine the impact on the rule 'equate marginal cost and marginal revenue' of introducing such real factors as oligopoly, consumer associations, natural disasters, and so on. It is arguable, presumably, that the tools of empirical economics could not have been forged or refined except in connection with such a simple model.

The main simplification afforded by my model of Scholesia is the abstraction of educational matters from wider socio-economic ones. We are able to face questions about educational distribution without the massive intrusion of the socio-economic factors which so often dominate what are supposed to be discussions about education. Our questions, moreover, take on a new precision. Instead of 'To what extent should there be equality within education?', we have 'Should the North/South system be abolished in favour of Centre (or East/West)?' To be sure, any answer we give to that question will be subject to alteration once we introduce various real factors back into the model. But the model, I hope, gives us genuine guidance as to what these factors, and their possible relevance, might be. How, if at all, will a negative answer be affected by the fact that, in the real world, attendance at certain schools does confer future economic advantage? How, if at all, will the fact that, in reality, there is a correlation between admission to certain schools and parental income going to affect it? And so on.

Would a negative answer to whether the North/South system should be abolished count as a standing answer – a negative one – to whether, socio-economic factors apart, educational inequality is unjustifiable? Not quite – for my model abstracts from more than these factors. In particular, we should have, at some point, to give up the myth that there can be totally accurate predictors of a child's educationally relevant abilities (as I do in chapter 3). Still, this and the introduction of various socio-economic factors are a long way off. The present concern is whether, under the conditions described, the educational inequalities of the North/South system are intolerable.

2 The egalitarian case

I take it for granted that there is a prima facie case for adopting that education system, among various alternatives, which most approximates towards an ideal of excellence in educational standards. I also take it – for the time being – that of the Scholesian systems mentioned it is the North/South one which most does this. This second assumption can be challenged, and that challenge will be considered in the next section. In this section I consider the egalitarian case which is pitted against the prima facie presumption in favour of North/South. Given that presumption, the main task facing defenders of the system is to counter the reasons urged against it by egalitarians.

More exactly, I want to consider and reject the reasons which Scholesian egalitarians cite in support of principle (A) – according to which the inequalities of North/South are not justified, since a more equal distribution would benefit the Southerners further. (Recall my strategy here: if this principle is too strong, then any more strictly egalitarian principle, applied to education, will of course be too strong as well.)

37

I speak rather charitably of 'reasons in support of' principle (A) – for it is fairly rare to find egalitarians in Scholesia, or elsewhere, actually citing reasons. It is much more common to find them describing the North/South system in such terms that to accept the descriptions is virtually tantamount to condemning the system. A large part of the defender's task consists in showing these descriptions to be unwarranted – to be, at best, question-begging. Here is a succinct and typical description of the North/South system found in one Scholesian egalitarian's writings:

> It is an élitist system in which some people, through the merest luck on their part, benefit at the expense of others. Hence it is not a system which rational men, choosing fairly, could conceivably opt for.

Four claims seem to be involved in this short passage. Each is taken to be critical of the North/South system; together they are taken to constitute a decisive case against it. They purport to serve as an answer to why educational inequalities which do not benefit the least educated as much as possible are intolerable. They are:

(i)   Some benefit *at the expense* of others.
(ii)   They do so, not through anything like *merit*, but *mere good fortune*.
(iii)   The system is *élitist*.
(iv)   It is not a system which men, *choosing in circumstances of fairness*, could *rationally* opt for.

Part of what I now want to show is that each point presupposes, and so cannot be used as a reason for, the egalitarian's conclusions. Let us take them in turn.

(i)   In Scholesia, we know, the better education of some does not work out to the maximum benefit of the least well-educated. But, described in this bare manner, it is hard to see what the criticisms could be. After all, the excellent health enjoyed by some people is of no great medical benefit to the illest. That is, you could maim or contaminate the healthiest without making the sick even sicker. Before an inequality which does not benefit the least advantaged can be subject to criticism, surely the following condition must obtain: if the better-off were less well-off then the worst-off would be better-off. If this causal condition does not obtain, it is impossible to understand the rationale for making the better-off worse-off.

Notice that, as they stand, neither Rawls's 'difference principle', nor its educational version (A), respects this condition – for they appear to condemn inequalities irrespective of any causal connection between the respective plights of the best-off and worst-off. But

38

let us charitably assume that such a connection is tacitly pre-supposed by anyone who mobilizes these principles. I also noted (see p. 27) the existence of some hard-line egalitarians who are seemingly willing to see the worst-off made even worse-off if equality is thereby promoted; who are, therefore, seemingly unconcerned with whether the plight of the worst-off is somehow caused by the advantages of others. But, again, I made the charitable assumption (which Flew thought was misplaced charity) that, on inspection, such egalitarians would usually wish to appeal to various hidden benefits (e.g. reduction of envy) which the equalizing steps would confer on the worst-off. So let us continue to insist that a rational deployment of the 'difference principle' (and of (A)) will presuppose a causal connection between the positions of best-off and worst-off.

But is this enough? Does the mere fact that if some people were doing less well others would be doing better constitute a prima facie objection to the former's advantages? Suppose you run slower than me, but faster than everyone else; so that, if I had not been in the race, you would have won. My being in the race, therefore, is a cause of your not getting the gold medal; but there can be nothing to criticize in that. After all, consider how inappropriate it would be for you to complain that I won at your expense, or that I was responsible for your losing, or that it was my fault that you did not win. Such complaints could, of course, be in order – if, for example, I had kicked your ankle at the last bend, or sent an irresistible blonde to your room the night before, or had been a favourite of the team coach who ordered you to exhaust yourself by setting a cracking pace in the first lap. But in the normal case, where I am faster, the causal connection between my entry and your losing the race can occasion no such complaints.

So our Scholesian egalitarian was quite right to insist that, for principle (A) to apply, the North/South system must be one in which some benefit at the expense of others, in which the advantages of some are responsible for the disadvantages of others. (By insisting on this sort of condition, there is something the egalitarian gains – namely a connection, otherwise missing, between inequality and injustice. I noted earlier (see p. 24) that an inequality is not even prima facie evidence of an injustice, since the justice or otherwise of a distribution has to do with how it came about. Now if it can be shown that an inequality, unwarranted by the 'difference principle', is one that has come about through somebody doing something at the expense of somebody else, it can clearly be a case of injustice too. My winning the gold medal is obviously unjust if I nobbled you on the last bend.)

But is the North/South system one in which some benefit at the expense of others? In the example of the race, what made my winning through nobbling you or being in cahoots with the coach a case of 'winning at your expense', while my winning because I was the faster is not, is that in the former case I did something reprehensible, wrong, unfair. And, in general, X gains at Y's expense only if both (a) X had not done as well, Y would have done better, and (b) X, in doing as well as he did, did something reprehensible, unfair, etc. Likewise, X is only (morally) responsible for Y's plight if he is (causally) responsible for it and did something wrong (or was culpably negligent).[6] So, the North/South system is one in which some gain at the expense of others only if there is a causal connection between the positions of the better-off and worse-off *and* there is something unfair, reprehensible, wrong, or whatever, about the advantages enjoyed by the Northerners. Well, we know that the first of the conditions is satisfied – matters could be improved for the Southerners by making the Northerners worse-off. But what about the second condition?

It is satisfied only if the egalitarian (or some other) condemnation of the North/South system is warranted. But this is no help to the egalitarian. He wanted to use the (presumed) fact that some benefit at the expense of others as a reason for condemning the system. This, however, is impossible; for it is only if the condemnation is warranted on other grounds that the system can then be described as one in which some benefit at the expense of others. Let us indeed grant that the North/South system is unjustified if it is one where some gain at the expense of others. But the egalitarian cannot convince us it is unjustified by showing that it is one where this occurs. Rather he must present us with reasons which, if well-taken, show us, at one and the same time, that the system is unjustified and that, in it, some gain at the expense of others. Hence we must proceed to the other objections in our Scholesian egalitarian's armoury.

(ii) Suppose that future Northerners, on meeting future Southerners, bash them on the head, thereby causing brain-damage which ruins their chances of passing the North entrance examination. In that case, North's alumni will have benefited at the expense of South's, for they will have done something analogous to my winning the race by kicking your ankle. But, of course, that is not the way things really are in Scholesia.

Perhaps, though, it is not required for some to gain at the expense of others that the former have done something reprehensible. It is enough, some might say, that in no way do they merit or deserve their advantages. Suppose I, the slower runner under ordinary conditions, win the race because, unknown to me, the ice-cream I ate prior to the race contained a powerful stimulant that turns me into a veritable Achilles. I did not do anything wrong, but perhaps your defeat was unfair. I did not do anything I ought not; but what happened ought not to have happened. In the best of all possible worlds, that sort of thing would not happen.

Things go as they should when the prizes, the benefits, go to those who deserve them. It is a requirement of justice, according to some, that those who do not deserve X should not get X. (Notice that this requirement does not follow from what clearly is a principle of justice – namely, that those who deserve X should get X. It only follows if, in addition, there is somebody who does deserve X: for if there is such a person, he should get X, and nobody else – the undeserving – should therefore get it.)

It may seem that our egalitarian critic can make nothing of this point in his criticism of the Scholesian system, for do not the Northerners deserve to go to North? After all, they are the ones with the talents which equip them to extract maximum educational benefit from going there. Yet he does try to make something of it – in the following passage, for example:

It is true that, at the age of 10, future Northerners display greater talent and ability than future Southerners. In a very feeble sense, therefore, they deserve to go to North. In this feeble sense, A deserves B if he possesses those features which the rules of a system require someone to have in order to get B. But in a truer and deeper sense, they are no more deserving than the future Southerners. They are the children, after all, of better educated parents; so, whether for purely environmental, or environmental-plus-genetic, reasons they enjoy a greater initial advantage. That they possess the features which admit them to North is not something they merit or deserve. The luck of having the parents they do is the sole cause. It is true that such children, before going to school, have worked harder, read more, applied themselves better, and so on: but such characteristics as industriousness and curiosity belong to them only as a result of environmental, or environmental-plus-genetic, factors. Either way, the children do not deserve to have the characteristics. Nor, therefore, do they deserve the advantages these characteristics confer. Since going to North school merely compounds these advantages, totally undeserved, it and the system to which it belongs should be abolished.

Our egalitarian has no doubt read his Rawls, according to whom

no one deserves his place in the distribution of native endowments . . . [or] initial starting-place in society . . . his

41

character depends in large part upon family and social circumstances for which he can claim no credit. The notion of desert seems not to apply to these cases.[7]

Rawls, too, admits a feeble sense of desert – if a person has done the things which a system announces it will reward, then he deserves those rewards. An important implication is this: desert always pre-supposes the existence of a system of distribution, and cannot be appealed to in support of that system. Certainly the fact that, within a system, a person deserves certain rewards, can do nothing to justify the system which confers such rewards. A man 'cannot say that he deserves and therefore has a right to a scheme of co-operation in which he is permitted to acquire benefits that do not contribute to the welfare of others'.[8]

What I first want to focus upon is a way, an illegitimate way, in which our egalitarian primes us to accept that the Northerners bene-fit from the merest luck on their part. He presents us with a dichotomy – 'Either something is deserved or it's the merest luck' – which, combined with the claim that the things which interest him are not deserved, forces us to see them as mere good fortune. But the dichotomy is false; let us see why.

Clearly it is not a matter of luck that some children, given their various characteristics, are equipped to get into North. They really are the more able, so it is not luck that they pass the entrance exam-ination. The 'luck', presumably, is meant to consist in their having those characteristics – industriousness, curiosity, etc. – which equip them to do well. But this suggestion needs to be taken very carefully. The less important reason for care is this: characteristics of the type mentioned feed on themselves over time. It is not a matter of chance that the more industrious, imaginative, thoughtful 7-year-old becomes the more industrious, imaginative, and thoughtful 8-year-old. Hence it is totally misleading to speak of the child's abilities as if they arrived, along with other gifts, in the last year's Christmas stocking. At any given point in his development, the admirable, educationally relevant qualities the child displays will, typically at least, be the result, *inter alia*, of previous exercises of hard work, application, imaginativeness, and so on. The import of this obvious fact, which the egalitarian none the less invites us to overlook, will emerge a little later.

The more important reason for suspicion goes deeper. One can certainly say of a young child that he is lucky to have perfect pitch or 'a good eye for the ball'. This is possible because such endowments are clearly accidental to his being the person he is. On no plausible account of personal identity could such features be taken as essential, identifying features. But it is far less clear that we can treat a person's intelligence and character (including his industriousness, imaginativeness, curiosity, etc.) as accidental appendages which he has sprouted – ones which he is lucky (or unlucky) to have. It is true that in some contexts, and for some purposes – census-taking, or fairy tales in which frogs are former princes – spatio-temporal continuity with a creature born of certain parents is taken as sufficient for identifying and re-identifying who someone is.[9] But the common conception of a person is richer than this. Without having to treat her words as metaphorical, we can understand the wife who insists that her inconsiderate, apathetic sot of a husband is not the person she married. (Whether we agree with her words will depend on many considerations – including ones which experts can provide. A psychiatrist may well persuade her and us that the charming man she married always displayed traits which, if the chips were down, would reveal him to be the beast he is; so that his present character is readily relatable to his former.) Again, most of us can be brought to accept a distinction between ways in which *we* might have been different and counter-factual circumstances in which there would be no force in saying it was *we* who existed. I can readily imagine that the creature born to my parents on the day of my birth should have become an illiterate, pious hermit. I see no force in saying that *I* might have become this, for no creature having the features I consider fundamental to me could at the same time be the creature just imagined. In consequence, it is not cogent for me to consider my lack of piety, or my need for social intercourse, as fortunate (or unfortunate) excrescences on my person.[10] It does not follow, of course, that these are features which I deserve or merit. To suppose that is to commit the same error as supposing they are matters of luck: the error of divorcing the person from his fundamental characteristics. There is no person, independent of these, who could either deserve or be fortunate in these characteristics. The dichotomy of 'merit or luck' does not apply, presupposing as it does an identification of the person who could have certain things in one or other of these ways.

The effect of these considerations is twofold. By insisting that the superior child's abilities stem totally from luck, the egalitarian is passing over what, for most of us, is the crucial consideration – namely that these abilities, typically, develop on the basis of work, application, inquiry, and so on. That is what makes the child deserving. Consider how different our attitude towards the North/South system might be if the success of the successful examinees were due entirely to their having taken a certain pill the night before the exam. The egalitarian is right, of course, to say that the child did not

43

merit whatever factors were prerequisites for the initial development of his abilities. But what sane man has ever denied this (necessary) truth?[11] It must always cause suspicion when someone bases his case on a claim which no one would dream of challenging. It causes the suspicion, realized in the present case, that he has misunderstood the concepts (in our case, merit and desert) which he is decrying. The import of the second consideration, concerning personal identity, is this: it reduces what looked like an argument to a bare, unsupported statement. The egalitarian wanted to say: 'Future Northerners shouldn't benefit, since it is the merest luck that they are future Northerners.' Such a claim, if I am right, is not cogent. So all the egalitarian is saying is: people should not benefit educationally through being the intelligent, industrious, imaginative, etc., people they are. One might want to subscribe to the statement, but there should be no pretence that any cogent reason is being offered.

I now turn to consider Rawls's important point that desert always presupposes a scheme of distribution and hence cannot be used to justify any particular scheme. Deserts, in the only sense he admits, are the rewards which, within a scheme, are guaranteed to those having certain characteristics. Whether the scheme which guarantees these rewards is justified is another matter. (For him, it will be justified only if it satisfies the 'difference principle' – if, in other words, the rewards given to some rebound to the benefit of the worst-off.) This is important because, if right, it scotches an argument some would want to use in favour of the North/South system – to the effect that some children, by virtue of their abilities, should go to a superior school. His reply would be that it is only if the system contains a superior school that it can make sense to say anyone deserves to go to it. In a different system, Centre for example, in which special benefits are not on offer, there is no sense in saying anyone deserves them. (He would add, of course, that since North/South does not satisfy the 'difference principle', it and its structure of benefits is unjustified.)

Rawls's general point is, I believe, fundamentally wrong. It is surely the case, very often, that considerations of desert serve to motivate a scheme of distribution; that judgments on desert are not always relative to some particular scheme. A testator, for example, might surely use the fact that some relatives have shown disinterested care for him, while others have not, as a reason for drawing up his will in accordance with one principle of distribution (say, leave an amount to each relative proportional to the amount of care he has shown) rather than another (say, consult the runes). And he will do so on the ground that the former principle is consonant with

44

people getting what they deserve. Indeed, I suspect that there are few realistic cases where a method of distribution is hit upon with no reference to prior considerations of desert. Even where this seems to happen, it is typically because of an assumption that no one is more deserving than anyone else – which is itself a consideration of desert.

Applied to educational systems, at any rate, the point surely fails. For most Scholesians, the North/South system achieves various educational purposes, and embodies high educational standards, to a greater degree than its alternatives. Only in this system are persons rich in the educational goods listed earlier (p. 34) produced. The system was not stumbled on by chance, but adopted for the above reasons. But, and this is the crucial point, neither these purposes nor therefore the rationale for the system, are unaffected by considerations concerning the differences between the children to be educated. On the contrary, it is precisely because some children display greater ability and potential than others, that the aim of producing some highly-educated persons is feasible. And it is because some children can take maximum advantage of the superior education at North, while others cannot, which has influenced the shape of the system. Scholesians would regard it as betrayal of such children, were their intelligence and other educational virtues not nurtured and developed to the maximum. It is not, then, that the Scholesians have first decided upon a system of education and then searched for a way of allocating children to the two schools in the system, so that the question of who deserves to go where pre-supposes the system. Rather, it is the thought that intelligence, imaginativeness, application, etc., deserve special benefit which has been a major factor in determining the very existence of the system. This thought could serve as an argument for introducing the system, even if it were Centre or East/West which was actually in existence.

To be sure, anyone who is persuaded that no children should receive a privileged education is likely to express his persuasion by saying that no child deserves to be better educated than another. But it is not available to such a person to use the (presumed) absence of desert to justify abolition of the North/South system. Rather, his denial of desert will be a function of, will presuppose, his condemnation on other grounds of that system. This is parallel to the conclusion we reached in the previous sub-section, as to whether it is a system in which some benefit at the expense of others.

In the preceding pages, incidentally, I have not challenged the principle on which the egalitarian bases his criticism – the principle that one should not get what one does not deserve. But, surely, that principle can be challenged. I do not deserve my inherited property;

nor does Adonis deserve his looks. But it would probably be wrong to take my property away from me, and certainly wrong to take his looks away from Adonis. Why? Because we are entitled to such things. So even if I were to be convinced that the ordinary notion of desert does not allow us to say that future Northerners could deserve their privileges, it would still be necessary to convince me that they should not have them. For it would remain to convince me that they are not entitled to them by virtue of their abilities.[12] Certainly you could not convince me of it by appealing to the trivial and obvious consideration that they are not responsible for the prerequisites of those abilities – for, whatever the connotations of 'desert', nothing like this is connoted by 'entitlement'. You might convince me by showing that the North/South system is intolerable, and hence a system to whose benefits no one is entitled. But then you must show me why it is intolerable.

(iii) I can be more brief with the predictable charge that the North/South system is 'élitist' – for, unfortunately, our Scholesian egalitarian shows no more sign of having thought about the meaning of this term than the angry student who accosted the warden of All Souls with the challenge, 'uttered in a . . . minatory tone', 'Are you in favour of an academic élite?'[13]

'Élite' is one of many words which, in and by recent debate, have become radically (in more senses than one) debased. It is often employed, in fact, as a mere boo-word with which to label any class of people of whose advantages the speaker disapproves. If, in this sense (or lack of sense), the Northerners are an élite then of course their existence is to be condemned. But calling them an élite is merely a way of expressing the condemnation, not an argument for it. Sometimes – and only slightly less feebly – the term is applied to people who, through their talents and merit, tend to achieve more and to gravitate towards the more 'responsible' positions in society. No doubt the Northerners are an élite in this sense, but it is difficult to see why – unless one has already swallowed the egalitarian conclusions yet to be supported – the existence of an élite is something to bemoan. As the warden said in reply to the angry student,

> If . . . 'being in favour of an academic élite' . . . means
> devoting special attention and giving special encouragement,
> special opportunities, and special rewards to pupils and
> students who are endowed with unusual gifts and show promise
> of outstanding achievement, then . . . I am not against an
> academic élite but in favour of it.[14]

What our critic must provide is a sense of 'élite' which has genuine empirical content, at the same time as making readily intelligible why the existence of élites is, prima facie, undesirable. Certainly the term has in the past had something of this sense. The question would then be whether the Northerners do constitute an élite in this sense.

The term is most at home, perhaps, in the military context, where historians frequently refer to élite regiments or units in the army – the Praetorians, Napoleon's Old Guard, or the SS Leibstandarte brigade 'Adolf Hitler', for example. But it is also at home in the legal context, where one speaks of, say, QCs forming an élite in their profession; or in the political context, where a group within a party constitute a party élite. It is important that, in these paradigm examples, 'élite' is prefaced by an attributive adjective like 'military' or 'legal'. For anyone referring to persons as an élite should be able to answer the question, 'An élite what?' In these standard cases, an élite is a special group, with a distinctive purpose, belonging to a wider organization – army, legal profession, party – which itself exists for an identifiable purpose.[15]

What, beyond having a distinctive purpose such as defending the emperor, makes a military unit an élite? It must, for a start, be deemed superior in relevant respects (fighting prowess, say) to other units in the army. And it must, presumably, be relatively small. It would be peculiar to call the artillery, as a whole, an élite despite its distinctive purpose and superiority over infantry and cavalry. Next, entrants into the élite must typically possess special features going beyond prowess. Particularly important are ones of an ideological kind; the soldiers must, say, be especially patriotic, loyal to the emperor, or wedded to the ideals which are officially being fought for. Next, an élite unit will standardly enjoy special privileges and advantages – in pay, for example, or in grandeur of uniform, quality of barracks, and the like. One would expect, further, the élite unit to be insular – highly protective of its privileges, jealous of interference from officers in less exalted regiments, ritualistic in the attempt to create and maintain a special identity. And, finally, one would expect it to enjoy protection from without – from the emperor, say. Like the Old Guard at Waterloo, or the Leibstandarte in 1945, the élite unit will only be thrown into battle when all else has failed. Otherwise, indeed, the élite's life would be brief.

No doubt there are characteristic features of élites I have not mentioned; and no doubt, too, one should not expect non-military élites to display all the features listed, at least not to the same degree. But it is not unreasonable to insist that any élite must display a sufficient number of the features to a sufficient degree.[16]

I do not inquire into why the existence of élites, in something

47

like the above sense, has been criticized by so many. But it is not difficult, I think, to guess what some of the criticism would be, and for the sake of argument, I shall accept it. (But it is worth adding that two of the most famous theorists of élites – Pareto and Mannheim – positively favour them, but with qualifications. Pareto insists that the composition of an élite change frequently, lest it become ossified and hidebound by tradition; while Mannheim insists that the composition come from several social classes.)

It seems clear to me that the Northerners cannot, for all the information we as yet have, be counted an élite in the substantial sense described. Before spelling this out, it would be useful to take, by way of contrast, what is a genuine case of a student élite. I have in mind the four SS Ordensburgen schools of the Third Reich.

> The ultimate destination for the élite . . . were the
> Ordensburgen, finishing schools for the future leadership,
> endowed with the mystique . . . of medieval orders of
> chivalry. . . . [Each] accommodated a thousand students . . .
> plus 500 instructors, administrative staff and grooms . . .
> Ordensburgen graduates were intended to provide the Third
> Reich's upper echelons. . . . 'The Ordensburg opens the door
> to political leadership' (Robert Ley) . . . [they] were
> impressively equipped. Vogelsang boasted the world's largest
> gymnasium.[17]

Here we have all, or almost all, the ingredients for a student élite. Special aims (future leadership), smallness, privilege, special entry requirements (racial purity *et al.*), insularity and ritual, protection by the state, superior ability and prowess (by Nazi criteria).

The contrast with North school – or English grammar schools – is stark indeed. The Northerners are not an especially small percentage of the student population (Scholesian educators reckon that the highest standards can be maintained with an intake amounting to between 20 per cent and 30 per cent of the young). There are no special entrance requirements, beyond of course the ability to benefit from the education (which is a *sine qua non* of any system in which there is selection, whether it is a system which gives rise to élites or not). There is nothing insular, and nothing protectively ritualistic, in the outlook and behaviour of the Northerners. Outside of school hours they mix freely with other students. And while, of course, the state protects the existence of North – after all, it is a legal institution – the state is not concerned to offer special protection to the students, by guaranteeing them jobs and the like. Most important of all, the Northerners do not constitute a genuine group, united by some distinctive purpose. True, they are at school for a purpose – to be educated; but the same applies to the Southerners. Certainly there is no special career which they are being trained to enter. The only features, then, which characterize the Northerners are their superior educational ability and the advantages they enjoy in the form of a superior education. These are surely not sufficient for labelling them an élite.

If you go into a certain Scholesian bar, you will find a clientele largely composed of ex-Northerners. They are dressed very differently from one another; they include teachers, lawyers, estate agents, pilots, soldiers, and people from many other walks of life; there is little similarity in their incomes or houses; few of them know one another, and an observer would not be struck by a sense of community or camaraderie among the individuals and small groups scattered about the bar. Such an observer would be struck by the contrast between this bar and a *Ratskeller* he visited in 1942, full of Ordensburgen alumni – uniformed members of a military/political élite, ritualistically drinking in a communal clique which our observer neither would, nor could, enter.

(iv)   I shall be brief with our egalitarian's final charge – but only because some relevant considerations are deferred until later in the chapter. Rawls's fundamental argument for the 'difference principle' is that it is one which rational men, judging fairly, would choose to govern the distribution of primary goods. It is presented through the heuristic device of imagining what rational beings, hidden behind a veil of ignorance, would opt for. The 'difference principle' would be opted for since it is dictated by the rational strategy of maximin – minimize how badly-off you might end up. It is to this argument our egalitarian appeals. Since the Southerners do worse in the actual system than they would in Centre (or East/West), then rational men, unbiased by knowing their own (or their children's) educationally relevant abilities, would opt for the latter – since they (or their children) cannot do as badly in it as Southerners actually do.

Rawls's argument has come in for many criticisms in its brief career. These include challenges to the coherence of his heuristic device (can people be ignorant of just those facts Rawls makes them ignorant of?) and to its relevance (so what if the 'difference principle' would be chosen by such ignoramuses?).[18] To some of these general criticisms, I will return; but for now I want to focus on the application of his argument to the educational case in particular.

Rawls is the first to stress two important points – first, that the maximin strategy is only rational in certain circumscribed situations, and second, that the 'difference principle' is only meant to govern the distribution of the total bundle of primary goods (and is not meant to apply, for example, to the distribution of cakes at a tea-party).[19] But given these points, and the known facts about Scholesian education and society, it is far from clear that there need be anything irrational in opting for the North/South system, even for Rawlsian ignoramuses. With respect to primary goods, the sole difference between Northerners and Southerners is that the former have more of those that consist in, or are immediate consequences of, good education. These do not, recall, take the form of income, power, status, and so on. So to opt for the North/South system is not to risk coming out badly in all, or most, primary goods. Nor is the difference between North and South vast: it is not as if Southerners receive no education, or nothing but the three Rs. What the two classes of students learn and receive in common greatly exceeds the difference. So to opt for the system is not to risk coming out very badly – or even badly – in the relevant primary goods.

It becomes unclear, then, that there is anything irrational in opting for North/South, precisely because it is unclear that conditions favour maximin as the rational strategy. In what way is a man irrational who says, 'I prefer the North–South system. Admittedly my children might do worse than they could do in an alternative system – but they might do better too. Their chances are not very small, and if they fail to get to North the consequences are scarcely disastrous. South is not such a bad school; nor does going there mean low wages or anything like that'? There is, I think, only one sense in which we might say a man is unreasonable to opt for North/South. Suppose there are powerful moral reasons for condemning that system: then anyone who nevertheless opts for it is being unreasonable in the sense of not being open to persuasion by good reasons. But, in the first place, this is a very different sort of unreasonableness from that involved in failing to obey some general strategy of reason, such as maximin purports to be. Second, and more important, such a consideration is of no help to our egalitarian critic. He wishes to condemn the system on the ground that it would be irrational to opt for it; but he cannot do this if the only reason for regarding the option as irrational is that the system is condemnable.

But let us imagine rather different conditions, so as to make maximin reasoning sound more alluring. Let us imagine that Southerners do very much worse, and that the chances of getting to North are really very small. Can we now conclude that rational men, choosing fairly, must reject the North/South system? I think not. Two of Rawls's deep presuppositions, which he does little to bring to the surface, are the following: his ignoramuses must be ignorant of any ideals they may have, and they must (in a sense to be explained) be individualistic in their concerns.[20]

Suppose I have, and know that I have, a certain ideal which I wish to see actualized in my society. We may assume – and it is a realistic assumption – that actualization of this ideal is not promoted by, and is in fact incompatible with, a distribution of primary goods in accordance with the 'difference principle'. It is quite possible, too, that if my ideal is very dear to me, I shall be relatively indifferent to how things are organized, how goods are distributed, should I come to see that there is little or no chance of my ideal being achieved or approximated to. Whether I am being irrational, in my initial adherence to the ideal and in my subsequent relative indifference, will depend, presumably, on what the ideal is. It is not clear that there is anything irrational in the ideals of, say, Taoism; and given the nature of those ideals, a quietistic attitude to what happens should those ideals be hopelessly unrealizable is intelligible. So a Taoist, who knows that is what he is, need not be irrational in rejecting or being indifferent to a distribution according to the 'difference principle'.

Suppose, next, that the good I am concerned to promote is one that belongs to a collective entity – to a social class, say, or the nation as a whole. Suppose, for example, that it is power and prestige for my country which concerns me. Such a good does not distribute – not in any obvious way at least – over individuals. (The USA is more powerful than Brazil; it does not follow that the representative American is a more powerful individual than the representative Brazilian.) If such a good is my concern, and I know it to be, there is no reason why a Rawlsian distribution will appeal to me. I am not interested, or not primarily, in how goods attach to individuals. Whether promotion of the goods, like national prestige, which concern me entails a Rawlsian distribution of other goods which attach to individuals is something I may doubt, and at any rate be fairly unconcerned with. Now, whether I am being irrational will depend, surely, on the nature of the collectivist goods I am concerned to promote. That is what I meant when I said that, for Rawls to condemn as irrational a distribution that does not accord with the 'difference principle', presupposes that his choosers are individualistic in their concerns. The goods which concern them must be those which attach to individuals.

Someone will perhaps say, 'But look: if people have and know they have various ideals and collectivist aims, then no doubt there is nothing irrational in their rejection of, or indifference to, a Rawlsian distribution. But the same is true if people have and know they have certain personal advantages over others – physical strength, for example. Just as it would be unfair to let people take such personal advantages into account, so it would be unfair if they

51

are influenced by their particular ideals or collectivist aims. So it is proper to put these behind a veil of ignorance if a rational choice under conditions of fairness is to emerge.'

I shall have a fair amount to say in the following section which is pertinent to this kind of point; but one's initial reaction is that there is a considerable difference between the two sorts of ignorance – of personal advantages, and of ideals or collectivist aims. Making people ignorant of their personal advantage is required to prevent selfishness creeping into the choice of principles of distribution. Putting considerations of such advantages aside might well seem necessary if the results of our deliberations are to be respected. But stripping a man of the knowledge of what his ideals are cannot be similarly justified. There is nothing selfish in wishing to see the ideals of Taoism pursued, so we do not make a man's deliberations less selfish by inducing in him amnesia concerning his Taoist beliefs. The same can be said of various collectivist aims a man may have.

Rawls is sometimes accused of setting up his conditions of choice so as to guarantee that it is his principles which will be chosen. As it stands, this is no criticism, since it is Rawls's stated purpose to do just that. The real criticism is that some of the respects in which he makes his ignoramuses ignorant cannot be independently justified as requirements for unselfish, fair choice. Ignorance of one's non-selfish ideals is a case in point. The conclusion must be, then, that even if the North/South system incorporates a very considerable loss of primary goods for very many people, it would only be an irrational option for men who are presumed not to have certain ideals and aims which that system satisfies. Of course, the fact that it would not be an irrational option for people does not show it would be a right option. But to show it is not the right one cannot consist in pointing to its irrationality.

Each of the charges against the North/South system we have looked at in this long section share a certain feature – they are all question-begging. When terms like 'at the expense of', 'irrational', 'élite', are used in genuinely substantive ways, there is no reason to suppose that the system is one in which an undeserving élite benefits, contrary to reason, at the expense of the rest. To be sure, each of these expressions gets used in an evaluative manner, more or less devoid of solid content. When so employed, of course, the propriety of the egalitarian's descriptions of the system presupposes his hostile conclusions, and can do nothing to warrant those conclusions. Hence he has done nothing to defeat whatever prima facie case there is for that system.

3   Quality and equality

The basic case for the North/South system is (almost embarrass-
ingly) simple. It permits a closer approximation to educational
excellence than its alternatives. The quality of education to be found
there is higher. It is not so simple, however, to show that this *is* the
case in favour, that the above claims made on behalf of the system
are warranted. But if they are, then given the egalitarian's failure in
the previous section to make his charges stick, then the system's
existence is justified.

What is one to say to someone who objects as follows? 'It is true
that in North/South, some get better educated than any would
otherwise be. But, equally, some get educated worse than anyone
would be in the alternative systems canvassed. So with what right
do you say that the quality of education to be found in North/South
is higher? All you are entitled to say is that it is higher for some – but
then you should add that it is also lower for others. So you are no
more entitled to say that the quality of the system is higher than an
egalitarian is to say the same of Centre or East/West.'

One may reply that there is a perfectly good sense in which a
move from the North/South system to one of the alternatives would
not involve a rise in educational quality in the way that a move to it
would. Let us distinguish 'distributional' from 'ontological' changes
in quality. If a Harrods representative says the quality of their
sausages has risen, he might mean one of two things – that more of
the sausages are now of the standard the better ones have always
been, or that some (or all) sausages are now of a better quality than
even the best had been before. The former rise would be 'distributional', the latter 'ontological'. In the one case, a certain quality
gets more widely distributed, so that some things come to enjoy a
standard which they had not previously enjoyed; in the other case,
a new quality or standard is achieved – one which no things had
previously enjoyed. An 'ontological' rise entails a 'distributional'
one – since if a new quality is created for some things then some
things enjoy a quality they did not have before – but not vice versa.

Whether we move to or from the North/South system, there will
be a 'distributional' rise in the quality of education – since whichever move is made some people will get better educated than they
otherwise would. By the same token, either move will entail a
'distributional' fall. However, it is only the move to the North/South
system which will incorporate an 'ontological' rise in educational
quality. For the Northerners will not only be better educated than
they would otherwise have been, but better than anyone would have
been. A new and higher level of educational transformation will

53

have been created. So the claim that the quality of education in North/South is higher than in the other systems, if taken 'ontologically', is correct.

But it is clear that the defence of North/South cannot rest here; for a critic will be quick to point out that while, in the relevant sense, a higher quality of education is to be found in North/South, a lower quality is also to be found there. For if we move to that system from another, then the Southerners will not only be worse educated than they would otherwise have been, but worse than anyone would otherwise have been. So while it is only the move to North/South which produces an 'ontological' rise in quality, it is only that move which also produces an 'ontological' fall. Why, the critic will demand, should this fall not constitute as much of a case against the system as the rise constitutes a case for it? Surely the defender of the system is being arbitrary.

It is good that this challenge is made, since the real nature of the case for the North/South system emerges in the way it is handled. The way to start handling it, perhaps, is to reflect that the criterion typically employed for there being a drop in the quality of some practice is not that some are now doing worse than any before, but that the standards at the top have declined. In other words, it is a 'distributional' fall – collapse towards mediocrity – which is typically connoted by the news that quality has fallen. If English football is in decline, this is not because 4th Division clubs are playing worse than ever, but because the top teams, and the national team, are not playing as well as of yore. If one says Italian painting decayed in the eighteenth century, one means not that the worst painters were worse than ever, but that there were no Leonardos or Titians around. Those who describe the move from North/South, but not the move to it, as marking a fall in the quality and standards of education, do so with justification. For while, as we saw, there is a sense in which the move to that system will involve a fall in quality, to describe matters thus, *tout court* and without qualification, will communicate the mistaken impression that, at the top, people are now being educated worse than before.

But is it any more than a linguistic accident that 'quality has fallen' or 'standards have declined' are typically taken to describe, not a worsening situation at the bottom, but a falling away at the top? I think not. It is one piece of evidence, if evidence is needed, of a fundamental human concern in myriad areas of human practice – the concern with the attainment, in whatever field, of excellence; the concern that some should scale the heights. By calling this concern 'fundamental', I stress that it typically outweighs the lesser concern that there should be an evenly spread, general improvement in the

54

quality of a practice. The prime concern of the lover of music or athletics is not with a general, marginal improvement in the amateur playing of string quartets, or the times clocked by run-of-the-mill club runners; but with seeing the highest standards of musicianship maintained or advanced, with seeing great athletes break new barriers. Indeed, it is hard to see how otherwise he can count as a real lover of music or athletics. Where there is conflict, as there must be, between attending to excellence and attending to an evenly spread, average improvement, there is rarely a serious question as to the preferred alternative. Such a question, in fact, is hardly met with in practice – for who would suggest that resources be diverted from encouraging musical or athletic talent to making the average violinist a bit more adept or the average sprinter a bit faster? Does anyone suggest that coaches devote just the same time and energy to enthusiastic tortoises as to the Achilles on the brink of Olympic victory? Or that the only available, high-quality violin be equally available to the prodigy and to the ordinary scraper?

When a practice, like building or education, has an important effect on everybody, another concern arises – that quality should not fall below a certain minimum. We want fine buildings, but we want not to have hovels; we strive to educate some excellently, but also to ensure that no one is without an adequate education. As I explained in chapter 1 (see pp. 3ff.), there is nothing egalitarian in this latter concern. It is not with whether some housing or education is worse than some other, but with its being bad, inadequate. The egalitarian shows his stripes by a quite different concern; to the effect that any improvement in bad housing, or whatever, must not be matched by a similar improvement in housing that is already all right. The point is obvious, though apparently it gets overlooked, that X can be worse than Y without being at all bad – just as one giant can be shorter than a second without being at all short.

I do not try to adjudicate contests between these two concerns; to measure, that is, the relative weights of the demand for excellence and for an adequate minimum. For in the case that interests us, Scholesian education, there is no suggestion that, by usual Scholesian criteria, the education at South does fall below an acceptable level. (There are, of course, those who adopt criteria by which the education at South is thoroughly awful, but by these criteria so is the education at North. Such people include, no doubt, the sort of writers I discuss in chapter 4.) What I do wish to stress is that in fields of human endeavour where it is relevant to establish an adequate minimum, then once this minimum has been attained, it is the concern for excellence, for scaling heights, that becomes dominant for most of us – dominant, that is, over the desire to see an evenly spread, average improvement. It is this kind of concern that is expressed by Herman Hesse, where the speaker (the 'magister ludi') is replying to the charge that playing 'the Glass Bead Game' is of value only for the few:

> We train them to an ever higher standard of perfection. You all know that in ours as in every art there is no end to development, that each of us . . . will work away all his life at the further development, refinement, and deepening of himself and our art. . . . The existence of our élite has sometimes been denounced as a luxury . . . [but] only here is our Game played properly, and correctly, to its hilt, and with full commitment.[21]

The passage also implies the obvious inconsistency between a concentration on excellence and a concentration on average, widespread improvement – an inconsistency due both to people's varied talents and to limitations on resources. Resources and methods devoted to fostering talent cannot, at one and the same time, be employed to raise the average person's performance or ability. The same point is expressed by Nietzsche in his attack on the egalitarian 'tarantulas':

> Life wants to build itself up into the heights with pillars and steps; it wants to look into vast distances and out toward stirring beauties: therefore it requires height. And because it requires height, it requires steps and contradiction among the steps and the climbers.[22]

Actually, there is more than an empirical point involved here. It is logically possible, I suppose, that every high-jumper of tomorrow should jump as high as today's record-holder – but the effect would merely be to shift the criteria for excellence in the sport upwards. And in general it is impossible that we should see excellence in the average performance. The horizon of excellence merely recedes as average achievement reaches the point at which it was formerly assumed to be.[23]

Suppose someone says he does not have the concern I have been drawing attention to – that, for him, it is the level of mean achievement that matters. One can do better, I think, than observe that he is an unusual person; for one can doubt, if he is a man with any enthusiasms, that he means what he says. For to have an enthusiasm for music or athletics, but to be indifferent towards the attainment of excellence in these areas, is hardly intelligible. The onus is, therefore, upon one who decries the advantages required for excellence in education to display that it is education, and its goods, which command his enthusiasm; that, in Oakeshott's terminology, it is

56

education which engages him, and not an obsession with an ideology that can only frustrate it.[24] (The one enthusiasm which the man mentioned at the beginning of the paragraph can be allowed is the second-order enthusiasm for frustrating those of others – an egalitarian enthusiasm.)

It is emerging, no doubt, that I write in the tradition of those who see a prime value of education to consist in the transmission and fostering of (certain kinds of) understanding, knowledge, critical appreciation, and the like for their own sake – in the tradition of Coleridge, Newman, and T. S. Eliot. Educational excellence resides in the transmission and fostering of these goods in depth and abundance. It would seem, indeed, that the ideal that some should excel requires something like this conception of education's prime value. If that value were seen to consist in equipping people to meet society's economic needs, or in producing 'autonomous' human beings, it is unclear that such an ideal could, so to speak, get a grip – for it is unclear that men can excel at being equipped for their economic roles or in being 'autonomous'.

There is no shortage, among the writers just mentioned, of elegant passages in which the intrinsic value of knowledge, etc., is extolled. T. S. Eliot's words are typical:

> It would be a pity if we overlooked the possibility of education as a means of acquiring *wisdom*; if we belittled the acquisition of *knowledge* for the satisfaction of curiosity, without any further motive than the desire to know; and if we lost our respect for learning.[25]

It cannot be said, however, that these writers have done much by way of analysis of the ideal – that of the intrinsic value of knowledge, etc. – which they hold dear. At any rate, there are ambiguities to note, and distinctions to make, which are of some importance, and of some bearing on the case for specially advantaged education. First, the demand that education contributes the goods just mentioned is ambiguous between the demand that education pass on already existing knowledge, understanding, etc., to those who have not yet encountered it, and the demand that education help foster the discovery of new knowledge, ways of understanding, dimensions of critical appreciation, and the like. Both demands are important, and it is unfortunate perhaps that influential writers on education, with their terminology of 'transmission', 'initiation', or 'transaction', have stressed (perhaps unintentionally) the former at the expense of the latter. For it is surely a criterion of an excellent education that among those who receive it, some will proceed to the discovery of new ideas, to creative innovations, to the advancement of knowledge. Numbering such men as Hölderlin, Herwegh, and Hesse among its alumni must create at least a presumption in favour of a school's, the famous Maulbronn Kloster's, excellence.

Second, there is, I think, a distinction – very obscure, I am afraid – to be made between the value that knowledge has *for* the person who discovers it or is 'initiated' into it, and the value it has independent of anyone's grasping it. The existence of true rather than false theories, for example, seems to me a good, which is not to be fully analysed in terms of the value *for* people of believing what is true. If the value of knowledge consisted solely in its value for the knowers – in the ways in which it sharpens critical powers, deepens perspectives, or broadens understanding – it is unclear why it should have to be genuine knowledge. For surely beliefs which are in fact false, 'knowledge' which is only so-called, could produce just the same benefits for people.[26] Good, but ultimately mistaken, theories can do as much by way of sharpening, deepening, and broadening as ones which are true. Yet most of us, I suspect, would want to agree with G. E. Moore that there is an additional good when the theories are true.[27] I cannot afford the time, I fear, to make this point, which will strike some as merely mystical, more persuasive.

The effect of the two points, I think, is to strengthen the case for advantaged schooling, like that at North. In fact, I take it as certain that, whatever the possibilities for a very widespread transmission of knowledge, etc., in some depth and abundance, the fostering and nurture of the ability to discover and to innovate requires specially advantageous conditions. So to the extent that this is a value, it must run counter to the value of focusing on an evenly spread, average improvement in education. The obscure implication of the obscure point about the value that genuine knowledge, etc., has independent of its value for people is somewhat as follows. It is the fact that knowledge, etc., does have a value for people that makes the question of its distribution a genuine one. But the additional good that resides in its being genuine knowledge, in the truth of theories, for example, is not a good of which it makes sense to ask, 'How shall it be distributed?' The only relevant question for someone with this good in mind can be, 'How do we best promote genuine knowledge and truth?' And if the answer to that is – as it surely is – that it requires some to be excellently educated, then it will not be to the point to complain that something valuable, a good, is not being generally and evenly enjoyed. That complaint is only relevant when the value in question is the one that knowledge, etc., has for people.

I want to end by considering Rawls's objections to what he calls

58

'perfectionism', which has enough in common with the concern for excellence for the objections to be pertinent. They are related, fairly clearly, to the last of the Scholesian egalitarian's charges discussed in the previous section. Perfectionism is the principle 'directing society to arrange institutions and to define the duties and obligations of individuals so as to maximize the achievement of human excellence in art, science, and culture'.[28] How perfectionist someone is will depend on the extent to which he is willing to sacrifice other desiderata to these ends. He is very perfectionist, for example, if he is willing to tolerate slavery for the sake of the Parthenon, Plato's *Dialogues*, and the tragedies of Sophocles. Rawls is hostile to the principle even in its mildest form; for example, he condemns 'subsidizing universities, . . . opera and the theater, on the grounds that these institutions are intrinsically valuable'.[29]

At a first reading, however, it is not entirely clear what the scope of Rawls's hostility is. The subsidies examples, as well as the wording in his definition of perfectionism, suggest that he is objecting, solely, to the allocation of public resources – by government, local councils, etc. – for perfectionist purposes. And his main objection to the principle, to be discussed in a moment, confirms this impression. But, if so, what is his attitude towards a distribution of goods for perfectionist purposes that has arisen, not through public policy or central institutions, but as a result of voluntary acts by individuals – of donations, private patronage, or covenants? The question is especially important when education is under discussion; for while it is clear that Rawls must object to the public subsidy of advantaged schools (unless this rebounds to the advantage of the worst-off), it is not clear what he should say about specially advantaged schools which are privately supported – about independent schools. Clearly it does not follow from the claim that there should not be favoured state schools that there should not be favoured schools at all.

Rawls's attitude, however, does emerge in one paragraph in the relevant chapter. While individuals may employ their resources for perfectionist purposes, this must all occur 'within a regime regulated by the two principles of justice'.[30] This must mean, I think, that if individuals so use their resources that the resulting distribution does not satisfy the 'difference principle', then this is intolerable. If this is his position, then Rawls must in consequence be opposed to any large-scale pursuit of perfection by individuals – for it is surely the case that such a pursuit generally, and certainly in education, results in a distribution which does not satisfy the 'difference principle'. The headmaster of the Yehudi Menuhin school recently thanked the Friends of the School for their financial help without which the highly favoured position of the pupils could not be maintained. It is quite clear that this help is incompatible with what the 'difference principle' requires of the distribution of wealth among schools.

Although this is Rawls's attitude, it is important to stress that his chapter is specifically devoted to attacking the public pursuit of perfection. And the main argument he deploys will succeed, if at all, only against this. (I return to the question of 'private perfectionism' in the appendix on independent schools.) The main objection is that 'in view of their disparate aims the parties have no reason to adopt the principle of perfection given the conditions of the original position'[31] (the original position, of course, includes the veil of ignorance). The point is this: people do not agree on the fields in which excellence is to be pursued, hence the pursuit of it in some fields but not others will constitute an intolerable denial of the wishes and liberty of those who would have preferred to see it pursued in the neglected fields. It is an intolerable imposition on philistine football fanatics if goods are taken from them to support advancement in the arts – just as the reverse policy would be unfair on the aesthetes. The first principle of justice, that of maximum equal liberty, requires that men be equally free and able to pursue excellence in the various fields which attract them – provided, of course, that the results of such pursuits do not fall foul of the distributions demanded by the 'difference principle'. Given this, then the initial choosers, ignorant of what their favoured pursuits are, will not opt for a situation in which they risk having these pursuits ignored in favour of others. They will not, if rational, opt for a perfectionist set-up.

I make three remarks (four, if you include the appendix on private schools). First: Rawls's argument is unpalatably relativistic. He writes as one who is a mere observer of men and their ideals, and not as one who is committed, who possesses certain ideals. To be sure, from the standpoint of a neutral observer, there can be no reason why some men's aims should be pursued at the expense of others. Precisely because he is without any commitments, it can only seem unfair, arbitrary, that excellence in one field is promoted over that in others. But why should the way things would appear to such a neutral observer be relevant to the attitude of one who *has* commitments and ideals? Of course, if the latter is ignorant of what these commitments and ideals of his are, then his position will be like that of the neutral observer: trivially, he will be unable to see any particular pursuit as more deserving of favour than another. But I have already discussed the impropriety of making men ignorant in this respect. A man with an ideal has a conception of how things ought to be; and he cannot abdicate that conception merely through the reflection that others may have differing conceptions. After all, an ideal – like that of excellence in education – is not a taste. He cannot see it as something which, through some whim, he happens to indulge in, and therefore as something on a par with the other tastes which men with different whims indulge in. The mere thought that, had my taste-buds been different, so would my taste in cakes, might suffice to prevent me imposing my particular taste on all my visitors. But the thought that I might not have been committed to excellence in education can do no more to make me absolutely tolerant of those who oppose such a commitment, than the thought that I might not have objected to murder can make me tolerant of murderers. Given this commitment, I cannot be tolerant of shifting resources away from education into staging ever grander fireworks displays or whatever. This does not make me a bigot, or 'intolerant' in a pejorative sense. It merely restates that I am committed to an ideal of excellence.

Second: educational excellence is a precondition for, or an important contributing factor towards, excellence in many of the fields where excellence concerns men. This becomes the more true as more and more practices – photography, for example, or even some sports – 'go scientific' and come under the wing of formal education. This means there can be agreement on the value of excellence in education among men who are otherwise disunited as to the fields in which perfection is to be the aim. The distinct possibility arises, therefore, that Rawlsian ignoramuses could agree on a perfectionist allocation of resources towards achieving educational excellence. All they need know is that, whatever other perfections they may desire, educational excellence is likely to be a prerequisite. (And this kind of general fact Rawls does allow his choosers to know.) No doubt the agreement on educational excellence could mask considerable differences over what such excellence consists in, on the shape education is to take, but it is nevertheless considerably greater than any agreement Rawls imagines emerging.

Moreover – and this is the third point – it will not follow from the plurality of conceptions of educational excellence that only one of these can be catered for. There is no reason why different schools, or different segments within one school, should not, in intention anyway, embody various such conceptions. The British system, for example, has managed to live with such disparate, but admired, institutions as Summerhill and Winchester, Dartington Hall and Manchester GS, and Oxford and the LSE. The battle between different conceptions of excellence in education is not like that between, say, free traders and autarkists, in which there can only

61

be one victor. So it should not be thought, as readily as Rawls seems to have done, that where there are 'disparate aims' the pursuit of any one must unfairly exclude the pursuit of the rest.

There emerges from this final point a positive consideration in the non-egalitarian's favour. Any egalitarian who can be taken seriously must desire not equality at any level, but equality at the highest level possible. But how does he identify the level which all are to be brought to? How does he tell which is the highest quality education that each may enjoy? Typically we identify what it is feasible for most to strive towards by first seeing some actually attain it. Yesterday's successes by the few set tomorrow's goals for the many. But such successes typically require not only that there be privileged, advantaged circumstances, but that there be a variety of these. In education as elsewhere, competition among different methods and projects may be the best breeding-ground for success. Not only, then, can various conceptions of educational excellence coexist, but this variety should be welcomed. In particular, it should be welcomed by those with an eye on a long-run, evenly spread improvement in education – for, to repeat, it is through favouring this variety that the goals to be set, if such an improvement is to occur, will be identified and tested.[32]

3   Education, equality, and society

The preceding chapter was a defence of a selective, mixed quality system of education. None of the egalitarian arguments considered were able to defeat the presumption – shown to be justified – that more able children receive a preferred education. The system described in that chapter, however, was an artificially simple one, from which many 'real-life' features had been abstracted. The question to be considered now is the following: is the provisional verdict reached so far vitiated once these 'real-life' factors are brought into play? Does egalitarianism gain a new strength once these factors are introduced?

To judge from contemporary debate, the most important of the features missing from Scholesia are ones of a broadly economic sort. In Britain, at any rate, it seems to be factors pertaining to social class which figure most prominently in debate. If 'economic' refers, *inter alia*, to kinds of work done (e.g. manual), as well as to income, then the notion of a social class is, usually at least, a primarily economic one. In the USA, it is a different social factor – race – which, perhaps, dominates debates to the greatest extent. But I shall give little separate attention to this, partly because my focus will be more on the British scene, and partly because it is economic factors that play a considerable role in the problems posed by racial differences.

There are, I think, three main socio-economic respects in which, it would be urged, Scholesia was unrealistic. First, it is not the case in reality that a child's going to one school rather than another is unaffected by his socio-economic background – and in particular, by the social position of his parents. Second, in the real world, of course, the type of schooling a person gets does strongly influence his own future socio-economic position. And, third, it is not usually the case, in actual societies, that where there is mixed quality school-ing, the different schools (or 'streams') are 'socially mixed': on the contrary, children from a particular kind of socio-economic background tend to be heavily concentrated in certain schools or 'streams'.

Each of these factors has been taken, by egalitarians, to vitiate whatever case there might otherwise be for selective, mixed quality schooling. Those who stress the first two factors are wont to invoke the slogan of 'equal educational opportunities', and to insist that this principle is doubly betrayed when there is educational inequality (in the sense of the previous chapter). Those who focus on the third factor are more prone to appeal to 'fraternity' or 'democracy' in their argument for educational equality.

It will be convenient, at certain points, to retain the terminology of North, South, and Centre: but we are now to think of Scholesia as incorporating the 'real-life' features just mentioned. Hence, the North/South system becomes a more convincing metaphor for actual systems (e.g. the post-1944 system) in which there is selective, mixed quality education; while Centre becomes a more convincing metaphor for actual systems (e.g. 'unstreamed' comprehensives) where differences in educational quality do not exceed those permitted by the 'difference principle'.

1 Selection

Although the bulk of this chapter will concern the impact of socio-economic factors, I begin by discussing a quite different one, from which we also abstracted in the original Scholesian model. We there assumed the existence of a test which, with complete accuracy, allocated to North just those children most able to benefit from going there. Had some clerical error resulted in Jack going to North while the more able Jill went to South, then although Jack might then be more educationally transformed than Jill, he will not be as transformed as Jill would have been had she gone (as she should have done) to North instead of South.

In the real world, of course, we do not find such accurate tests and predictors. A common complaint against the 11-plus was that some children who failed it were of equal or greater educational potential than some who passed it. It is important, here, that this complaint be distinguished from a number of others. It is not relevant, at this stage, to consider the complaint that 11-plus 'favoured' middle-class children. That is a point about the direction in which alleged errors tended, and goes beyond the complaint that the test was prone to error. Nor is it relevant, here, to attend to the radical charge that 11-plus failed to test educational potential at all, but only the potential to do well in what bourgeois teachers label 'education'. Such objections will be considered, indirectly at least, later on in this chapter and the following one.

There are, of course, many well-known difficulties in assessing

64

the accuracy of an educational selection procedure. Most famous of all, perhaps, is the degree to which such procedures are self-verifying; and certainly 11-plus and the like serve not merely to predict, but to influence, future performance. It is, I should think, easy to exaggerate the importance of the self-verifying mechanism to which attention is most often drawn – the so-called 'stigma' or 'labelling' factor. Tell a child he has failed, and that will encourage him to continue to fail – or so the story goes. A more important aspect of self-verification is the tendency to adjust the level of future performance expected to the nature of the intake determined by the selection procedure. One will not, on the whole, pitch standards so high that too many of those who passed the test fall below them, nor pitch them so low that too many of those who failed soar above them. One is therefore unlikely to get in the position of saying that a selection procedure is hopelessly inaccurate on the ground that very many 'passes' later did badly while very many 'fails' later did marvellously.

Another difficulty is this: by the time children who have been divided by the selection have their abilities reassessed (at 'O' level, say), too many factors have intervened for the later performance to count as a sure guide to the accuracy of the original predictions. If a child's later failure is the result of family difficulties, chronic acne, or an unforeseeable obsession with football, his performance is no adverse reflection on the selection criteria.

These are but two of the many difficulties in assessing a selection procedure. Given such difficulties, the question arises as to how we are in a position to judge, as we generally do, that such procedures are, to a degree, inaccurate. The basis, it seems to me, is largely rough and ready, and intuitive. Teachers at one type of school will sometimes notice the child who displays an enthusiasm and talent for the more demanding work he would have been encountering, as staple diet, had he gone to an academically superior school. The reasonable guess is then made that, for each such child who is noticed, there are others who would have displayed the enthusiasm and talent if they had actually gone to the more demanding school. The child who is noticed is one whose enthusiasm and talent shows through despite the relatively unfavourable scholastic context. There are surely others whose qualities remain latent because of this context.

If this point is taken to be a criticism of selection, it will be no reply to it to stress that, in a properly organized system, there will be adequate machinery for transferring the 'late developers' where they belong. Of course there should be such machinery, but the problem being raised does not concern the children whose abilities get noticed, but those whose abilities remain latent. Clearly there can be no machinery for correcting undetected mistakes.

Nevertheless, I cannot see that the criticism is sufficiently powerful to suggest, by itself, that selection and, with it, mixed quality education, be scrapped. T. S. Eliot sardonically refers to this criticism as the 'undiscovered Milton' objection.[1] A method of selection, the objection goes, is intolerable if, among those who are selected for inferior education, are children whose hidden abilities would have flourished had they gone to a superior school. (Actually, the objection requires something stronger: namely that these abilities would have flourished at least as much as those of some (most ?) children who are actually at the superior school.)

The weakness in the argument is that it invites an immediate, parallel counter-argument, which we might dub the 'undiscovered Simple Simon' argument. Undiscovered Simple Simons are those children who do well at more demanding schools, but whose abilities would have remained thoroughly hidden, or would have atrophied, had they gone to a less demanding school. There is no reason I can think of to suppose there are fewer undiscovered Simple Simons than undiscovered Miltons. It was presupposed by the original argument, after all, that there are children whose abilities will only show under relatively favourable conditions. This must suggest that there are children whose detected talents would have remained buried under conditions less favourable than those they actually enjoy. It would be unwarrantedly optimistic to think that favourable conditions are usually sufficient – but not necessary – for bringing out abilities; for supposing, that is, that favourable conditions would bring out hidden abilities while unfavourable ones would not suppress detected ones.

Nor can I see any reason why a case for Centre, based on undiscovered Miltons, is not completely balanced by a case against, based on undiscovered Simple Simons. Let us grant that, if Centre came into being, the abilities of some of those who would otherwise have gone to South will unexpectedly flourish. But we must surely grant, alongside this, that the abilities of some of those who would otherwise have gone to North will unexpectedly atrophy. If so, I cannot see that the balance works out in Centre's favour. (Perhaps I should stress that Centre is, as before, assumed to be educationally superior to South but inferior to North. Without this assumption, egalitarian considerations would not even be relevant. They could add nothing to the already overwhelming case for Centre if that school were better than both the others, and nothing to counter the already overwhelming case against it if it were worse than both the others.)

2   A slogan – and its perversions

Two of the socio-economic considerations which, some urge, should make us reverse our provisional approval of North/South were these: socio-economic position influences which school a child will attend, and is in turn influenced by that. Before I tackle the import of these considerations directly, in section 3, I want to say something about a slogan which is bound to be heard whenever such matters are discussed – that of 'equal educational opportunities'. The rough idea seems to be that when factors like those mentioned obtain, the system is one of unequal opportunities, and hence intolerable.

Our interest is the connection between equal opportunities and educational equality as understood in the last chapter. What sort of case, if any, can be made against a system like North/South on grounds of equal educational opportunities? My answer will be that the notion of equal educational opportunities is in too much of a mess, frankly, for it to make any useful contribution to the discussion. We shall be better-off directly tackling the question of whether the socio-economic factors mentioned vitiate the case for selective, mixed quality schooling, and by-passing the question of whether these factors make for unequal opportunities. The mess, I believe, is due partly to a serious ambiguity in the slogan, partly to various perversions it has undergone in the hands of egalitarians, and partly to the fact that the notion of opportunities has become irretrievably 'value-loaded'. I hope to spell all of this out.

Doubts about the clarity of the slogan set in as soon as one reflects on the simultaneous existence of two fashionable, but countervailing, views on the connection between equal opportunities and equality of whatever opportunities are for (especially the 'levelling' equalities of chapter 1, as well as educational equality). One tendency is to pit them against one another – to see the pursuit of equal opportunities as incompatible with 'true' egalitarianism.[2] This tendency is found among egalitarians and their opponents alike; but whereas the former like to see the demand for equal opportunities as a thinly disguised apologia for the continuing existence of important inequalities, the latter prefer to see the demand for 'levelling' equalities as a bastard and deformed son of the only sensible demand – that for equality of opportunities. But there is a growing and opposed tendency to suppose that equality of opportunities requires equalities of a 'levelling' sort; to suppose that, unless outcomes are pretty much equal, then there cannot have been equal opportunities. At its crudest, this tendency is reflected in attempts (soon to be encountered) to define 'equal opportunities' in terms of similar outcomes.

For such discrepant tendencies to arise, the notion of equal opportunities must be a pretty murky one. One difficulty, of course, is of a sort already encountered – that of specifying respects. When do people have an equal opportunity to take a holiday in Spain? Well, consider the following quartet: a very poor Englishman, an astronaut on the job, a Spanish political exile, and someone too late with his holiday booking. It is senseless to ask of these people whether they have the same opportunity unless a relevant respect is specified. None except the exile are legally prevented from going; none except the astronaut are geographically excluded; none but the poor man are financially prevented; none but the latecomer are prevented by the over-popularity of Spanish resorts. Since opportunities exist, roughly speaking, when preventing, interfering factors do not, then the various members in the quartet share opportunities in some respects but not others. For example, three of them have the legal opportunity, but those three do not all have the physical opportunity. I shall return to this kind of difficulty later. I want, first, to concentrate on some others.

Place an adjective before 'opportunities' and a syntactical ambiguity is typically created. An F-ish opportunity may be one for something F-ish, or it may be one deriving from something F-ish. A man's financial opportunities, for instance, may be those he has for obtaining finance, or those he has by virtue of his finances. Educational opportunities may be ones for education, or ones provided by education. Let us refer to the 'access' and 'provision' senses. This ambiguity creates one in the slogan 'equal educational opportunities'. When the Forster Act is said to have promoted equal educational opportunities, it is the 'access' sense which is on show – for what that Act did was to remove obstacles in the way of primary education. Whereas it is a version of the 'provision' sense which is on offer when Floud, Halsey, and Martin define 'equality of educational opportunity' as 'equality of economic and social opportunity through education in a secondary school'.[3]

It is important to stress how independent these senses are, for it is clearly possible for a policy to equalize opportunities in the one sense while making them less equal in the other. By increasing the percentage of blacks able to enter certain professions, quotas for blacks in universities will make opportunities more equal, across races, in the 'provision' sense; but by discriminating against white students these quotas clearly contradict, in an important respect, the principle of equal opportunities in the 'access' sense.

Syntax surely favours the 'access' reading as the more natural – and so does history. The demand for equal educational opportunities, originally, was the demand that various obstacles in the way

68

of education be removed – one's religious beliefs, for example. No doubt it is regrettable that this did not remain the only sense. Aside from the fact that it is permitted by syntax, I imagine two factors account for the currency of the other, 'provision' sense. A crucial element influencing access to education at any but the earliest stage is the student's earlier education. Good preparatory schools win lots of scholarships to good public schools which in turn win lots of scholarships to Oxbridge. Any discussion of opportunities for education is therefore bound to involve a discussion of the opportunities provided by (earlier) education. The habit is thereby acquired of talking about opportunities in terms of what is provided by education – a habit which persists even when these opportunities are no longer ones for yet further education. Educational opportunities then get understood in terms of the social and economic prospects which the latter stages of education provide.

The other process is rather less savoury. It was an undoubted tenet of faith among those, like Tawney, who earlier insisted on various policies in the name of equal opportunity, that by widening working-class access to education a massive boost would be given to the socio-economic prospects of working-class children. Rightly or not, the impression has grown that no such massive change has been wrought. Rather than concede that equalizing opportunities can fail to achieve such a change, a common radical reaction has been to insist that the policies earlier advocated – direct grants, for example – do little or nothing to make opportunities more equal; to insist, that is, that a policy is only affecting a 'real' equalization of opportunities if it considerably boosts the economic prospects of the worse-off. It is not unusual to find that an emotive slogan has its meaning altered instead of being scrapped when the policies based upon it fail to meet expectations.

Whatever the historical origins of the ambiguity, it surely goes a long way in accounting for the existence of the two countervailing tendencies noted earlier – that of pitting equality of opportunity against 'levelling' equality, and that of seeing the former as requiring the latter. For to stress equality of access in education is to presuppose the existence of differences in education and its equality. Reference to opportunities for an education of a certain sort would be idle if it is an education that everyone is bound to get anyway. The more, on the other hand, one stresses the provision of equal socio-economic opportunities through education the more likely are people to advocate educational equality as an alleged prerequisite in this process.

These remarks need some qualifications, however. First, it would be misleading to portray the educational egalitarian as opposed to

69

equality of opportunity in the 'access' sense. What he opposes is
what is presupposed by policies for equalizing – or, come to that,
unequalizing – opportunities, namely qualitative differences in
education. Second, it is quite possible for someone to base his case
for educational equality – for Centre, say – on grounds of equal
opportunities in the 'access' sense. Such a person, of course, cannot
look on Centre as embodying (in a non-trivial way) equality of
opportunities, any more than he can look on the graveyard as
embodying the equal opportunity to some day die. His point, rather,
may be this: North/South would be justifiable if, and only if,
children had equal opportunities to get to North. Since, he argues,
they do not and cannot, then Centre is to be preferred. So it would
be a mistake to think that those who pit the notions of equality of
opportunities and educational equality against one another cannot,
nevertheless, base a case against North/South on the former notion.
People who do so, of course, must be distinguished from the breed
of egalitarian met in the last chapter, for whom the inequalities were
to be condemned irrespective of equality of access.

It would be misleading, too, to think that the demand for more
equal opportunities in the 'provision' sense carries with it an automatic commitment to educational equality. Indeed, those most keen
to use education as a means for increasing equality of socio-
economic prospects favour so-called 'reverse discrimination', or
more euphemistically 'positive inequality', or more euphemistically
still 'affirmative action'. Such people will no doubt prefer Centre
to North/South, but nicest of all would be a system in which those
who would otherwise be least likely to succeed in the outside world
have their 'life-chances' massively boosted by preferential
education.

The ambiguity discussed constitutes a serious impediment to a
clear use of the slogan of 'equal educational opportunities' in serious
discussion. Different people mean different things by it, and there is
continual, unannounced criss-crossing of senses. But there is worse
to come. Both senses lend themselves to perversions which, in recent
years, social scientists – and those they manage to persuade – have
not been shy to practise.

Both perversions are conveniently illustrated in a single passage
on p.1 of the editors' introduction to a collection of essays on the
Coleman report (entitled *Equal Educational Opportunity*):[4] ' "equal
educational opportunity" is meaningless for a large number of
American schoolchildren. Recent social science research supports
this contention, revealing huge gaps in educational achievement
between racial groups and social classes'. The two perversions are
those of (a) taking achievement as the measure of opportunity, and

70

(b) taking equality as a relation between social classes (or racial groups). It is surely obvious, once pointed out (which it rarely is by egalitarians), that differences in achievement do not in themselves imply anything about differences in opportunities, however liberally that word is used. And it is scarcely less obvious that by evening out opportunities across classes or groups it does not follow that individuals' opportunities have been equalized in the slightest degree. (To suppose it did follow would be like thinking that you reduce differences in people's weights by moving fat people into a town full of thin people so that the weight of the average resident in that town becomes more like the weight of the average man in the country as a whole.)

Let us first of all focus on (b). People have become so habituated to discussing equality of opportunity as equality across classes that the identification is more often implicit than otherwise. A writer who raises the question of the extent of inequality of opportunity will typically proceed, without further ado, to those familiar figures showing how few working-class children go to Eton, how many middle-class children go to grammar schools, and so on. Even if we assume such figures show anything about opportunities, the assumption that equalizing opportunities is a matter of evening them out across classes is an extraordinary one. Suppose North's admissions policy was changed, so that henceforward only those whose names begin with 'A' can go there. Presumably no social class will now be significantly over- or under-represented at North – but it would be ludicrous to suppose people now have an equal opportunity to go there. Or suppose a college opens its gates, free of charge, to anyone who wishes to study there. This would surely mark a significant equalization, in several respects, of the opportunity to attend that college; and it would do so even if, as a result, the student body became more predominantly middle-class or white (or working-class or black) than before.

One would not want to deny that some opportunities may be heavily concentrated among people belonging to a particular class, so that, as a matter of fact, equalizing people's opportunities will tend to even things out across classes. But it remains absurd to identify the equalizing with this evening out. It must be a contingent truth, at best, that an unequal distribution of opportunities is unfavourable for children from a certain social class – rather than children with a particular name, from a certain location, of a particular religious background, political colour, skin colour, height, temperament, or whatever. The perverse identification in question has several pernicious consequences – for instance, the tendency to ignore differences within social classes which, in the case of some

71

opportunities, would surely be greater than differences between classes; or a myopic dismissal of factors other than social class which affect differences in people's opportunities. Worst of all, perhaps, is the impression which gets created that everything would be all right if only members of one class did not, generally, enjoy more opportunities than members of another – even if this result can only be brought about by taking away opportunities from those who have them. This would indeed be a perversion of the slogan, for in its heyday that slogan was a demand for removing obstacles, not for removing opportunities, so as to get equality.[5]

If defining 'equal opportunities' in terms of differences between social classes is the pathological version of the 'access' sense, then understanding the expression in terms of achievement is the pathological version of the 'provision' sense. This is the preferred way of understanding the slogan in the Coleman report – whose 600 or so pages, therefore, are not about what they are advertised to be about. Coleman, in fact, offers us two definitions in terms of achievement. The weaker one defines 'equal educational opportunity' as 'equality of results, given the same individual input', while the stronger one defines it as 'equality of results, given different individual inputs'.[6] This is mere, and bad, stipulation; for however vague 'equal educational opportunity' may be, it cannot bear either of the senses provided by Coleman. This follows immediately from the simple reflection that results are influenced by plenty of factors other than opportunities – by ability, luck, and the desire to make use of opportunities, for example.

Notice that Coleman's definitions go well beyond the (already suspicious) 'provision' sense – according to which equal educational opportunity requires progress, through education, towards socio-economic opportunities. Clearly progress towards that goal does not necessarily involve equalizing educational achievements. Some people object to private schools on the grounds that their alumni are unfairly advantaged in the job market – in which case, getting rid of them will help equalize opportunities in the 'provision' sense. Nothing is implied about equality of educational achievement: for all I know abolition of private schools would produce wider differentials in results. Again, it must remain a contingent truth, at most, that policies which would equalize socio-economic opportunities through education would do so through equalizing educational achievement.

Coleman does in fact have an argument, feeble though it is, for understanding 'equal educational opportunity' in terms of equal achievement:

Suppose the early schools had operated for only one hour a week and had been attended by children of all social classes. This would have met the explicit assumptions of the early concept of equality of opportunity since the school is free, with a common curriculum, and attended by all children in the locality. But it obviously would not have been accepted, even at that time, as providing equality of opportunity, because its effects would have been so minimal . . . [and] additional educational resources . . . would have created severe inequalities in results.[7]

Let us by-pass the fact that the argument begs the question, since it takes 'severe inequalities in results' as the mark of unequal opportunities; as well as the fact that it is far from obvious that the system imagined is one where opportunities are unequal (after all, we have not been told – and are never told – what opportunities are). The most the argument can show – if we grant that the system imagined is not one of equal opportunities – is that equality of opportunities requires a good deal more than free, universal schooling in a common curriculum. There are any number of factors, other than lack of money or physical distance, which can provide obstacles in the way of getting or benefiting from schooling. Equalizing opportunities may well require that these obstacles are removed. But this has nothing to do with results being equalized. Even if, as a consequence of removing the various obstacles, differentials in achievement were reduced, it is not this consequence – but the removal of the obstacles – which makes it legitimate to speak of opportunities having been made more equal. (It is surely worth stressing that the least serious objection to the system Coleman imagines is that it contains inequalities. What is wrong with it is that many children do not get decently educated – and what is wrong with that is what it says, not the fact that some get less well-educated than others!)

It is surely not feeble justifications such as Coleman's which account for the perversions. Indeed, when they are put together to form one grand perversion – so that 'equality of educational opportunity' becomes defined as 'comparable educational achievement on the part of minority and majority groups (or social classes)'[8] – the motivation becomes very clear. It is patently ideological. The honoured banner of equal opportunities has been seized, and is being waved, by those whose objective it is to eradicate all (and perhaps only) those differences among men which correlate with social class or ethnic membership. The seizure is understandable: nearly everyone wants what they call 'equal opportunities', so

73

to label one's objective with that slogan is to confer upon it a veneer of almost universal respectability. It is not my purpose, for the moment at least, to pass comment on that objective which the slogan, through its perversions, now thinly disguises. It is, rather, to stress that because of these perversions the slogan has become virtually unusable in serious debate. Too many have been successfully persuaded by 'persuasive definitions', like Coleman's, for there to be any safety in invoking it.

I have so far said almost as little on what do or should count as educational opportunities as those who go about clamouring against various systems on the grounds that they do not equalize whatever they are which are supposed to count as opportunities. In none of the articles in the Harvard collection on *Equal Educational Opportunity* does an author pause to distinguish opportunities from, *inter alia*, abilities, capacities, strokes of fortune, taking advantage of one's opportunities, or wishing to do what one has an opportunity to do. Clearly the non-performance or non-achievement of X could be due to any one of these latter factors being missing, rather than to lack of opportunity to do X. In most discussions of which I am aware, moreover, an earlier point I drew attention to is completely overlooked – the point that it is idle to ask what opportunities someone has independent of a context, of a specification of respects. This was the point made in the example of the holiday in Spain (p. 68). It applies, naturally, to education as much as to anything else. Whether a child now has an opportunity he previously lacked to study physics depends on context. In one context, the fact that he is now allowed to study physics will be relevant, while the fact that he does not have an adequate background in mathematics will not. In another context, the order of relevance may be reversed.

I shall not pursue these matters further, and will not, therefore, have much recourse to the notion of opportunities in following sections – for I would not wish to be numbered among those who steam ahead with the notion without doing anything to explain it. The reason I shall not pursue matters is that the notion of opportunities has become too irretrievably 'value-loaded' for a serious, neutral analysis of it to be of more than Laputan irrelevance. While it would be possible to provide such an analysis, which made the sort of distinctions I just made, for instance, the attempt to then employ the notion in accordance with that analysis would, I am sure, be overwhelmed by the irreversible tendency of people to use the term 'opportunities' to reflect their moral and ideological stances. Disagreements about the opportunities, and the degree of their equality, to be found in North/South would, at a fair guess, merely reflect moral or ideological rivalry over the system, and not be substantive differences serving in any way to explain why there is that rivalry. (Rather as a person's willingness (unwillingness) to call the National Front a 'Nazi' organization reflects, rather than accounts for, his antipathy (tolerance) towards that organization.) If so, one will not get very far in discussing the pros and cons of that system by first trying to settle questions about the opportunities found in it.

That nearly everyone unhesitatingly claims to want opportunities in education to grow is only explicable if they are using the term 'opportunity' in a strongly evaluative way. For if 'opportunity' were being used in a neutral way, it is not difficult to think of any number of opportunities which no one could want to see extended. Children have a golden opportunity to pass exams if invigilated by senile, blind teachers – no one, I take it, advocates a growth in this opportunity. The expression, these days, appears to denote the absence of whatever factors, in the speaker's view, ought not to influence achievement and results. In the slogan 'equal educational opportunities', the expression gets used to refer to whatever it is that the speaker wants to see equalized. How else does one account for the claim, made by a 'Rank and File' author, that only when everyone actually receives a university education will there be equality of educational opportunity?[9] Someone who finds it intolerable that access to a certain school should be influenced by how well-educated a child's parents are is more than likely to express himself by saying that children do not have an equal opportunity to get to this school: whereas someone who finds it perfectly reasonable, and tolerable, that a child should benefit from his parents' knowledge, is less likely to describe matters in that way. He is more likely to tie the existence of equal opportunities to the existence or otherwise of legal, or institutional, barriers to access. No doubt one could press the question of whether, in the light of a sober, neutral analysis, the fact that one's parents are very well-educated gives one, in itself, an opportunity that others lack. But to press the question would misconstrue the nature of the issue which divides the parties in the argument – the issue, namely, of whether it is tolerable that there should be mixed quality schooling in which selection favours children with well-educated parents. Better, then, to tackle that issue directly – circumventing the question of whether such a system, tolerable or otherwise, is one in which opportunities are, *ipso facto*, unequal. Given the ambiguity of the slogan, the perversions performed on it, and the irreversible tendency for 'opportunity' to become a mere value-word, we shall surely be advised to ignore word and slogan in what follows.

75

3 'The cycle of inequality'

There exists a legion of familiar figures which, in countless tracts
and tomes, are dragooned in order to demonstrate the connections
between socio-economic and educational factors mentioned at the
beginning of the chapter. Such figures are often said to display a
'cycle of inequality', in which education serves as the hub about
which it revolves. Here are some examples: in 1973, apparently, 59
per cent of children at grammar school came from 'white-collar'
homes, although children from these homes constitute only 38 per
cent of the relevant population; according to UCCA in 1968–9, only
28 per cent of university students were sons or daughters of manual
workers, although 60 per cent of the working population were in
manual jobs; according to the 1973 *General Household Survey*, 59 per
cent of secondary modern alumni earned less than £1,500 and only
0.8 per cent of them earned over £3,000 – while the corresponding
figures for degree-holders were 11.1 per cent and 33.3 per cent
respectively.

But what exactly is supposed to be wrong with what such figures
show? Or, more to our purpose, how exactly can what is wrong,
if anything, suggest a case against selective, mixed quality education of the North/South variety? Against, for example, a system
in which there are both grammar and secondary modern schools,
and in which a relatively small percentage of people go on to
university?

I imagine, and hope, that there will be readers who are stopped
in their tracks by the very act of raising such questions. For it is
taken for granted, in the countless tracts and tomes, that the figures
do reveal something terribly wrong – but it is rare indeed to find
anyone trying to identify just what this is. One writer, having
pointed out that gaps in the educational attainments of different
social classes grow during secondary education, at once concludes
that 'this finding rightly brought into doubt the 11-plus examination and the tripartite education system . . . which results from it'.[10]
But why does this 'finding' bring these matters 'into doubt'? No
reason at all is suggested by the author. Another writer, having cited
figures like those above, then announces: 'Deficiencies, discrimination, distortions have been pointed out in the previous pages. Each
deformity invites a solution separately, usually as part of the general
thesis that the whole lot cries out for replacement.'[11] But apart from
some rhetoric about the system being a capitalist plot for the 'sub-
ordination and future exploitation' of the proletariat, no reason is
offered as to why it is 'deficiencies, discrimination, distortions'
which the figures reveal, let alone why 'the whole lot cries out for

replacement'. Even those who are, on balance, favourable to selective, mixed quality education tend to regard it as an unfortunate blemish on such a system that quality and attainment are so correlated with socio-economic factors.

Before I try to tackle the questions raised, a couple of brief comments on certain of the figures frequently marshalled by egalitarian critics – those familiar tables showing how few working-class children become, *inter alia*, bishops, Tory cabinet ministers, university professors, doctors, or lawyers. First, these figures are peculiarly selective; for I have never seen them set off against figures showing how few upper-class children become, *inter alia*, 'pop' stars, England footballers, or trade union leaders. Second – though this is really what the first point is driving at – these figures are uninteresting unless accompanied by information on what jobs people want to have. Unless it is assumed that nearly everyone wants to be a bishop, Tory minister, to 'wear bowler hats or read *The Times*',[12] etc. – or unless it is assumed that there is no concentration of such ambitions among certain classes – it is unclear what there is to bemoan in the figures. The first assumption is, of course, absurd, while the second is surely wildly false. It would certainly be both paradoxical and obnoxiously snobbish for egalitarians to join with the Victorian father or Jewish mother of comic portrayal in thinking that every son ought to have ambitions as bishop, doctor, or lawyer.

Let us turn, then, to the questions of whether there is something intolerable, and if so what, revealed by the figures mentioned at the beginning. One thing can be conceded: such figures, for all the information they provide, could and in certain circumstances would signify something seriously wrong with the system in which they obtain. But let me add at once that the evils I have in mind (a) do not exist on a large scale in modern Britain – and to the extent that they exist at all, are incapable of accounting for more than a fraction of the socio-economic/educational correlations in question, (b) do not call, by way of remedy, for the abolition of selective, mixed quality schooling, and (c) are not targets which only the egalitarian is privileged to shoot at.

Twin evils, which could in some circumstances account for the 'cycle', would exist if admission into selective education and then into jobs were determined on the basis of class membership. These evils[13] might take different forms: it might be, for example, that the formal criteria for admission explicitly insist on a certain social class background as a qualification; or, without being as blatant as this, they may lay down conditions which only those from a certain background could, with any likelihood, meet.[14]

I postpone until an appendix the issue of private schooling. This

77

done, it is clear that admission into selective education in Britain is, neither in form nor effect, based on criteria which qualify people according to social class. Entry into grammar school and university is on the basis of observed ability; and those with the ability are not prevented, financially or otherwise, from accepting the offer of places. (This is not to deny that there may be a degree of unconscious bias, favouring children from a certain social background, in the tests of ability. The following chapters, however, contain warnings against hysterical exaggerations of this kind of consideration.) So much, indeed, was admitted as far back as 1957 by authors usually regarded as belonging to the egalitarian ranks: 'Virtually the full quota of boys with requisite minimum IQ from every class was admitted to grammar schools and the distribution of opportunity stands in closer relationship to that of ability . . . than ever before.'[15] The story is generally the same when we consider entry into professions. The Bar, medicine, academia, and the Civil Service, for example, select on the basis of ability, and qualifications that have nothing to do with parental occupation. There are murkier areas, no doubt, where who one's parents are counts for a lot; but, if anything, fashion has veered towards 'affirmative' preference for people from the 'wrong side' of whatever the tracks are now supposed to be.

It would be unclear, moreover, why abolition of selective education would be the appropriate remedy, even if the evils in question remained with us to a far greater degree than they in fact do. A change in the criteria for selection would seem the obvious panacea. Indeed, one immediately associates ferocious criticism of such evils with the 'meritocratic' attack on the disutilitarian results of taking anything but ability as a relevant criterion – an attack, of course, which presupposes the value of mixed quality education.

Finally, it can scarcely be an egalitarian privilege to complain about irrational or unfair criteria for selection. What is wrong with such criteria is that they are irrational or unfair, and not – or not mainly – that they work to the advantage of one class rather than another. A law forbidding lawyers' sons from entering 'A' streams would be no less objectionable, as I see it, than one which enjoined it.

A quite different evil that the figures could, in certain circumstances, reflect would be the existence of genuine poverty and deprivation. Children in families locked in a struggle against poverty could, failing private charity, hardly be expected to equip themselves for entry into the more demanding schools and professions. A trio of comments on this possibility needs to be made, similar to those made on the other possibility.

First, there is no widespread poverty and deprivation in contemporary Britain. While, no doubt, pockets are to be found, they could not begin to account for the extent of class discrepancies in selective education and the professions. Eliminate all cases of genuine poverty and the effect on, say, working-class representation at university would be small. Second, it is unclear why 'unstreamed' comprehensives, 'open door' universities, etc., would be expected to help, if ours was a society of widespread poverty. Indeed, one might expect remedies to tend in the opposite direction – as they do in most really poor Third World countries, in which education is highly selective and of intentionally mixed quality. Rawls, we saw in chapter 1, was willing to postpone implementation of the 'difference principle' in circumstances where poverty was so great that the premium should be on increasing total wealth before concentrating on its 'fair' distribution. It is in such terms, one might think, that even the most egalitarian-sounding Third World leaders would justify concentrating educational resources on producing a corps of well-trained engineers, doctors, etc. Finally – as we also saw in chapter 1 – it is no egalitarian privilege to condemn (alleviable) poverty and deprivation. What is wrong with being poor is that one is poor – not that one has less than others. In some conditions, equalization can be a means towards curing poverty, but this has not been a significant weapon in the radical reduction of poverty in this country. As egalitarians never cease to remind us, despite this radical reduction, '*differences* in income . . . have remained roughly the same since the war, giving us one more link in the cycle of inequality'.[16]

At this stage I fear that I cannot avoid a digression on an objection that is bound to be raised against my most recent remarks (Those who are satisfied by these remarks can skip this and the next two paragraphs.) It will be objected that my remarks run counter to what Robinson describes as the 'now almost universal agreement that poverty is not an absolute but a relative concept'.[17] Whether they run counter to this depends on what it is that there is 'now almost universal agreement' upon. It is certainly true that the reference of 'poor' is governed by criteria that are subject to change, and that the tendency is for these criteria to become more relaxed over time, so that some who would not previously have been regarded as poor come to be so regarded. This is partly because 'poor' is an effective word for drawing attention to those whom one wants to see helped – so there is a tactical advantage in calling 'poor' those who, by the criteria in force, are not really poor. This helps shift the criteria. And it is partly because words are sturdy plants: threatened with extinction by the possibility of having nothing to refer to, they stay alive through the criteria for their use altering at the same time as the changing facts which would otherwise put them out of business. But I fear that the 'almost universal agreement' Robinson has in mind is upon something quite different and much more suspicious.

The idea seems to be that 'poor' is relative in that it always refers to the relatively worst-off X per cent (10 per cent?, 15 per cent?) of the relevant population. It would be difficult, otherwise, to understand Robinson's point that, according to the 'relative concept' of poverty, poverty is inevitable wherever there is inequality of wealth. Put technically, the idea seems to be that 'poor' is an adjective with only an attributive, and not a predicative, use. That is: 'a poor X' is always something that is poor for an X, rather than something which is both an X and poor. ('Large' is attributive: a large minnow is something that is large for a minnow, not something which is both a minnow and large. Contrast 'square': a square figure is not something that is square for a figure, but something which is both a figure and square.) But this idea is perverse. If 'poor' and 'rich' were purely attributive, there should be no irony – which there is – in expressions like 'poor Millionaire' or 'rich beggar'. Certainly someone can be poor for a millionaire (he has only got £1,000,001) or rich for a beggar (he has a blanket as well as newspapers to sleep under). Again, it would become the merest tautology – which surely it is not – to refer to the least well-off sections of society as being in poverty. If the least well-off were all as well-off as Croesus the reference would be straightforwardly false. Needless to say, what sounded like a deep truth of sociology – 'poverty is inevitable without equality' – would emerge as a dull truism. *Of course* there will be poverty if 'the poor' are those with less than others. (It is interesting to contrast 'poor', when used in connection with standards of living, with 'poor' when used in connection with quality – as in 'poor violinist' or 'poor speaker'. Here the use really is purely attributive. A poor speaker is someone who speaks poorly, not someone who speaks and is poor.)

'Poor' refers to those who have insufficient to meet certain needs. That, you may say, does not help much, for is not the concept of need a 'relative' one? Certainly 'need', like 'poor', refers in virtue of criteria that tend to become more relaxed, so that some of today's needs are the caveman's luxuries. But it would be silly to over-react and conclude that needs are whatever wants there are which the worst-off X per cent are unable to satisfy. Otherwise, once more, there could then be no irony in referring to the 'needy millionaire' who cannot buy some of the things – a second yacht, say – which his wealthier jet-setting friends can. Clearly there are limits on what wants can count as needs. Among those which can are various wants for nutrition, sanitation, shelter, social intercourse, recreation, and

80

mobility. When I say there is relatively little poverty in contemporary Britain, I mean there are relatively few people unable to satisfy these needs. Indeed, our welfare state does not permit people to be unable to satisfy at least the most urgent of these.

It is worth stressing that if one does insist on using 'poverty' in the perversely relativized way, it will no longer follow from the existence of poverty that there is any evil to complain about. In particular, it will not follow that there is anything to complain about in the correlation between poverty, so understood, and representation at certain sorts of schools. Or rather, such a complaint will now presuppose an egalitarian commitment, and can do nothing to justify such a commitment – for, as we just saw, poverty so understood is a definitional consequence of inequality.

It remains, in fine, to identify the nature of the egalitarian complaint; for we have found that some of the evils the figures might reflect are not to the point. It is high time we distinguished between two broad categories of critic: between those whose complaint against selective education is a function, essentially, of a deeper, general antipathy towards the very existence of social classes, and those whose complaint is compatible with an acceptance, not necessarily grudging, of distinct classes; between those whose educational polemic is incidental to a wider polemic against classes, and those whose critique is independent of any such general polemic.

I do not have very much to say to the first kind of critic. I do not want to become embroiled in reviewing the merits or otherwise of class society; so I shall confine myself to showing that if these critics' educational polemic really is incidental to their wider polemic then, *qua* a criticism of mixed quality education, it entirely misses its mark. So much, indeed, is surely implied in the preceding chapter. From what I said about it, Scholesia could well be a country without social classes (it was a 'Rawlsian paradise', education apart) – yet a case can be made out (I made it out) for selective, mixed quality education in Scholesia.

It is difficult to fill this point out without refining the crude and lumpy notion of social class that keeps cropping up. Whether an educational critique flows from a critique of social classes will presumably depend on what these are, with some degree of exactitude, taken to be. It is, of course, commonplace for sociologists to stress the ambiguities in the notion, but this does not always, or often, prevent them from using it without due warning as to its sense, or from slipping, without giving notice, from one sense to another.

Often, in everyday conversation, a person's education is counted among the criteria of social class. When this is done, it will become, of course, trivially true that an objection to classes carries with it an objection to mixed quality education – for the former objection will have the latter built into it *ab initio*. Another popular tendency is to associate, inextricably, social class with what we might vaguely call a 'style of life' (something I say more about in chapter 5). Eat some fish and chips on the way from the football terraces, then drink in the public bar while your wife is at Bingo to brace yourself for a drive to the coast the following day – and you will probably be characterized as belonging to a certain class. There are those, no doubt, who object to there being distinct 'styles of life', of the type just caricatured – indeed, a related objection will be looked at in the following section. But presumably it is not class in this sense that is the present concern: if it were, all those figures showing how few manual workers' sons go to grammar school, etc., would be of opaque relevance.

A more academic notion of class is the one supplied by Marx – in terms of the ownership of the means of production and distribution. Masters were those who owned other human beings as productive means; proletarians were those who owned nothing but their own labour. Those who fulminate loudest against classes frequently demand the abolition of classes in this sense: frequently, that is, they are socialists. But despite recurrent invocations of Marx's name, it is hard to see that this can, or should, be the notion of class paramount in the minds of those who found their attack on selective education on the sort of figures mentioned earlier. Abolition of classes in Marx's sense would do nothing, in itself, to remove distinctions between professional, clerical, and manual workers – and nothing, in itself, to eliminate income differentials. But it is distinctions and differentials of these sorts that the figures were all about – *not* differences in ownership of the means of production and distribution. Or put it this way: suppose all manual workers became – as many of them are – capitalists, through being given shares in their industries. It is hard to believe that those who complain about the under-representation of manual workers' children in 'A' streams or universities would now be appeased – although, *ex hypothesi*, this would no longer be under-representation of a class in the marxist sense.

The notion of class being used by our first kind of critic must surely be that of groups engaged in different kinds of work, to which different status and, above all, different remuneration is attached. Within the polemic against classes in this sense there can be several variations. The complaint may be against the division of labour as such, or only against the higher pay that professional work is supposed to command – and, if the latter, the objection might be to any pay differentials, or only to those which exceed what the 'difference principle' permits, or only to those which exceed what something stronger than that principle permits, or. . . .

Surely it is now clear that hostility towards classes, in the relevant sense, need not and should not carry with it any hostility towards selective, mixed quality education. For Scholesia was 'classless' in the sense that there were no differences in income or status exceeding those allowed by the 'difference principle'. Yet the whole thrust of the last chapter was in favour of selective, mixed quality North/South system. (It could make no difference, if to appease more extreme egalitarian appetites, Scholesian equality, in matters of status and income, went further than the demands of the 'difference principle'.)

The point, very simply, is this: if it is social classes you are against, then get rid of them. There is no reason to get rid of selective, mixed quality education as well. The only possible reply could be that such an education system helps to create or maintain the different social classes. But, given the present sense of 'class', this would be a remarkably implausible reply. No doubt a system like North/South will help determine which people will occupy which jobs, and therefore which people will receive a certain income. But it is not the education system which creates the different sorts of job, or the differentials in income and status attached. The important message of both the Coleman report and the Jencks study is that egalitarian policies in education have done little or nothing to reduce income differentials. (It is worth adding a second important message these studies have: these policies have done much less than imagined to determine which people will receive which incomes.)

Let us turn to the more serious business of identifying and assessing the complaint of the second kind of critic – he who, without being committed against social classes in the sense just discussed, nevertheless sees in unequal education an obnoxious feature of class society; who sees in it an ugly face, not just its face; and who thinks a fair education system is possible in the boundaries of class society.

The complaint – to be found in a host of writers[18] – tends to go something like this: what is intolerable is the rigidity of classes (work/income/status sense), the powerful social forces which make it so likely that members of a social class in one generation will be sons or daughters of members of that same class. What makes this intolerable is precisely that it is a social matter, and not one of natural necessity. One of the most powerful, and therefore least tolerable, processes making for this rigidity is a selective, mixed quality education system. It is true, by and large, that selection into better schools or higher streams is on the basis of ability – but children from different classes have widely different chances of acquiring the relevant abilities. By conferring advantages on their children both before and during schooling, parents from the better-off classes increase the children's likelihood of acquiring those abilities which, finally, make it so likely they will remain in the class of their origin. Such, I believe, is the familiar line of complaint – softened though it may have been by the findings of Coleman and Jencks.

Two (reasonably important) asides before tackling the complaint. First, there is a sense of 'social class' in which the complaint could be read as an attack on the very existence of classes. When it is said that the USA is 'classless', what is meant, typically, is not that there are insignificant gaps in income or status, but that there is a high degree of social 'mobility': people born into one class (in the earlier sense) are not so likely as in the Old World to remain in that class. The day is long gone when it is useful to ask, 'What is the proper meaning of "social class"?'; so let me just reiterate that, for present purposes, I shall use the term to refer to groups distinguished by kinds of work done, status, and remuneration, irrespective of 'mobility'. Second, it is common for those who level the above complaint to wave the slogan of 'equal educational opportunity'. Crosland, for example, defined 'opportunity' in terms of the likelihood of acquiring intelligence and other educationally relevant abilities: so, for him, a selective system, within class society, was bound to be one in which educational opportunity was unequal. For the reasons given in the previous section, I shall not discuss matters using this terminology. I shall ask if there is something wrong with a system in which better-off parents can increase the likelihood of their children's educational and professional success without worrying if such a system is to be described as one of unequal opportunity.

Is it supposed to be self-evidently wrong that better-off parents have, and exercise, this power? I am not sure what to reply to someone who thinks it is, beyond retorting that I, and many others, do not find it so. (Depending on what is meant by 'self-evident', this might be a knock-down reply.) But perhaps the following reflection helps: no one, outside of Erewhon, objects to children enjoying some of the benefits they have, in part, through having the parents they do. Good health and an attractive appearance, for example. No one thinks the children ought not to take advantage of these benefits, by swimming, dating the opposite sex, and so on, on the ground that other children have parents who, culpably or otherwise, have failed to confer these benefits. There are, to be sure, differences between good health and its advantages on the one hand, and education and its advantages on the other. But if there is a difference relevant to the point at issue – whether, namely, it is improper for children to benefit educationally from their parents' position – it surely needs to be spelled out. Such a difference, if there is one, is hardly evident.

It is surely time to go onto the offensive, and lay down a challenge which, I believe, our critics are unable to meet. In chapter 1, I quoted with approval Nozick's point that if we are to condemn a distributional set-up as unfair it is incumbent to specify what wrongs or injustices have occurred on the path leading to that set-up. If, in particular, we are going to condemn the distribution of social classes in schools, streams, or colleges, then the onus is on specifying the injustices in the process whereby this distribution occurs. Clearly it is not by magic that children from one social class are over- or under-represented in a certain kind of school. The mere fact that one's father is well-off cannot explain how one landed up in a grammar school.

What then is the process whereby, through one's parents belonging to a certain class, one's likelihood of acquiring educationally relevant abilities is increased? My point, following Nozick, will be that unless one can identify something wrong in this process, there will be no right to complain about the injustice of the result. There are, of course, any number of factors playing a role in this process. Of almost no significance, however, are those expensive aids – private tutors, for example – bought with the express intention of furthering the child's chances in the selective system. The most significant factors are not those bought, planned, or arranged with selection in view. As John Lucas stresses, the experiences which awaken, and then sustain, the interests and dispositions which blossom into educational ability are too varied, too unpredictable, too much a matter of the chance encounter with a line of a book or with a painting, for the idea of planning, beyond a very limited level, to be feasible.[19] Where the advantaged child is educationally favoured is, primarily, through his being put in the way of the experiences which will spark, foster, and reinforce his abilities. A number of elements in this process can, crudely at least, be distinguished. There is, for a start, his parents' behaviour – especially their verbal behaviour. *Ceteris paribus* the child of professional parents will find himself in a rich linguistic environment; one in which, moreover, he is likely to pick up the bits of information, the kinds of stories which will set off his educational interests. Then there are the surroundings his parents are able to supply him with – books, a room of his own, a large range of (one hopes) stimulating toys, and so on. Finally, and very importantly, there is – to use the horrible jargon – the child's 'peer group'. By mixing socially

85

with friends enjoying similar advantages, a dynamic interplay is set up, in which each friend further stimulates and reinforces the interests and enthusiasms of the next. From a book like *The Railway Children* one can see how infectious curiosity and learning among a group of initially disposed children can be.

This is all very brief: many other factors could doubtless be mentioned, but I suspect that most of these – travel abroad, for example (travel, notice, not sunbathing) – would share this important characteristic of putting the child in the way of rich experiences. Now I find it impossible to see what is supposed to be wrong with all of this. Are linguistically competent parents supposed to remain taciturn on the ground that other parents are less talkative or fluent? Are parents who can afford them supposed to refrain from buying books or toys that might be of educational benefit to their children, because other parents either cannot afford them or prefer to spend money differently? Are parents to ensure that their child's circle of friends includes a sprinkling of dullards so as to keep down the intellectual dynamic that might otherwise grow up? Such questions, I hope, answer themselves.

The egalitarian likes to give the impression that the advantaged child's abilities are bought for him. But this, we see, is crude to the point of total falsity. Perhaps one would object to a system in which those who pass the selection exams do so because, in the preceding weeks, they all go to an expensive 'crammer' or have private tutors. But this, of course, is not how things work.

Of course, if selective, mixed quality education were condemnable on independent grounds, the fact that individual parents do nothing improper by conferring advantages on their children could do nothing to justify the system. But in the previous chapter I tried to show there are no such independent grounds (of an egalitarian sort, at least) for condemning the system. What I have been looking at over the preceding pages is the idea that, even if such a system were otherwise justifiable, it is not to be tolerated given the under- and over-representation of social classes in the various sectors of the system. But if I am right in arguing that there is nothing improper in the process whereby this distribution obtains, then I cannot see that any case has been made out against such a system.

Everyone, of course, would think it nice if all children could be put in the way of educationally enriching experiences – so there is nothing characteristically egalitarian in thinking this. What is characteristically egalitarian is the demand that – given the existence of social classes, and of limited resources, and of parents who are not in fact going to put their children in the way of the relevant experiences – children of better-off parents be prevented from enjoying the benefits their parents are able to confer. But can anyone seriously advocate preventing this, when it would involve, *inter alia*, preventing these parents from talking so much?

It is interesting, I hope, that in all of this long discussion, no mention has been made of the notorious nature versus nurture issue. That issue indeed seems to be a giant red herring in the ethical debate over the justifiability of selective, mixed quality education. If two children of, say, age 10, have different abilities, and there is nothing to complain of in the way the first child came by his superior ability, then the question of whether they had the same innate potential (whatever that might mean) is irrelevant to the question of whether the first should be allowed to benefit from his superior ability. Atkinson is being too mild when he writes, 'even if all human differences were social in origin, they would remain real, and it would not be self-evidently absurd to hold that account should be taken of them in framing social policies'.[20] Someone will declaim, no doubt, that if there was no innate difference then the first child does not deserve his superior abilities. (Would he if the difference had been innate?) I have tried to deal with this sort of point already, in section 2 of chapter 2.

4 'Social mix'

Because neither Northerners nor Southerners, in general, came from a distinctive socio-economic background – because, in a certain sense, Scholesia was 'classless' – there is a favourite egalitarian criticism which does not apply to the Scholesian system, but which is often levelled against selective, mixed quality systems in the real world. The criticism is that the schools, streams, or colleges in such systems display an insufficient degree of 'social mix'.

In some mouths, the demand for 'social mix' merely repeats one or more of the demands already encountered in this chapter. For example, it may be valued solely as a means towards preventing the bias for people of one's own social sort which, it is alleged, infects the job-market: in the truly mixed society neither the old school tie nor the old cloth cap would pull strings. Commonly, though, 'social mix' is held to be valuable in its own right, irrespective of any role it may play in breaking the 'cycle of inequality'. Certainly some of the reasons adduced in its support have little, directly, to do with preventing the passing-on of advantage; and it is not hard to think of systems which might appease the egalitarians encountered earlier in the chapter but which would not satisfy the principle of 'social mix' – a system, for instance, in which 'reverse discrimination' had gone so far that manual workers' children completely dominated the better schools. Advantage would now be disinherited, but there would be no more 'social mix' than before.

It is best, perhaps, to think of those radicals who demand total 'social mix' as constituting a distinct breed of egalitarian – for their interest is not, or not primarily, in how goods (educational ones included) are distributed, but in fostering a way of life, a society in which, as they see it, fraternity and democracy are truly manifested. (It might be possible, with a bit of juggling, to place the demand under the general rubric of egalitarianism described before – but I shall not try.)

What is 'social mix', and why should anyone find it desirable (other than as a means to other egalitarian ends)? The idea is certainly a vague one, but sufficiently powerful to be invoked in defence of a huge number of multifarious policies and measures. These range from the trivial (undergraduate objections to 'high table') to the serious (comprehensivization). Sometimes the policy defended is the removal of some barrier to the free intercourse of different groups – as when a previously all-male college opens its gates to women. Sometimes, more radically, what is defended is the encouragement or even enforcement of greater intercourse – as when, through 'reverse discrimination', the admission of ethnic minorities is favoured. A minimum ingredient in such policies is the allowance or encouragement of greater physical contact between people of the relevantly different sorts. They are to be put in the same classroom, or on the same campus, or encouraged to visit one another's homes as part of a 'community school' project. But physical contact, of course, is not the point. The point, it would seem, is of the 'learning how the other half lives' variety. Physical contact will create an acquaintance with the lives, interests, activities, tastes, or hobbies of 'the others'. The relevant sense of 'acquaintance' here is not 'knowing about' – the sense in which I am well-acquainted with the history of the Punic Wars. Acquaintance of that sort can, and usually has to, be gained through reading about 'the others' – as when one becomes acquainted with exotic styles of life by reading Evans-Pritchard or 'William Hickey'.

What is wanted, apparently, is the sort of acquaintance that involves sharing the activities, interests, etc., of 'the others'. 'Participant' understanding rather than aloof 'observer' understanding. The true devotee of 'social mix' wants to see a reduction in the differences among the ways different groups live, and a corresponding increase in the number of activities, etc., which, through greater contact and exhortation, they will come to unite in. Hence the importance of a measure typically advocated by these devotees – the removal of symbols of difference. These are to be removed either because they act as conventionalized barriers in the way of easy intercourse or, more vaguely, because they encourage feelings of difference that thwart the communal sense which 'social mix' requires. School uniforms, famously, are often defended as a levelling device which makes it impossible for children from different classes to display their stations, literally as it were, upon their sleeves.

It is, perhaps, worth noting an ironical, even paradoxical, feature which many demands for 'social mix' have. What appears as a demand for this, at one level, can at another level appear as a demand for social autarky. Ethnic minorities, these days, are often encouraged to maximize 'fellow-feeling', to become, irrespective of social class, 'soul-brothers' or whatever. But at the same time they are encouraged to maximize the distance between themselves and everyone else. 'Family', even a 'soul-family', requires there to be people who are 'not family'. Within the enclosure barriers are to be torn down, while around it the fences are to be raised.

Why are people so keen on 'social mixing'? For lots of reasons, of course – not all of them compatible. One consideration appeals to the 'enrichment' that people of one sort will obtain through increased acquaintance with others. This is a favourite consideration in the case for 'reverse discrimination' in the USA[21] – and belongs in the same general camp as some ideas of John Dewey, which I shall be looking at in some detail. Another argument is that a 'socially mixed' society – especially one where there is plenty of mixing at school – will be a more harmonious society. The less contact people of diverse sorts have, and the fewer their range of shared activities, the less 'understanding' will they have of one another – in which case, they will be less likely to agree upon, or even communicate about, the problems which face them all.

Sometimes the principle of 'social mix' figures centrally in quasi-philosophical social theories according to which lives are not being properly led, or 'realized', unless sunk in the communal pool. Here 'communal' has two senses. Not only must community be encouraged in the sense of increasing the number of generally shared activities and interests, but these activities must be directed towards the good of the community, conceived of as some entity transcending the individuals that compose it: the Nation, the Volk, the Proletariat – or whatever. The 'style' of social mixing prompted by such views does not seem to vary much with the particular 'communal' end in view. Climbing the Zugspit with one's whistling 'Kraft durch Freude' colleagues, or taking a mass dip in the Yangtse – the picture is similar and familiar. Not every ideologist, it would seem, would concur with Meredith's judgment that 'as out of an undrained swamp, there steams the malady of sameness'. But it is not with such heady doctrines and philosophies that I shall concern myself.

I shall start by looking at some ideas of Dewey, which intimately relate education and 'social mix'. *Democracy and Education* contains a genuine argument for 'social mix', based on educational considerations. For Dewey, 'democracy' does not refer, primarily at least, to a form of political organization, but to a form of society – one in which two characteristics must be manifested. A society is the more democratic if, first, there are 'more numerous points of shared common interest', and second, there is 'freer interaction between social groups'.[22] It is in virtue of these characteristics, moreover, that democracy is the preferred social form, for they provide 'the measure for the worth of any given mode of social life'.[23] It is no surprise, therefore, to find Dewey insisting that it is 'the office of the school environment to balance the various elements in the social environment, and to see to it that each individual . . . come into living contact with a broad environment'.[24] For only then will education be helping to forge a society in which 'interests . . . are shared by all its members' and in which there is 'fullness and freedom' of interaction between different social groups.[25]

Left like this, Dewey's argument looks like one from the value of democracy, in his 'social mix' sense, to the importance of a certain educational function. But at a deeper level he wants to argue that the value of democracy – including its manifestation in schools – is itself educative; so that the argument becomes one from the value of education to the importance of democracy. This is as well, since otherwise we should have been offered no reason why 'social mix' is a 'measure for the worth . . . of social life'.

Dewey's central point is that knowledge, learning, understanding, and communication – the aims of education – require the democratic mode of life, for the sake both of their extent and their quality. This is not, or not mainly, because democracy furnishes institutions and an environment which are conducive, as means, to education. The point is a conceptual one: knowledge, etc., require, by their very nature, the democratic life. Without it, they cannot, as a matter of logic, expand and flourish to any degree. Learning, for Dewey, is coming to grasp meanings – not of words, simply, but of practices, things, processes, and events as well. And to grasp meanings is to recognize uses. For something to have a meaning, it must have a public, social use. 'It is the characteristic use to which a thing is put . . . which supplies the meaning with which it is identified.'[26] The significance of a chair, for example, is that it is used to sit on. Words have meaning not simply through being used in discourse, but through calling to mind the uses of the things they refer to. So, 'the one who understands the words "Greek helmet" becomes mentally a partner with those who used the helmet'.[27]

It follows, for Dewey, that there cannot be private, individual learning and understanding. A congenital Robinson Crusoe might discriminate between helmets and non-helmets, in that he can put them in different piles, but he will not understand what he is doing, since he has no grasp of the public use to which helmets are put. If, by chance, he were to label them by the noise 'helmet', he would not understand the meaning of this term.[28] Again, I may be trained to respond physically to certain stimuli, but I would not have learned anything. To have learned, I must have been brought to grasp the point of my responses within some shared activity. I have learned a ball-game, say, only when I grasp that my response of catching the ball plays a role in a joint, purposeful activity.

Education then, for Dewey, must consist in introducing the young to the shared activities found in their society. For it is these activities alone which confer meanings and, thereby, provide the fodder for learning and understanding. It is now supposed to follow that education will be at a maximum in a thoroughly democratic society: for, *ex hypothesi*, this is a society in which there are many generally shared activities. The more shared activities, the more meanings there are to be created: the more, therefore, there is to learn and communicate about.

Supposed to follow. Unfortunately the supposition is false. The whole argument is fallacious, depending as it does on equivocation over expressions like 'more shared activities', 'greater mutual interests', etc. If you place 'more' in front of a noun phrase consisting of an adjective followed by a noun, you typically create a syntactically ambiguous expression. 'More' may qualify the noun-phrase as a whole, or only the adjective (thereby forming a comparative). 'Put on more colourful clothes!' may mean 'Put on more of the colourful sort of clothes you already have on!' or it may mean 'Put on clothes more colourful than those you are wearing!'. Likewise, a demand for more shared activities may either be a demand for more activities of the sort that are shared, or a demand for activities that are more shared (i.e. more widely shared). It is only when the demand is read in the first way (with 'more' acting as a quantifier ranging over activities) that it is supported by Dewey's analysis of knowledge and learning. For what that analysis entails is that a person's scope for learning is increased by participating, actually or vicariously, in more activities that are shared by some people or other – for he is then encountering new meanings. Unfortunately, though, it is only when the demand is taken in the second way (with 'more' as an adjectival modifier) that it serves as a demand for democratization and 'social mix'. For only when taken this way is it a demand that more and more people should get together in the same activities.

Two things are clear. First, the demand for more shared activities in the first sense does not entail this demand in its second sense. Just as someone can put on more clothes of a colourful sort without putting on clothes that are more colourful than his present ones, so a person may widen the range of shared activities available to him without encountering activities that are more widely shared in than those he has already encountered. Second, Dewey himself is guilty of the fallacious move. For we see him moving from the claim that there should be 'numerous . . . interests which are consciously shared' to the quite different claim that there should be 'interests of a group [which] are shared by all its members'.

Not only does the one demand not follow from the other, but there are good grounds for thinking them to be at odds with one another. A policy designed to encourage just those activities or interests which everyone, or a very large number of people, can unite in would surely conflict with a policy designed to encourage a large number of activities and interests. For there is not likely to be more than a few activities for which mass enthusiasm can be drummed up. One might reasonably think that it is the highly fragmented society, in which there is any number of barriers to 'fullness and freedom' of intercourse, where activities and interests will be most numerous and varied.

My point is at its clearest, perhaps, in connection with communication. Dewey appears to argue that since communication requires shared activity among the communicators, then the more sharing there is the more communication there will be. This is like arguing that since mates must share various characteristics then the more characteristics they share the more they will mate – an inference whose invalidity is demonstrated by the normal man's antipathy towards chest-hair and a bass voice in his prospective mate. Not only is the argument fallacious, Dewey's conclusion is surely false. Given the minimum amount of sharing presupposed by successful communication about the everyday world we all encounter, further communication requires ever more diversity in people's interests and activities. For then there are more things for people to communicate about. How it is that, on the basis of a shared language adequate for dealing with the mundane, people with radically different, often esoteric, very unshared, interests can communicate these to one another, is a complicated and remarkable story. But that it happens is beyond doubt.[29]

92

Dewey, I noted earlier, argues that it is not just the extent, but the quality of knowledge, etc., which is increased in democracy. This claim is so far untouched by my point. Still, Dewey's remarks on quality and 'social mix' are wildly implausible. Writing of societies in which there are rigidly distinct social classes, he says: 'The evils . . . affecting the superior class are less material and less perceptible, but equally real. Their culture tends to be sterile . . . their art becomes a showy display and artificial; . . . their knowledge overspecialized; their manners fastidious rather than humane.'[30] Does he really think that Periclean Athens, Renaissance Florence, Elizabeth I's London, or 'Wittgenstein's Vienna' were characterized by cultural sterility, showy art, over-specialized learning, and mere fastidiousness? And would he really find the easily whistlable tunes Zdhanov forced Prokofiev to compose 'fertile', the mass-culture programmes of television 'genuine', or the manners in Pol Pot's thoroughly 'mixed' Cambodia 'humane'?

It is clear we must look elsewhere if we are to find a good reason for putting a premium on 'social mix' at school. The most frequently heard reason is the one that appeals to social harmony. Harmony, in serious matters, means the relative absence of conflicts of a crippling sort. Either such conflicts do not arise, or if they do the will and the means exist to contain them. Such harmony, it is conjectured, is fostered by mutual understanding. The more men understand one another's aims, problems, and points of view, the less likely are they to be torn apart by irreconcilable conflicts. Mutual understanding, it is further conjectured, requires greater contact with and, ideally, greater participation in, the activities and interests of all by all.

Such is the story told by generations of political thinkers. Democracy, as a form of political organization, is often advocated on such grounds, for a democracy, so it is said, is a system in which differences, though they exist, can be harmonized without the body politic being destroyed. (Despotism often gets argued for on the same grounds: an 'iron man' is needed to weld people together in an harmonious whole. Rousseau manages to get himself quoted in both traditions, which does not mean he was inconsistent: if 'particular wills' do not merge into a common will of their own accord, someone – the 'divine legislator' – must do it for them.)

Political and social harmony, the story continues, is made that much easier if, at a young age, people are brought up in the mutual understanding it presupposes. Hence the demand for 'social mix' at schools – for an early demolition of those barriers that would otherwise threaten the social harmony which is a prerequisite of civilized society. It is often said, for example, that the Irish 'troubles'

would be less acute had the young from different religious backgrounds been more thoroughly mixed during schooling.

It would be silly to deny the element of good sense in this story.
Some failures of understanding, and subsequent conflicts, are due to
lack of contact and acquaintance. What at first seem the risible or
obscene habits of 'the others' may, on closer acquaintance, emerge
as perfectly intelligible, even laudable. Still, the story is much too
general, and the case for radical, thoroughgoing 'social mix' in
schools, based on considerations of understanding and harmony, is
unproved. Certainly it would have to be a powerful case if it is to
defeat the presumption in favour of which I have been arguing – the
presumption in favour of selective, mixed quality education which,
in a society like ours, is bound to involve a fair degree of social
separateness.

What I shall do is pit against the case described a number of
considerations which run in the other direction – ones which should,
at the very least, make one hesitant about the merits of a swingeing
policy of 'social mix'. These considerations are not desperately
original. Most of them can be found, elegantly expressed, in John
Lucas's sensitive paper 'Equality in education'.

First: it is a mistake to assume, in general, that it is increased
contact, mixing with one another socially, or levelling in outlooks
and tastes, which is required for that sense of solidarity and
community which fosters harmonious relations. Many examples, at
macro- and micro-levels, can be given of harmonious collectives
composed of extremely disparate and socially hived-off groups. For
long stretches feudal society was stable and harmonious, and the
main conflicts occurred between people of the same social status.
A knight governed by a code of chivalry needed another knight
governed by the same code to fight with. Many political thinkers
of the time, indeed, followed St Augustine in thinking that the feudal
structure presented that harmony which was the earthly reflection
of the divine order. At a more micro-level one thinks of the traditional army regiment in which – despite a rigid hierarchy of
authority and status, and thick barriers to 'full and free' social intercourse – a strong sense of solidarity and community can exist. To be
sure, there are examples of organizations where it is the very similarities among the members that bind them into an harmonious
whole – the early trade unions, say, or the 'Broederbond'. There
is simply no generalization to be made here. Harmony or community can as well flourish through the complementarity of very different
purposes and styles of life as through a basic similarity among them.

Second: the story went that harmony is promoted by mutual
understanding which, in turn, is promoted by the demolition of

social barriers, by increasing common activities. But care needs to be taken, here, with the notion of 'understanding'. In one sense, I understand you better if I know more about you – and this is knowledge I can often get from books or other sources of information. In another sense, I only understand you well if I am in living contact with you. I come to sense your moods, feel what is likely to upset you, see what 'makes you tick'. It is in this sense that a good wife can understand her husband better than an army of psychiatrists. Finally, there is the affective sense of 'understand' in which, very roughly, to understand is to sympathize. To have this understanding is to *be* understanding.

Presumably it is in this final sense that understanding can be directly instrumental in promoting harmony. The more sympathetic I am towards your aims, motives, and activities, the less likely am I to ride roughshod over you. Now there is no reason to think this sort of understanding will be encouraged by greater understanding in the first, 'knowing about', sense. The more information I gather about your sadistic motives, the less tolerant shall I become of your behaviour. Nor, as I see it, should it be presumed, in general, that sympathy and tolerance will be promoted by understanding in the second, 'living contact', sense; though advocates of 'social mix' appear, so often, to make this optimistic presumption. Surely it depends on who is brought into contact with whom. Familiarity can as well breed contempt as respect. Social anthropology is full of charming stories of field-workers whose attachment to initially alien peoples grows warm with time. But it is also peppered with stories where it is antipathy that grows. Margaret Mead's Samoans may have been delightful, but what about the Manus she later lived among? Malinowski could not stand the Trobrianders; and one anthropologist's disenchantment with the Ik was deemed worthy of staging. If people are repulsive, it is unclear why further contact with them should produce tolerance and sympathy. Indeed they may come to appear more repulsive than they really are through enforced contact with them.

Hostility which grows with familiarity may be due, of course, not to the defects in those who are the target of the hostility but to the defects in those who display the hostility. At the time of writing, the press is full of stories – most notably the 'Little Miss Posh' case – of the cruelty exhibited by working-class children, in comprehensives, towards children from more genteel backgrounds. Differences in accent, manners, and appearance do not necessarily become less marked, or less remarked upon, through mixing: the result, too often, may be to make these differences all the more abrasive. Perhaps working-class children have suffered, in their morale, from the 'separateness' or 'aloofness' of middle-class children. But it is surely time we shared Bantock's concern with the way 'the crudity of working-class manners and habits can be terrifying to children bred in a different and on the whole gentler atmosphere'.[31]

Third: there is another way an over-stringent policy of 'social mix' in schools can backfire. There are those, many of them, whose reaction to being pressed to conform with the activities and interests of the rest is one of rebellion. He who would otherwise have been an individualist is forced, by such pressure, to become a rebel – to the possible detriment of himself and his relationships with others. Such is the message of many of the great *Bildungsromanen* – of Musil, Alain-Fournier, and Hesse. The less scope the individualist youth has for doing those things that set him apart, the greater is the danger that he will do only what is negative – that, perhaps, he will swell the ranks of one of those recent breeds, the 'drop-outs' or the anarchist, juvenile terrorists. The great *Bildungsromanen*, of course, were set in private schools – often of a theological or military variety. But, as John Lucas reminds us,

> comprehensive schools could be far more divisive than public or grammar schools were ever even alleged to be, because enforced juxtaposition in accordance with an egalitarian ideology which denies the right of people to be different is liable to breed in those who are or want to be different a far more intense resentment than an enforced differentiation among those who want to be the same.[32]

Finally: there is yet another way in which a zealous programme of 'social mix' could boomerang, and result in divisions more sinister than those which are to be broken down. As every good demagogue and dictator knows, the most effective devices for achieving harmony and solidarity are not those which stress the similarities among members of the community, but those that stress wherein the community as a whole differs from some other. It is unnecessary to reiterate examples of whole nations, or whole sections of society, being welded together in a sense of oneness by the presence of a common enemy, real or phantom. On a smaller scale, the communal enthusiasm of fans on the football terraces is due less to their all being supporters of team X than to the presence, on the opposite terraces, of team Y's supporters.

This powerful tendency to unite, most of all, when there is some-thing to unite against can, perhaps very often does, take sinister turns in education. There is, to begin with, the danger that attempts to weld the young together in one big family, by stressing what they have in common – in particular, their youth – will only succeed if a sense of opposition to the 'non-young' can be excited. As Lucas, once more, puts it: 'The final result of forcing equality on the young could be that they found a sort of unity in a universal hostility to the middle-aged who had, in the name of equality, insisted on treating them not as individuals but as units.'[33] Can egalitarian educational policy be totally unrelated to the iconoclasm of so many young people, their cynical scoffing at traditional values, their worship of unscrupulous 'pop' stars whose trademark is an *insouciant*, flippant nihilism? The other danger is this: the attempt to demolish some of the familiar distinctions between groups will, if the tendency I mention is as strong as I fear, merely produce new, more worrying divisions in schools. Flatten the bulge in one place, and it pops up in another. A not too serious example can be furnished by sport, when this is used as a levelling device by those who encourage activities in which children, regardless of social class or whatever, can be brought together. If my school experience is anything to go by, the effect of too thorough a concentration can be to create a new class of pariahs – the athletic 'duffers', easy targets for those who have been coagulated on the playing-fields. The 'weed' can be more a victim of scorn and laughter than the boy from the 'wrong side of the tracks' (or, more common these days, the 'right side'). A more serious example is this: academic attainment is a virtue that must necessarily be underplayed in a stringent programme of 'social mix' – partly because exceptional attainment is heavily concentrated in a certain social class, partly because the whole paraphernalia of 'mix' (unstreamed classes, for example) favours the average. A consequence can be that those who remain 'academic' become objects of opprobrium, the 'grey men' of the school. The more academic attainment is played down, the more the exceptional student stands out as 'peculiar', and peculiarity, we know, can spawn prejudice.

The least that the considerations offered over the last few pages suggests is that far more needs to be known about the short-term and long-term consequences of thoroughgoing policies of 'social mix' in schools before, on the basis of slogans of 'democracy', 'fraternity', and 'equality', educationists blindly forge ahead in these policies.

The upshot of this long chapter is that introduction of 'real-life' factors into the Scholesian model has not overthrown the case, made out in the previous chapter, for selective, mixed quality education.

Appendix: Private schooling

I have not postponed discussion of private schooling to an appendix because I think the issue to be minor or peripheral. Indeed the issue promises to become more urgent as an increasing number of parents come to view private schooling as the most viable alternative to the comprehensive schools they find so unpalatable. The father who ten years ago would have been content to see his child at the local grammar school is now forced to choose between the local comprehensive, moving house, and paying for his child's education. This, together with (slowly) growing affluence, augurs a continued expansion in the private sector. I postponed the discussion only because it would have been tedious to have kept lacing the text with the caveats and qualifications that some rather special considerations concerning private schooling call for.

Let me make three preliminary points. First, when I speak of private schooling I do not have any particular kind of institution in mind – Headmasters' Conference schools, say, or direct grant schools. Parents pay to have their children educated in a variety of institutions, and it is with the propriety of this payment that I am concerned, and not with the pros and cons of particular sorts of institutions in which this goes on. Second, I stipulate that private schooling is of above-average standard. How closely or generally that stipulation corresponds to reality, I do not know – though I do take it that some of our private schools provide a first-rate education. I make the stipulation for the, by now, familiar reason that it gives the egalitarian something to be egalitarian about. If it were endemic to private schools to be so many Dotheboys Halls, or William Morris's 'boy-farms', then of course they should be got rid of. Egalitarian considerations would not enter into the case. Parents do not have the right – or, if they have it, should not be allowed to exercise the right – to pay for a rotten education. Third, I shall not touch on all, or even many, of the arguments advanced for or against private schooling, since they have nothing to do with the egalitarian case. I shall not, for example, have anything to say about Anthony Crosland's polemic against public schools – to the effect that, well though they may have served the building of Empire, they now produce quite the wrong kind of 'gentlemen' to captain industry or administer a government department.

My interest is in identifying the egalitarian's special objection to private schooling. Even those who are not opposed to selective, mixed quality education *per se* often baulk at the idea that the better schools should be private. And those who are against selective, mixed quality education in general seem to harbour extra venom for a system in which parents pay for a good education. Unsurprisingly, it is usual to find the venom unaccompanied by any clear statement as to why it is harboured. But unless a special objection can be identified, the case for private schooling is strongly supported, if not actually entailed, by what I have already said in the text. For I concluded that selective, mixed quality education is perfectly proper, and (in chapter 3) argued that this conclusion is not vitiated by the fact that some parents, in part through their financial position, are able to benefit their children educationally – by buying books, for example. In lieu of a special objection, it is hard to see how, if it is deemed proper for parents to benefit their children in that sort of way, one can then deem it improper for them to benefit their children by paying fees at a good school.

As before, I shall adopt the strategy of first discussing the issue in maximum isolation from various socio-economic factors bound up with private schooling, and of then seeing how any conclusions reached are affected, if at all, once these factors are introduced. Official writings on private schooling, such as the 1944 Fleming report or the 1968 Public Schools Commission report, make depressing reading by their continual muddling of socio-economic considerations with those of a more strictly educational sort. (When, that is, the latter considerations manage to get a look in at all. One might have thought, for instance, that a relevant consideration in favour of certain private schools would be their special suitability for high-calibre pupils. But this is breezily ignored in the 1968 report which, as part of its insistence that private schools shall not be 'exclusive', demands that the larger schools be open to pupils from the whole ability range. Smaller schools are excused: they only have to cater for three-quarters of the ability range!)

So let us return to the Scholesia of chapter 2 – that little country whose education system exists in almost splendid isolation from socio-economic factors. The Scholesia we visit has, however, changed in one crucial respect. The egalitarian critics of the North/South system won the day, and it has been replaced by the single school Centre – in which the only differences in educational quality permitted are those blessed by the 'difference principle'. Within a short time, however, parents of those who had been, or would have been, at North – the would-be Northerners – rebel. They band together, pool funds or raise loans to set up a new school, Arctos, in which they then pay for their children's schooling. (This requires them to spend more than they had previously spent in the form of taxes – since North had been financially favoured in the public system. But they think the sacrifice to be worthwhile.) After a while, Arctos becomes a replica of North: it is not difficult, for example, to attract former North teachers away from Centre or away from the non-teaching jobs they had gone into.

If this is what happens, I find it impossible to see what objection, on egalitarian or other grounds, there could be to the Arctos/Centre system over and above the objections, which I rejected, to North/South. If anything, there must be less objection – for no one can now complain that they are 'exploited' by taxes which were disproportionately spent to the benefit of North.

This is important, for it shows that the objection to private schooling cannot simply be that it is private. For if the effect of 'going private' were merely to replicate the system that anyway existed, there could be no special objection to the change. If all and only parents of grammar school children decided, under threat of comprehensivization, to pay for replicas of the grammar schools, these would be as justifiable, or unjustifiable, as the originals.

But, as that last sentence reveals, there is a very unreal assumption made about the Scholesian development as I described it. In reality, it would not be all or only the parents of would-be Northerners who would send their children to Arctos. Some of these parents would not be willing to pay, while some parents of would-be Southerners would be willing to pay. The result must be that entry into Arctos and Centre would not be rational in the sense that entry into North and South was defined to be (see p.33). There will be children at Arctos less able to benefit from the superior education offered there than some children at Centre. There are, of course, limits on how far the entry can stray from being rational: for, if too many would-be Southerners went to Arctos, educational standards could not be maintained at a sufficiently high level for a sufficient number of parents to make the financial sacrifice involved in sending their children there. Still, the effect of 'going private' will be to deviate from the rational selection that prevailed in North/South. (Of course, in any real system, mistakes will be made in selection – but I tried to deal with that problem in section 1 of chapter 3.) Ignoring socio-economic factors, this must be the crucial difference between mixed quality education in a completely public and a partially private system respectively. This must be the feature on which the egalitarian founds his special objection to the latter system. Certainly my defence of mixed quality education was premised on the selection methods in the system being rational. That defence must be amended if the new, special objection is to be met.

What we are to assess, then, is the charge that mixed quality education is justifiable, if at all, only when selection is, in the relevant sense, rational. It is grossly unfair, so the charge goes, when variations in parents' willingness to pay create a situation in which children most able to benefit from the better schools do not go to them while children do go to them who are not most able to benefit.

100

If this charge is valid, then my earlier point – that parents do not act wrongly by financially aiding their children educationally – will not serve to rebut it. For it could be argued that a system is unjustifiable even though individuals who take advantage of it are not to be condemned for so doing. Fee-paying parents, perhaps, are like Marx's individual capitalists caught in the 'vortex' of the profit system: it is not they, but the system in which they are allowed to operate, which is to be criticized.[1]

But the charge is not valid, since it contains a fallacy of *ignoratio*. What it ignores is that, although, because it is private, entry into the better school, Arctos, is not thoroughly rational, there would not be a better school unless it were private. A distribution of desirable goods which is not thoroughly rational is only to be condemned when a thoroughly rational distribution exists as a genuine alternative. Where the only alternative is the destruction of the desirable goods, it is obviously preferable to opt for the partially irrational distribution. Loaves of bread should go to the neediest, perhaps; but it would be absurd to object to people making their own loaves, which do not always go to the neediest, if those loaves would not otherwise have been produced at all. Again, it is perverse to criticize a private sector in medicine on the grounds that those who pay for treatment are not always the sickest if, without that sector, the medical resources necessary for the treatment would not otherwise have been called into existence at all. Since Scholesian egalitarians, by abolishing North/South, have removed the option of a thoroughly rational distribution of educational goods, then the irrational element in the Arctos/Centre system constitutes no objection to it.

A common response to the point I just made about medicine is that the existence of a private sector has an adverse effect on the public sector. I do not know how true this is in the case of medicine. In the educational case, there is reason to think that the existence of Arctos would have a slight adverse effect on Centre – partly through admitting a disproportionately large number of more able pupils, and partly by seducing some better teachers away from Centre. But it is worth remembering, in connection with this second point, that many teachers would prefer to leave the profession rather than teach at Centre – so some of the good teachers employed at Arctos are ones who, otherwise, would be altogether lost to the profession. (A similar point could be made about medicine. It is no good critics of private medicine producing examples of doctors seduced away from the public sector into the private unless it can be ascertained that there would be as many doctors available in the absence of a private sector and the resources it calls forth.) But certainly Arctos does not adversely affect Centre in the significant respects that North was supposed to adversely affect South – by taking a disproportionately large share of limited public resources.

At various points in the text, I have said (over-optimistically perhaps) that thinking egalitarians would not wish to see the position of the better-off worsened unless this could significantly benefit the worse-off. If so, thinking egalitarians could not have the same objection to Arctos that they had against North. Not only, then, does the special objection against private schooling evaporate, but there is one line of egalitarian criticism which is not available against private schooling.

Our critic will by now have become impatient, for it is clear that various real-life socio-economic factors are missing from the Scholesian situation. Most obviously, it is not the case in our society that all parents have the financial ability to send their children for private schooling. (In Scholesia, recall, wealth is distributed according to the 'difference principle' – so that it is reasonable to assume that if any can afford school fees, all or almost all can. This does not, of course, mean that all will be equally willing.)

But what is the import of this fact? People are wont to take it as vitiating a favourite defence of private schooling in terms of parental freedom. This defence, so the objection runs, pastes over the fact that very few parents have the freedom to educate their children privately, so that proscription of private schooling would not constitute a denial of any general freedom but only of a freedom enjoyed by the financially privileged.

There is, undoubtedly, confusion here.[2] There are many important respects in which everyone is free to educate their children privately. Reference to freedom, like reference to opportunity (see pp. 68f.), must be tied to context, for one is free to do X when one is not prevented by some factor which, in the context of discussion, is relevant. For example, a radical Labour MP may be free to send his son to Ampleforth in so far as he is not prevented from doing so on legal or religious grounds – but not free in so far as his credentials as a radical would be destroyed by such an act. Of course, if in the context one means by 'free' no more than 'unhindered by financial shortage', it will become a tautology that not everyone is free to privately educate. But in that case one would add nothing morally significant to the bare statement that some people are financially short by saying that they are not free to privately educate their children.

This said, it must be admitted that telling a man who is financially unable to do X that he is, nevertheless, perfectly free in a number of respects to do it, could be as cynical and comforting to him as the 'Arbeit macht frei' banner must have been to new arrivals at Auschwitz. It would be a feeble defence of a system in which only the richest accused could procure expert counsel to point out that no one is actually forbidden from procuring expert counsel. But there is a vital difference between this case and the educational one. While each person accused of a crime has the right to expert counsel, he does not have a right to be defended by the very best lawyers in the country. Charged with a crime, I have a right to be defended by a competent lawyer, but not to be defended by a Clarence Darrow or Norman Birkett. To get them, I must, reasonably enough, pay. It is, equally, a right of each child in a civilized society to receive adequate schooling; but there is no right – and could not be – to receive the best schooling to be found. (This is not the same, of course, as saying the child has no right to the best schooling that the school he attends is able, given its resources, etc., to provide. He has that right, just as I have a right to expect the best defence my lawyer, who is no Darrow, can plead.)

In some instances, when read in the proper way, the principle that some shall be free to do, or get, X only if all are is reasonable. It would be unjust, presumably, to let some candidates resit an examination during which they suffered migraine unless one allowed all such candidates to do so. But here it is important to distinguish 'being free to' in the sense of being allowed to, from having the effective ability to. The reasonable principle is that if some are allowed to resit all shall be allowed to. It would not be reasonable to hold that some shall be allowed to resit only if all are effectively able to resit. This would have the absurd consequence that if one migraine sufferer goes abroad, or is otherwise prevented from resitting, none of the sufferers shall be allowed to resit. Similarly, it is reasonable to insist that if any parents are allowed to privately educate their children, all should be allowed to. But if the principle, that some parents shall be free to privately educate only if all are, is taken to mean that, unless all are actually able to then none shall be allowed to, it is not reasonable. Or rather, it will only be reasonable if one has already decided against private schooling. For the principle of equal freedoms, when so stated, presupposes, and cannot therefore be used to support, a case against private schooling.

Critics of private schooling will no doubt want to stress a number of other 'real-life' socio-economic factors, which were missing from the Scholesian system – but these do not, I think, raise any fundamentally new considerations. It will be stressed, for example, that private schools are not usually havens of 'social mix', or that there are very significant correlations between private schooling and

103

future professional and financial position. To the extent that one is committed to 'social mix' and to breaking correlations between schooling and later socio-economic position, one will be especially hostile to private schooling. I have little to add to what I said about these commitments in chapter 3, but the following observations might be useful.

While vestiges of the 'old boys' network' no doubt remain, it is clear that selection into what the 1968 report called 'the most important positions in society' is less and less based on the mere fact that someone went to a private school. It is increasingly based on qualification. One might want to challenge the criteria for qualification in force – but that is another matter. Moreover, it is hardly apparent that the only, or the best, way of dealing with the old boy's network is the Augean policy of getting rid of the old boys.

Second, the hackneyed figures showing how many privately educated persons go on to fill 'the most important positions in society' are opaque in their significance unless accompanied by information as to who wants to fill them. One would surely expect a disproportionately high number of privately educated children to be ones who anyway, in virtue of their upbringing and parental expectations, consider such positions to be viable and desirable options. This simple, but frequently ignored, factor of desire is one of several which make it doubtful that the effect of abolishing private schooling would be a massive one in breaking the 'cycle of inequality' that runs from parental station to the child's future station.

Third, while considerations of 'social mix' militate with special force against private schooling, it is equally the case that some of the counter-considerations mooted earlier (pp. 95f.) have special force in the other direction. It is to be expected, for example, that many privately educated children will be ones who, as Bantock put it, might suffer cruelly from enforced, continual social contact with children of cruder manners – partly because, on recent evidence, so many of the latter would 'have it in for them'.

One thing these points suggest, I think, is that private schooling is best seen as, at most, a fairly vivid reflection or symptom of a general state of our society. There are those who find our state of society intolerable – who find it execrable that it is one in which, *inter alia*, jobs can sometimes depend on 'who you know', children's futures are often laid down for them by who their parents are, and considerable distances in manners and interests separate different social groups. Such people, if they have their way, will no doubt get rid of private schooling along with whatever else they see as reflections of the society they loathe. What I find peculiar is the mounting of a vitriolic offensive against private schooling within our society as it actually is. The polemic against private schooling should surely be a relatively incidental ingredient in a wider diatribe against our kind of society – and one to act upon only on the day, if it should come, when those who hate the society in which they write and speak of their hatred are in a position to overthrow it. To do otherwise, as one writer puts it, is surely to confuse the spots with the measles.[3]

4　Epistemological egalitarianism

1　Education and the sociology of knowledge

The egalitarian ideas so far encountered have, in broad outline, been formed in the traditional mould. In chapter 2 it was the familiar idea that educational goods, like others, should be more evenly distributed. And, in chapter 3, we met with such old friends as equality of educational opportunity, the idea that education should neither reflect nor promote inequalities in wealth, and the demand that schools should serve as 'social mixers'. The ideas to be discussed in this chapter and the next, however, do not belong to a long-established egalitarian tradition. Indeed they have largely grown out of a disillusionment with that tradition and are, in several respects, at odds with it.

These new brands of egalitarianism are based on claims about matters that, so far, I have said very little about; on claims about what constitutes a good education, about the nature and value of knowledge and truth, and about cultural standards. I have said little on these matters so far because their relevance would have been unclear. In chapter 2, it was enough for me to assume some normally uncontended criteria for what count as educational goods, and get on with the question of their distribution. Nor would it have been clear what relevance to essentially ethical matters an analysis of the nature of knowledge could have had.

Still, the nature of knowledge and learning did make a brief appearance – when I discussed Dewey's claim that their scope is widened through 'social mix'. That appearance was instructive, for Dewey's claim does illustrate how someone might (in his case wrongly) infer, in a direct way, egalitarian conclusions from an epistemological premise. The authors to be discussed in this chapter wish to go far beyond Dewey, in basing a thorough-going egalitarianism on claims about the nature of knowledge and truth. I shall dub these authors 'radical egalitarian critics of knowledge and educational reality' – or, for short, 'Reckers'. You will all know who I mean by the Reckers when I tell you that the *locus classicus* for their doctrine is the book, edited by M. F. D. Young, entitled *Knowledge*
106

and Control. It is fair to say, I think, that at present Recker egalitarianism is overtaking more traditional brands in academic educational circles. If it has not yet had a big impact on educational policy, that is due to its extremely radical nature; but as new generations of education students who have fallen under its spell permeate the education system, one fears that this impact may not be too distant. (It is worth noting that, to judge from some of their prescribed course reading, educationalists at the Open University appear to have adopted Recker egalitarianism as an official doctrine.)

In the Reckers' doctrine, equality figures in two different ways. Not only is their radical critique of knowledge supposed to yield various egalitarian demands, but it is plainly an ideological commitment to equality which has stimulated and sustained the critique. In their introduction to a recent Recker volume, the editors make it plain that their aim is to explain the 'why' of the school system's ability to 'perpetuate social inequalities', and that their target is 'those liberals and social democrats' who 'could not comprehend that the education to which they sought to widen access might itself be involved in perpetuating the inequalities they were concerned to overcome'.[1] The story they tell of the genesis of epistemological egalitarianism is roughly as follows: until recently (1971 presumably, the date of the first Recker manifesto, *Knowledge and Control*) the basic demands had been for equality of educational opportunity and for the more equal distribution of education (in the sense discussed in chapter 2). Attempts to implement the demands – direct grants, EPAs, comprehensives, etc. – failed, as noted in the previous chapter, to deliver the expected goods. Upper-class and middle-class children still do much better at 'O' and 'A' levels, and continue to dominate the universities. The standard 'liberal' reactions have been either a disillusioned acceptance of so-called Black Paper élitism, or an equally gloomy realization that attempts to implement the demands require far more swingeing policies than hitherto. According to the 'Reckers', both reactions are misguided and result from the failure 'to have recognized that we need to examine "what counts as education" . . . [and] the way in which prevailing definitions of it sustain just that form of society which those on the Left . . . wish to change'.[2] Once this need is recognized, the story continues, it will be seen that educational 'failure', so highly correlated with social class, is a function of the very criteria of education, knowledge, intelligence, and so on – and is not due to insufficient doses of the social engineering designed to equalize matters within a system governed by these criteria. As one leading Recker puts it, 'innovation in schools will not be of a very radical kind unless the categories teachers use to organize what they know about pupils and to determine what counts as knowledge undergo a fundamental change'.[3]

There is no doubting, then, the Reckers' faith that their investigations into 'what counts as education' will yield radically egalitarian dividends. But what is the nature of the claims which are supposed to yield these dividends? There can be no short answer, since it is going to take several pages to uncover even the rough structure and meaning of the claims. But very roughly, the Reckers' idea is this: the sociology of knowledge has revealed that what counts as knowledge, and its various kinds, is a function of socio-historical construction and definition. As such, current criteria of knowledge, truth, and validity are rooted in particular social conditions and lack objectivity. Many of our firmly established educational practices – such as the subject-based curriculum – presuppose a different, and mistaken, view of knowledge. Hence these practices, along with their inegalitarian consequences, are to be abolished.

In various, and more-or-less extreme, forms this is the doctrine espoused by most of the contributors to *Knowledge and Control* and the recent stable-mate it sired, *Society, State, and Schooling*. Such a doctrine is also found in other well-known radical writings – by Illich and Freire, for example. As a number of anti-Reckers have noted, it is also the predominant doctrine of recent generations of B.Ed. students of sociology. (Some comfort might be derived from one Recker's observation that there tends to be little connection between the doctrines subscribed to by teachers and their actual classroom practice.)[4]

The preceding, very rough sketch suggests that the Reckers' doctrine contains three components – sociological, epistemological, and educational. For the idea is that certain sociological claims entail, or at least support, a number of philosophical theses which, in turn, imply or strongly suggest the baselessness of various educational practices. To a degree, I am idealizing here – for the three components are rarely distinguished with any rigour by the Reckers themselves.[5] But such idealization or interpretation is essential if assessment is to be made possible; for, frankly, the writings in question are too ambiguous, confused, and conceptually crude for mere description to serve the purpose. Indeed, I regard the task of interpretation as the central one. Interpretation of muddled doctrine will here, as elsewhere, take us more than half-way towards critical rejection.

I shall examine the three components in increasing order of difficulty, beginning with the educational critique. There are three practices which, more than any others, draw the Reckers' fire. First, the division of the curriculum into distinct subjects or disciplines thought to correspond to distinct kinds of knowledge; second, the standard and deep-rooted distinction between teachers and taught, givers and receivers of knowledge; and, finally, the whole apparatus of assessment, particularly examinations, with its consequential partitioning of students into successes and failures.

It is worth pausing to attend to some of the obvious and less obvious inegalitarian aspects of these practices, which Reckers stress and condemn. The teacher/learner distinction, with its concomitant and asymmetrical authority relation, is in itself a form of inequality, and one from which other inequalities inevitably flow. By bringing up children in the belief that teachers have rightful authority over them, it is alleged, we condition them to accept, as adults, the élitist hierarchy of social life. For Illich, 'the safeguards of individual freedom are all cancelled in the dealings of a teacher with his pupil'.[6] Examinations, too, foster inequalities beyond the immediate and obvious one. By failing, a child is not only prevented from continuing his education in certain ways, but is likely to feel a sense of inferiority – an attitude which will further encourage servile acceptance of the social hierarchy, one of whose lower levels he is likely to occupy.

The real villain of the piece, for many Reckers, is the first practice mentioned – the division of the curriculum into distinct subjects – for it is this which largely serves as the basis for the other practices. The very existence of a subject or discipline implies the existence of experts in it – hence of individuals with a special authority to tell others what is and is not the case, and to assess when they have succeeded in mastering the knowledge imparted to them by the experts. But the practice has its own special inegalitarian consequences. For one thing, the experts associated with a discipline will form themselves into a professional clique, jealous of privilege, and resistant to democratic challenge from junior ranks. For another thing, the everyday, street, 'folk' knowledge which cannot be allocated to any of the official subjects will find no place in the school and will, for that reason, be treated as inferior. This 'discontinuity between their knowledge of the world and what they experience in school orderings, subjects, topics, etc.', is especially prejudicial to working-class children who, allegedly, are peculiarly rich in such extra-curricular knowledge.[7]

Inequalities, one is told, require justification. The inequalities just mentioned are not justified since they belong to, or stem from, educational practices with no rational justification, resting allegedly on huge mistakes about the nature of knowledge. Such is the Reckers' position.

It is more difficult to identify, with any precision, the sociological claims embroiled in the doctrine. There are, I think, three of them, and they derive from two important sources in sociology. One source is the tradition stretching from Marx, through Mannheim, to Schütz and Berger, of the sociology of knowledge – the investigation of intellectual life in relation to its socio-historical conditions. The other source is phenomenological sociology, with its stress on the reference that must be made, in explaining social behaviour, to the significance which the agents themselves attribute to their actions. As we shall see, tension can arise between the two traditions but, to an obvious degree, they must converge. The phenomenological sociologist, after all, cannot avoid a concern with the knowledge of agents, since this must mediate any explanation of their behaviour. It is no accident, therefore, that several sociologists – Schütz, for instance – should combine the phenomenological approach with a primary interest in the social conditions of knowledge.

Before I outline the claims which stem from these sources, a cautionary word. The claims, as I present them, will sound relatively tame – tamer, certainly, than in Recker presentations. This is partly because I omit the superfluous and dramatic terminology which often accompanies them, but partly because I insist on distinguishing the claims from some radical philosophical theses with which they are typically fused in the literature. Unless we heed this distinction, we shall be in no position to assess the sociological backing which the other components in the doctrine are supposed to receive. I intend no disrespect, incidentally, to the fathers of these traditions in describing the claims as 'relatively tame', for it is perhaps due to their important insights that the claims have become domesticated into the conventional wisdom.

The first claim, in essence, is the platform of phenomenological sociology. (Though several features of the claim are to be found in the views of John Dewey, which I mentioned in the previous chapter.) Men are active interpreters of the natural social world about them. The concepts in terms of which they classify that world are a function of their activities and not passive imprints from mechanical observation on a mental *tabula rasa*. Moreover, since social action is typically rational – genuinely guided by men's beliefs – then any explanation of such action must appeal to these actively created concepts and classifications. It is essential to note, as well, that when men categorize they are, generally, lending meaning and significance to what is categorized, for their ways of classifying relate to their interests and purposes. To classify certain objects as tools, for example, is not simply to conceptualize, but to imbue things with a significance relative to discernible human

110

purposes. It is a corollary that men with different purposes might have conceptualized the world in very different ways. Most of these points are built into Schütz's remark that 'all scientific explanations of the social world *can*, and for certain purposes *must*, refer to the subjective meanings of the actions of human beings from which social reality originates'.[8]

The second claim is one subscribed to by most influential sociologists of knowledge. Many of the beliefs and concepts espoused by individuals or groups are ones which serve to enhance their social positions. In the case of Marx, notoriously, the dominant ideas of an age are those which reflect and promote the economic interests of the dominant class. In a number of ways, later sociologists have widened Marx's horizon, while remaining faithful to his general point about the ideological nature of thought. For one thing, the emphasis is no longer confined to the economic class basis of beliefs; the ways in which professional groups, such as teachers, develop advantageous ideologies have also come under study. Nor is the emphasis so squarely upon moral and political ideas. One finds sociologists of knowledge now investigating the social role of concepts such as intelligence, insanity, or violence. ('Violence', I read recently, is a middle-class boo-word for labelling what is more neutrally described as placing fists on jaws, or boots in groins.)

The third claim is best seen as one which is required to reduce an apparent tension between the first two. The phenomenologist's picture is one of free, active men creatively constructing the concepts in terms of which they lend significance to their world; while the picture suggested by Marx and Mannheim is of men apparently condemned to operate with certain concepts and beliefs – those which reflect dominant economic interests or whatever. The disparity can be alleviated to some degree by what we might call the 'Coppélia' claim, or more officially the doctrine of 'reification'. In the ballet, an old man creates a doll which he then believes to have power and life of its own, an illusion which is cruelly exploited when a village girl impersonates the doll. The illusion was in attributing to a human creation a reality, power, or value beyond that imparted by the creator. The creation became 'reified'. Money, according to Marx, is falsely treated by men as having a value of its own. Concepts, classifications, and criteria can become 'reified', too, and appear to have a validity, objectivity, or 'out-thereness' (to use a favourite Recker expression), which belies the fact that they are mere instruments to be used, modified, or scrapped as men will. So, to some extent, the phenomenologist's freedom is reconciled with Marx's compulsion: men's intellectual creations come, through the process of 'reification', to constrain their future intellectual activity.

111

I want to make two remarks, at the present stage, on the connections between these sociological claims and the educational critique. First, it is fairly easy to see what links someone is likely to try to set up. It will come as no surprise to find Reckers treating the division of the curriculum into subjects as an instance of the 'reification' mentioned in the third claim. What are really human inventions appear to men as objectively separate bodies of knowledge. Nor will it be any shock to find the criteria of assessment employed by middle-class teachers condemned as reflections of class interests. But second, it is or ought to be perfectly obvious that in no sense do the sociological claims entail the educational critique. There is not, for example, the faintest inconsistency in holding both that curriculum subjects are human inventions and that the distinctions so produced are rational ones which any sensible curriculum must respect. Nor is there any logical difficulty in maintaining that, while certain criteria of assessment do as a matter of fact further some social interests, they are nevertheless valid criteria which any rational man must accept. (The rules for judging high-jump competitions favour tall people, but it is unclear what other rules could be seriously proposed.) Someone might, of course, want to abolish the criteria simply because certain interests get favoured; but this is not the Recker point. They want to show the criteria to be unfounded.

What my second remark implies is that the sociological claims need to be mediated by further claims, of an epistemological nature, if they are to support the critique. It must be the philosophical theses which provide the direct backing for the critique. Most Reckers see this and proceed to proclaim the philosophical theses which might do the trick. There are, though, some unfortunate exceptions. Thus we find Gorbutt arguing that 'particular educational activities *can* no longer be justified in absolute terms once the social basis of such justifications is recognized'.[9] This cries out for the insertion of a missing, epistemological premise establishing that what has a 'social basis' cannot therefore be 'absolutely' proper. As it stands, Gorbutt's argument is a grotesque *non sequitur*.

2 Sociology and epistemology

Identifying the philosophical component in the Reckers' doctrine is a Herculean task. Breathtaking logical leaps, the constant use of unexplicated but highly ambiguous terms, and amazing naïvety about the nature of epistemological problems all contribute to our difficulties. What I shall first do is present the theses in the Reckers' own words, and then proceed to interpretation. The interpretation

112

of these ambiguous words will not be guided, primarily, by the aim of discovering what the authors 'really mean', for I doubt there are any particular real meanings they have in mind. Rather – and in a spirit of charity – I want my interpretation to satisfy two constraints. First, I want the theses to come out so that they are not totally implausible ones. Second, I want them to come out so that we can see how they might, intelligibly, receive some support from the preceding sociological claims. If no such interpretation can be imposed then either the educational critique rests on totally implausible grounds, or the sociological component in the doctrine is superfluous. Either way, the boast of the 'new' sociology of knowledge to have established epistemological egalitarianism would be revealed as idle.

I detect three theses (yet again) in the epistemological component, which I shall dub the 'Subjectivist', 'Monist', and 'Relativist' theses respectively.

(A) 'Subjectivism' is the denial of so-called 'objectivism', which, according to Esland, is the thoroughly wrong view according to which the 'individual consciousness recognizes objects as being "out-there" ', as 'co-ercive external realities'. It sees man 'not as a world-producer, but as world produced'. Such a view is to be discarded in favour of one which treats the world as 'the products which [man] has created'; which stresses that human subjects are 'co-producers of reality and the survival of this reality depends on its continuing plausibility to the community'.[10] In an example to which I shall return, Young illustrates the thesis by unfavourably comparing the 'objectivist' view of mathematics, by which mathematical reality exists independently of human belief or construction, with the view (which he attributes to Wittgenstein) that mathematics has only 'social reality', that it is an 'invention, not a discovery'.[11]

(B) 'Monism' is the thesis I attribute to Young when he attacks 'the absolutist conception of distinct forms of knowledge which correspond closely to the traditional areas of the academic curriculum'. We should see these areas as *no more* than the socio-historical constructs of a particular time'.[12] Gorbutt echoes the theme when he writes that 'the apparent self-evident justification for education into particular forms of knowledge is laid bare as an ideological statement'.[13] Knowledge, or belief, is a seamless whole which ideologists of the time have artificially tried to divide into distinct forms.

(C) 'Relativism' is nicely illustrated in a passage Reckers are fond of quoting from C. Wright Mills. 'There have been, and are, diverse canons and criteria of validity and truth, and these criteria . . . are . . . open to socio-historical relativization.'[14] Or, as Esland

113

expresses it, 'truth and validity are not absolutes but derived through certain relevances and legitimacies'.[15]

Only the philosophically insensitive could think these theses, especially the first and last, to be at all clear. For one thing, each is ambiguous in scope. Are the 'objects' which are not 'out-there', but 'produced', *all* objects, including sticks and stones? – in which case, we are being offered extreme Idealism. Or is the point restricted to theoretical entities, such as electrons or superegos? – in which case it is perhaps some kind of Operationalism that is on offer. And what distinctions are being denied by the thesis of Monism? Fairly particular ones, such as a distinction between historical and geographical knowledge as distinct forms; or very general ones, such as that between *a priori* and *a posteriori* knowledge? Again, is it all or only some principles of logic – which, I take it, are included among the 'canons of validity' referred to by Wright Mills – which may be revised or scrapped in a different socio-historical situation?

Besides these problems of scope, a number of crucial expressions are left unexplicated by the Reckers. 'Out-there' is a good example. Is any form of Realism, according to which a world exists external to the mind, supposed to be mistaken? Or only a 'Naïve Realism' which takes the external world to be just about as it appears to be? And when our authors talk of 'criteria for truth', do they mean definitions of 'truth' (e.g. Tarski's semantical definition of the predicate 'is true') or, quite differently, the ways in which people actually test for the truth and falsity of sentences?

One thing is clear: there are ways of interpreting the theses, as so far expressed, which would have either or both of two results. Either the theses would carry little plausibility, or there could be no way they are supported by the sociological claims – or both. Suppose the Subjectivist thesis is interpreted as an espousal of extreme Idealism. Not only is such a theory unappealing, but it bears no relation to the sociological point about men being active constructors of concepts and interpretations. That men construct concepts can hardly entail there is no external world for them to conceptualize. Or suppose the Relativist thesis is interpreted to mean that any currently rejected proposition might be regarded as logically true in other socio-historical circumstances. Such a claim is absurd; for while there can, I believe, be genuine disputes as to the logical truth of some sentences, there can be no disputing that some sentences – including the negations of all classically accepted logical truths – are not logically true, nor capable of being believed true in whatever 'socio-historical circumstances'.

It would be fruitless, as I said earlier, to delve into what the authors 'really mean' by the epistemological theses. So let us

114

proceed to offer interpretations which lend the theses some plausibility and some intelligible connections with the sociological claims.

The Subjectivist thesis, I shall interpret as a pretty thoroughgoing version of a view associated with some philosophers in the Pragmatist tradition, and which I will label 'Strong Pragmatism' for lack of a better title. (But readers are advised to concentrate on how *I* characterize the view, putting behind them the associations the word 'pragmatism' normally has for them.) The central claim is that all truths – or far more than usually suspected – are, in a rather special sense, theoretical ones. By theoretical truth, I mean one whose criteria include the success of the theory to which it belongs; success, that is, in the explanatory and predictive, and perhaps other, purposes for which the theory is designed. That some truths are theoretical in this sense is not contentious. The statement that certain tissue contains DNA will only be deemed true, presumably, to the extent that the relevant biochemical theory works. If that theory is overtaken by a more successful one, in which there is no room for DNA, such a statement will no longer be counted true. The Strong Pragmatist wants to claim, however, that even such humdrum sentences as 'That is my pen' are theoretical; their truth depends on the success of a theoretical framework in which we postulate things like pens and people. Such sentences do not report pre- or extra-theoretic encounters with reality, but belong to a scheme we have constructed for explaining and predicting the course of experience. Pens, no doubt, belong to such a well-tried and well-grounded theory that we are apt to forget there is a theory lurking at all. But it is essential to stress that theory always is lurking, especially when we turn to statements which belong to less well-grounded schemes – ones about social classes, persons, intelligence, or meaning, for example. Statements like 'There are three social classes', 'Intelligence is on the wane', 'He is the same person who killed Smith', or 'x means the same as y', might not look theoretical – but, in fact, they are only as secure as the theories in which we postulate such entities as classes, persons, intelligence, and meanings.

This Strong Pragmatist viewpoint is clearly far from immediately absurd.[16] And it accords reasonably well with some of the quotations from Recker literature cited earlier. There is, for the Strong Pragmatist, a sense in which entities – electrons, social classes, meanings, etc. – are not 'out there', if being 'out there' means that the criteria for their existence are independent of the role they play in human purposes. And there will be a sense in which the world does not 'coerce' us to describe it this way rather than that; for how we describe things will depend, in part, on which of our constructed concepts best serve our purposes.

It is important that this Strong Pragmatist thesis is not confused with, or inflated into, certain others. For one thing, it is not an ontological thesis concerning the 'real' existence or otherwise of the entities postulated in theories. It is compatible with both a realist and anti-realist attitude towards theoretical entities. That the criteria for the truth of a statement about DNA involve the success of a theory does not show that DNA molecules are 'fictions', operationally reducible to whatever one favours as the 'real' constituents of the world. It would also be quite wrong to graduate to the view – which might be given the label Subjectivist as well[17] – that reality must somehow remain unknowable, because always hidden behind a veil of human interpretation. Even the admirable Schütz seems guilty of this move when, having stressed that a description of social behaviour must make reference to the conceptions of the agents, he concludes that it is impossible to 'exactly know what reality is'.[18] His conclusion is doubly unwarranted. For a start it is incompatible with his stress that social action *can* only be described with reference to the agents' own conceptions; for, if that is so, these conceptions do not veil reality, but are essential parts of the social reality the scientist is describing. More generally, there is no inconsistency in holding both that the concepts in terms of which we describe are constructed by us for theoretical purposes, and that things are just as our concepts portray them. Indeed, to the extent that the concepts belong to particularly well-grounded theories, that is the natural, if not inevitable, conclusion to draw. (Sometimes, it is worth adding, the fact that things *are* conceived of in a certain way would count as part of the reason why they are properly conceived of in this way. Friends are only friends, presumably, because they see each other as such (well, almost).)

The second thesis, Monism, I shall interpret as at least the denial of the traditional distinction between *a priori* and *a posteriori* knowledge. Given the familiar assumption – which is debatable, though I will not discuss it here – that these two kinds of knowledge correspond to two classes of proposition, necessary and contingent, then the Monist must at least be denying a genuine distinction between these two classes. I say that he must be at least denying these distinctions, since otherwise he could not have the complaint he does against those, like Hirst, who base a curricular division between 'formal' disciplines, like Maths, and 'empirical' disciplines, like Biology, upon the existence of distinct kinds of knowledge and propositions. No doubt there are somewhat finer distinctions he must also be wanting to deny – that between knowledge gained through observation and knowledge got through a process of *Verstehen*, perhaps; but my focus will not be upon these.

116

It is worth remarking that Monism is a natural, though not compulsory, bedfellow of the pragmatic Subjectivism just described. For having denied the traditional distinctions, it is natural for one to treat them as misleading reflections of the different ways in which we treat various propositions. On such a view, for example, the traditional 'necessary truths' might be thought of as those, merely, which for some reason or none we are peculiarly reluctant to revise in the face of possible experiences. It is also worth adding that Monism of this sort has been urged by some of the most influential analytic philosophers of the century – making nonsense of the Recker habit of lumping all such philosophers into one derisible heap.[19]

The Relativist thesis, judging by the quotes from Wright Mills and Esland, makes claims about both truth and validity. I shall take the claim about truth to be part and parcel of the Subjectivist thesis, on my pragmatist interpretation of it. For one could, presumably, take the claim that truth is not 'absolute . . . [but] derived through certain relevancies and legitimacies' as a misleading restatement of the idea that the acceptability of concepts and descriptions is related to the explanatory success of the theories in which they are embedded. The claim about validity, I shall take to be at least the claim that there can be *limited* alternatives to standard logic; that there can be coherent and viable challenges to at least some standardly accepted principles of inference. I stress the word 'limited' here, for we saw (p. 114) that it would be unintelligible to propose certain non-standard principles as genuine principles of inference.

This third thesis combines fairly well with the other two. The idea that even logic is revisable, within limits, seems a natural outcome of the stress upon all truths being judged by pragmatic criteria. Putnam has argued, forcibly, that where logic and physical theory (e.g. quantum physics) conflict, the logic should be as much up for revision as the physical theory.[20] And this idea connects up with the one we saw emerging in Monism, to the effect that so-called 'necessary truths' (of which logical truths are the traditional paradigm) differ from others only in the degree to which we would be content to give them up.

There is another thesis that lurks in Recker literature, which might also be described as relativistic. It is the claim that whenever we assess – whether by canons of logic or other criteria – a framework of assessment is presupposed, which is not itself up for assessment. Any assessment, therefore, is relative to some framework. This modest point must not be confused with the radical one which emerges if it is then insisted that these presupposed frameworks are not themselves capable of being assessed rationally. This radical point is, no doubt, intended by many Reckers; but it is not one they are entitled to on any possible sociological grounds, and nor is it one I can see any reason to take seriously.

I have now completed my charitable interpretation of Recker epistemology. We are faced with three theses none of which is implausible, and which can be made to hang together in a coherent outlook. Shortly, I want to show that these theses can receive some modest support from the sociological component. Before that, though, it is worth pointing out how the philosophical theses, on my interpretations, escape some of the more popular criticisms which have been levelled against the Reckers by other philosophers.

A favourite objection has been the *tu quoque* one. If there is no objectivity, what is the status of the remarks made by the Reckers themselves? As John White puts it, 'If truth and falsity do not exist in any absolute sense, then obviously the thesis about the relativity of all knowledge cannot be true in this sense.'[21] But if the attack on Objectivism is the Strong Pragmatist one described, then the Reckers face no real problem here. Their sociological concepts, like those of physical theory, will not be 'objective' in the relevant sense, since both are governed by pragmatic criteria; but they do not thereby become any more spurious than the physical concepts are. Parenthetically, it seems to me that the *tu quoque* charge is too quick, even when levelled against much more extreme claims – such as that no knowledge other than that possessed by sociologists of knowledge is well-founded. One would have to ascertain that the sociologists' assertions do not have a privileged status. No doubt it would be a pretty Herculean task to make out a case for such a privileged status, but attempts have been made, and they deserve some attention. I have in mind, for instance, Habermas's idea that it is only after a cleansing process of introspective reflection, by which one examines and liberates oneself from the influences which have formed one's beliefs, that a man is entitled to treat the surviving beliefs as genuine knowledge.[22] The idea that belief only becomes knowledge after some kind of internal cleansing has a long history. It can be found in Plato and Descartes, for example.

Another popular objection, levelled especially against the Relativist doctrine, is that doubts about logic and rationality shortly become unintelligible. Richard Pring writes that

> where basic canons of rationality are treated as 'problematic' and 'open to enquiry', it is not possible to understand what such an enquiry might consist in. For example, if the principle of contradiction is 'problematic', it would not be possible to engage in an enquiry about it. Any enquiry presupposes that self-contradiction is unintelligible.[23]

Even if Pring's point is correct, it will not worry the limited kind of logical relativism I described. A proponent of this view might distinguish more and less 'basic' principles of logic and admit that some of the most 'basic', such as the law of contradiction perhaps, do not allow of alternatives. In fact, though, it is hardly clear that Pring's point is correct. Wittgenstein, Tarski, Gödel, and many others have 'questioned' the law of contradiction, with at least an appearance of intelligibility. Certainly there are formal systems in which there is no such law and which do not seem, obviously at any rate, to be incapable of coherent interpretation. (It is important to stress two things here. First, it does not follow from the fact that there are many propositions which could *not* be intelligibly regarded as logical truths that there is any standardly accepted logical truth which cannot be challenged. Second, the alternative to dropping the law of contradiction is *not* to regard some contradictions as true, but to regard some as truth-valueless or having a value other than True or False.)[24]

The three sociological claims described earlier do, it seems to me, lend modest support to the three epistemological ones as I have interpreted them. Indeed, the interpretations were largely adopted in order to guarantee this result. There are at least two ways in which sociological observations, whether banal (Wittgenstein's 'reminders') or otherwise, can help out a philosophical claim. A typical philosophical conflict arises when one person denounces as impossible what another thinks is possible. The latter's case is helped by his being armed with putative examples of the 'impossible' actually occurring. Such examples may well come from sociology. What the examples do is to put the onus upon the opponent of explaining them away as spurious. Thus it will be encouraging to the proponent of the Relativist thesis to read of Lèvy-Bruhlian tribes who, prima facie, adopt, without talking gibberish, the deviant logics he deems possible. Another kind of philosophical confrontation occurs when someone denies what is very generally and ordinarily held to be the case. The burden is upon him to explain how common men can persist in what is mistaken. That burden is lightened if he is provided with an account of a psychological or sociological sort which shows that the beliefs in question are ones men are likely to have, irrespective of whether they are true or not; for then the presumption in favour of common sense is defeated. It is in this way, perhaps, that the doctrine of reification can buttress the Monist attack on distinct kinds of knowledge. The common tendency to suppose there are these kinds, and that they correspond to historically evolved disciplines, will be seen as an aspect of the general tendency to reify what are in fact purely human creations.

One can dimly see how, in both these general ways, empirical support for the Subjectivist thesis might be offered. Presumably it is pertinent to that thesis to draw attention, in the way Kuhn has, to the manner in which scientists suddenly forge new concepts which then dictate to them how to describe, in fresh terms, what might otherwise have appeared to be hard, given data. And one can see how the doctrine of reification might help to explain away the common failure to perceive the theoretical nature of even such humdrum entities as pens and trees. Because the theory to which such concepts belong is so well-established, the idea that the entities are postulated rather than passively encountered gets masked from view.

Let me close with a couple of dampening remarks. First, I stress that these sociological observations lend only some, and not very much, support. Clearly there is no substitute, in establishing a philosophical claim, for philosophical argument. The philosopher who insists that something is possible must show this, and not rest content with putative examples of the thing's actual occurrence; for he must be able to meet the challenge that the examples are spurious. Second, let me stress again that the sociological claims will lend no support to theses much more radical than the ones I offered the Reckers. There is a general reason for this: the more radical the epistemological conclusion argued for, the more justified is the suspicion that the sociological claims are not sociological at all, but have built into them the contentions they are supposed to support. Sociological research, says Young, has revealed 'the obvious empirical possibility of different sets of criteria of validity'.[25] Well, how different could the sets 'discovered' by sociological research be? Someone convinced that it would be unintelligible to employ certain criteria as criteria of *validity* will simply reject the sociologist's description of societies in which these criteria are allegedly employed. In particular, he will query the translations which the researcher must have employed in order to have foisted such criteria on the natives. It is only someone who already accepts the intelligibility of accepting contradictions who can accept Lèvy-Bruhl's description of his 'prelogical' peoples. Anyone else must either think Lèvy-Bruhl has mistranslated, or think he has confused the literal and the metaphorical.[26]

3 Epistemology and education

The sociological claims, we saw, were insufficient to warrant the educational critique. Do the epistemological theses warrant it? If they do, the Reckers' doctrine deserves serious attention, for not

120

only do those theses get some sociological backing, they also form a pretty coherent, and far from absurd, conception. At any rate, the doctrine would deserve this, even if my charity has been misplaced in ascribing it to any Recker.

Unfortunately, I see little or no connection between the epistemology and the educational practices being condemned. Whatever points in the critique may be valid do not require the epistemological backing; and the epistemological theses lend no support to them. Actually, it seems to me rather obvious, once the components are distilled as they have been, that there cannot be any interesting connection. How, for example, could the very deep thesis of Monism touch on the practical propriety of taking biology, say, as a distinct classroom subject? Unfortunately, we are in an area of debate where the obvious needs to be spelled out.

My method will be to first display the lack of connection in the case of mathematical knowledge and education; and then draw some general lessons from that case. On p. 113 I noted how Young illustrates the Subjectivist thesis by rejecting the 'realist' view of mathematics in favour of the view that mathematics has only *'social reality'*. He does so in the context of attacking the ' "curriculum as fact" or commodity view of knowledge', which he takes to underpin the various educational practices that all good Reckers decry. So his point seems to be that immediate educational implications do flow from a proper understanding of the nature of mathematical knowledge, from realizing that it is not 'out there' as a distinct body of truths to be transmitted and assessed by those 'in the know'.

To focus upon mathematics, then, is to focus on one of the few examples actually provided by a Recker as illustration. Moreover, charity towards the Reckers makes it an especially apposite case for other reasons. For one thing, each of the epistemological theses may seem to be at its strongest in application to mathematical knowledge. That mathematical entities – sets, series, etc. – are not encountered, but entertained only so long as they serve explanatory purposes or practical aims; that mathematical truths are not *sui generis* but either very well-confirmed empirical ones (as Mill held) or distinguished by our refusal to amend them in the face of apparently recalcitrant experiences (as Wittgenstein held); that non-standard logic is required for handling inferences in certain areas of mathematics (as the Intuitionists hold in connection with non-denumerable sets) – each of these claims has been made with some force. Moreover, it might seem that theses of a more radical kind – ones which, therefore, fit Recker terminology better than the ones I offered them – are not without some plausibility in application to mathematics. By his salute to Wittgenstein, I imagine that

121

Young intends to embrace a radical kind of so-called 'Constructivism'. According to this idea, mathematical entities are literally created by us, as we add, continue series, construct sets, or whatever. For example: until we have actually continued a series to the point where *n* is included or excluded, there is simply no truth of the matter as to whether there is such a series containing *n* or not. The series does not pre-exist for us to inspect; rather it is invented by us as we continue it. The illusion of pre-existence is created by the fact that, typically, there is general and automatic agreement on whether a certain number is to be included. Fairly clearly, if even this view of mathematics does not yield the Reckers' educational conclusions, nothing more moderate will. So, for the sake of argument and charity, we shall accept the plausibility of such a view. (Not that many mathematicians or philosophers do. It is merely swashbuckling of Young to treat as self-evident, or as something immediately implied by some banality about men being creative, a view which has been dismissed by, among others, Cantor, Frege, Russell, Hardy, and Gödel.)

It seems clear to me that none of the Recker educational criticisms begin to follow from such a conception of mathematics. The general reason is that this conception, and its rivals too, are at too deep a level to have an effect on mathematical practice and thinking, except at the most advanced stages. The exception is unsurprising, since these advanced stages are characterized by the intrusion of such conceptions into the topics of debate. They are the stages where mathematics merges with philosophy of mathematics. The vast bulk of mathematical practice and learning can and should proceed unhindered by worries as to which of these deep conceptions is correct. (Which is not to say that children should not be encouraged to discuss such conceptions, i.e. to philosophize about mathematics. Personal relationships should not be hindered by philosophical theories of personal identity; which does not mean people should not discuss the theories.)

In the first place, there is nothing in the above conception to encourage the idea that there are not experts in mathematics, with the authority to transmit what they know to the inexpert; nothing, that is, to gainsay the standard view, reviled by Young, that there is 'a body of knowledge to be transferred from the teacher who has it to the pupil who has not'.[27] That mathematical entities are 'created' not 'discovered' cannot belie this, for (a) what have been created are things about which there can be considerable expert knowledge, and (b) considerable knowledge may be required for the creation. Let us grant that what Euclid or Gödel proved did not, in some sense, exist before the proofs. Yet it requires a good bit of

122

understanding to follow the proofs, let alone to have originally produced them. Nor can Wittgenstein's idea, that before we give an answer to a mathematical question, it has no true or false answer, go against the standard educational view. For that idea is obviously compatible with there being established rules and procedures – often matters of expert knowledge – for constructing the answers.

It might be replied, I suppose, that these rules and procedures are not matters of knowledge, but of convention and decision. But, in the first place, there will remain the important, often expert, knowledge that these are the conventionally adopted rules and procedures. The rules, syntactic or semantic, of German or French are, in the main, conventional: clearly that does not prevent there being experts who know a great deal about, and can teach a great deal about, these languages. Second, dubbing these rules and procedures 'conventional' only has force if it is possible to conceive of genuine, viable alternatives to them. By a 'genuine' alternative, I mean one which is not equivalent to the original (in the way that multiplying by 2 is equivalent to the procedure of multiplying by 4 and dividing by 2). By 'viable', I mean the proposed alternative must be intelligible, with results that can be taken seriously. Now it is far from clear that there are such alternatives to the rules and procedures of elementary mathematics, or of the great bulk of advanced mathematics. (The weakest passages in *Remarks on the Foundations of Mathematics* are those in which Wittgenstein tries to imagine genuine, viable alternatives to standard mathematics.) Moreover, even if there are such alternatives, it would take a mathematician of some genius to convince us of them. Not only would he have to be thoroughly grounded in standard mathematics, but those of us who were able to understand him could hardly be mathematical duffers.

It would be ludicrous, finally, to treat the Relativist point about the possibility of alternative logics in mathematics as suggesting the impossibility of unprejudiced assessment of students' powers of ratiocination. The following considerations about alternative logics need to be kept in mind here: the use of such logics only becomes a desideratum, if at all, at advanced levels (e.g. to block Dedekind's definition of real numbers); these logics introduce no new principles of logic, but deny the universal applicability of some standard ones (applicability, in particular, to propositions for whose truth and falsity we have no decision procedure); and last, the vast majority of standard principles are left unchallenged. In short, the proposed alternatives are highly restricted in scope and content. It is surely worth keeping the following two points to the fore as well. Even if it is hard to assess the relative merits and demerits of standard versus deviant logic in mathematics, there need be no difficulty in assessing if someone is operating properly within a given logic. Second, it should make all the difference in our attitude towards our budding mathematician whether he is refusing to draw a standard inference, because of his Intuitionist commitments, say, or failing to draw it because he is very muddled. It is one thing for Heyting or Brouwer to resist the move from '*n* is not in the set A̅' to '*n* is in the set A' on the basis of a theory about negation in mathematics; quite another for our budding student to fail to make it, on the basis of no theory whatever.

The other Relativist point, about mathematicians employing presuppositions which are not up for assessment, is equally incapable of prompting a negative attitude towards the possibility of objective assessment. Contentious assumptions – as to whether mathematical entities exist independently of our constructions, say – are not required by ordinary mathematics. Counting, calculating, dividing, etc., can go on quite happily whichever of the contentious assumptions are made. No doubt even pretty simple mathematical activity presupposes something – but there is no reason to suppose that what is presupposed is either contentious or incapable of being given some justification. I have in mind, for example, the assumption that the symbols we use in a calculation do not change shape each time we look away from the paper. Would an examiner be *prejudiced against* the duffer if he refused to entertain the possibility that the symbols he reads on the exam paper have no resemblance to those the student actually wrote down?

Someone might say that, by taking mathematics as the focus, I am meeting the Reckers on ground particularly favourable to me. Had the ground chosen been history, would not the Reckers' educational complaints sound much more powerful? – such complaints as those against the notion of historical 'expertise', the separation of history from other areas, or the 'bourgeois' bias exhibited by history teachers when assessing students' work. Perhaps they would – but the point is irrelevant. My case is not against the Reckers' educational critique – or not primarily – but against the idea that such a critique can be derived from the sociologically-backed epistemological theses uncovered. There is, after all, little that is original in the complaints made by the Reckers. The whole interest of their doctrine resides in the attempt to support these complaints sociologically and epistemologically. Given this, we can see that mathematics ought to be a specially favourable case for the Reckers, since, as we saw, the epistemological theses seemed especially plausible in this area. (It is, I take it, more plausible to hold that mathematical entities are theoretical constructs than that historical

124

entities, such as past kings, are.) Yet, as we also saw, the educational critique gets no backing from the epistemology. Perhaps the complaints levelled against history are justified; but this will not be because of the truth of the epistemological theses. If history does not deserve a separate place in the curriculum, this will not be because there is no *sui generis* kind of historical knowledge, *Verstehen* or whatever. And if there cannot be historical 'experts', this will not be because of the much too deep point about the pragmatic, theoretical nature of all the historian's concepts.[28]

The discussion of mathematics ought to have appeared laboured since, it seems to me, the lack of connection I was concerned to stress is rather obvious. I would like, however, to draw some general lessons from that discussion; for most of the points made are by no means confined to mathematics.

The first lesson is that creation and construction are perfectly compatible with knowledge, truth, and objectivity (in the sense of rationally well-founded agreement). That is: the fact that an entity is postulated – or even literally created – for human, explanatory purposes in no way conflicts with these virtues. That certain entities – mathematical series? moral values? – are literally brought into being by human intellectual action does not mean there are not strict rules governing how they are brought into being; even less does it follow that 'anything goes' as far as their future handling is concerned. Perhaps people have been misled by Romanticist accounts of artistic creation. Yet even here it is not the case, in general and outside of the very *avant-garde*, that there is total liberty in the construction of a fictional creature, or in what can be said about it once created. No one, not even Dickens, writing a sequel to *Pickwick Papers*, could have Mr Pickwick spending his Swiss holiday bounding up the North Face of the Eiger for exercise. The reason for this loss of liberty is not that our creatures, like the ills in Pandora's box, somehow become automotive. Rather what we build into the creations commits us, for the sake of consistency and coherence, to proceed in certain directions and not others. What is built into a mathematical entity, such as the number 7, of course commits us far more rigorously to what we may then go on and say about it than what Dickens builds into Mr Pickwick in chapter 1.[29] Nor is there anything in the Strong Pragmatist idea that all our concepts are constructed within a theoretical, explanatory frame to endorse a *laissez faire* attitude towards these concepts. Whether concepts are succeeding in their allotted roles; whether they are better replaced by another set; whether it is time to abandon a whole scheme of explanation in which the concepts are embedded – these are not questions beyond rational decision, or at any rate the sway of

125

rational considerations. The doctrine of reification might be salutary against those who fail to register the degree to which entities are created or theoretically postulated. But the opposite doctrine (anthropification?) can be equally salutary against those who ignore the severe constraints both on how we can create or postulate and on what can be done with our creations and postulates.

The second lesson is really a cluster of lessons about that family of notions, 'alternative', 'convention', 'custom', 'habit', and so on. (It is related to the first lesson for, as we saw in the mathematical case, one of the things which (mistakenly) appealed to the Reckers about Strong Pragmatism and Constructivism was the (non-existent) implication that 'our knowledge' must be a matter of convention and custom to which there are ready alternatives.) The first thing to learn is to insist on those distinctions, ignorance of which encourages a grossly exaggerated picture of how convention enters into knowledge, and hence of the possibility of alternatives to 'our knowledge'. One distinction is between the conventionality or otherwise of a practice which is in force, and the conventionality or otherwise of there being some practice having the same effect. From the fact that the choice between X and Y may be more or less arbitrary, it does not follow that our doing one or the other is an arbitrary quirk. It may not matter if we drive on the left, or drive on the right, but it matters very much that we all do just one of those. Many practices in intellectual areas are conventional in the sense that a different practice would have done just as well. It does not follow that there is any conventionality in our having to adopt at least one of these practices. For example, physicists have to use some method of measurement – even though it may not matter much which of various alternatives, all having the same practical results, it is they opt for. Another, more crucial, distinction is the semantical one between what refers or expresses and what is referred to or expressed. Of course the symbols and words we employ are employed by convention; but it does not follow that the propositions so expressed are 'true by convention'. (Roadsigns are conventions, but not the locations of the cities to which they point.)

Respecting this latter distinction must also discourage an over-facile view as to the possibility of genuine alternatives to well-established theories. If two theories have incompatible consequences, then testing between them is not ruled out in principle – so the choice of one against the other is not mere convention. If, on the other hand, their consequences are identical, the idea that we have two theories, rather than one theory variously expressed, must come under serious scrutiny. For example, a teleological theory about X, having exactly the same consequences as a mechanistic one, might

126

plausibly be held to be translatable into the latter. The teleologist's 'X occurs in order that Y' might, as a crude first shot, be regarded as a notational variant of the mechanist's 'The influences on Zs which lack Y, through lacking X, are such as tend towards their extinction'.

A related distinction to attend to is that between a subject or discipline as an institutionalized study, and a subject as what is studied in that study. A student doing history is studying the past, but his degree in history is not a degree in the past. Failure to mark the distinction encourages the idea that theories, concepts, etc., must be matters of convention or custom – for to be sure, the ways in which the study of such theories and concepts is organized and institutionalized bear the mark of convention and custom. It also encourages the reverse error of supposing that if our theories and concepts naturally separate into discrete kinds of knowledge, these divisions must be reflected in discrete institutionalized studies, with their special slots in the curriculum. In connection with the latter point, it is worth recalling that the great Newman's defence of a liberal education, comprising a number of distinct subjects, is in no way based on there being kinds of knowledge distinguished on philosophically significant grounds. On the contrary, he insists in almost Hegelian or Quinean terms that knowledge is the apprehension of

> one large system or complex fact . . . there are no natural or
> real limits between part and part . . . [the sciences] proceed
> on the principle of a division of labour, even though that
> division is an abstraction, not a literal separation into parts . . .
> sciences are the results of mental processes about one and the
> same subject matter, viewed under its various aspects.[30]

So Newman's grounds for the existence of distinct subjects are not epistemological. Rather, the obvious differences between the propositions we entertain, such as that one is about past battles and another about the inside of the human body, warrant the distinctness of subjects because (a) a division of labour here, as elsewhere, yields increasing returns, and (b) specialists in different subjects mutually check on another's excesses, thereby promoting a more sober overall science or philosophy than would emerge without such a separation of powers.

Another lesson, in the same area, concerns what may be inferred from the fact, if it is a fact, that even our most strongly embraced beliefs and concepts are not rooted in necessity, so that it is at least conceivable that what they represent might have been otherwise. In a fairly sober piece of 'Reckage', Whitty rightly points out that because there may be conceivable circumstances in which the beliefs would not be rightly held, it does not follow that the existence of the beliefs is explained by the machinations of interest groups or 'epistemic communities' engaged in 'legitimizing activities'.[31] For, he says, these beliefs may be explicable in terms of underlying socio-historical factors whose effects are not under the control of such groups. But although this trichotomy offered by Whitty – 'Beliefs are either rooted in necessity or in underlying historical circumstances or they are foisted on us by "legitimizers" ' – is better than the dichotomy which misses out the middle alternative, it is not sensitive enough. What needs to be added are those beliefs, which Kant had so much to say about, that without being subject to historical factors or 'legitimization', but without being rooted in 'the nature of necessity', nevertheless require us to hold them. They are the beliefs which, as far as we can tell, must be held by any creatures remotely like ourselves if they are to make sense of and communicate their experiences. Although we can perhaps conceive *that* there should be creatures without these beliefs, it is an impossible or at best gargantuan task to conceive *of* such creatures. Blindness to this important possibility has been encouraged, possibly, by a misreading of Wittgenstein's remarks on 'forms of life' (an expression which one must now wish had never been coined). Too many writers glibly assume that when Wittgenstein relates the truth of beliefs to the form of life of the believers, he is proposing some kind of anthropological relativism; what is true for us is false for the Azande, etc. But 'our' form of life for Wittgenstein is the human form of life – not that of a twentieth-century Englishman as against that of an eighteenth-century Frenchman or even a fifth-century aboriginal. Reflection on the examples he gives of what characterizes this form of life – taking the existence of the past for granted, treating certain other creatures as persons, taking it that things do not keep doubling in size, etc. – should discourage the view that 'our' form of life is one to which there are readily available, coherent, and pursuable alternatives.

Yet another lesson in the area is to be on guard against supposing that what might be a genuine alternative for another society can be a genuine alternative for an individual within a given society. That a certain belief or piece of behaviour may be intelligible or acceptable in some society does not entail that an individual in our society can intelligibly or acceptably adopt it. Hence, it would be no sign of prejudice or parochialism on the part of, say, a teacher if he is dismissive of such beliefs or behaviour among his students. Let us grant that Samurai ethics formed a coherent system in which actions could be intelligibly evaluated. Such a system, however, is not a genuine option for someone in our society, for the whole set of institutions against which such an ethic was situated does not obtain among us.[32] In 'Patriotism', Yukio Mishima describes, and gets us to understand, a Japanese soldier who regards it as his, and his wife's, duty to commit *hara-kiri* when ordered to arrest his best friend for mutiny. Would a headmaster who condemns as absurd a prefect's judgment that he should take cyanide (and force some on his girl-friend as well) rather than report the misdemeanours of some class-mates therefore be guilty of narrow, Western parochialism? Again, we might admit for argument's sake that the primitive's system of spirits, demons, and the like constitutes a coherent alternative to the Western explanatory scheme of particles, bacteria, etc. But since the whole background in which the primitive's beliefs are set – invocation of spirits, spells, appeasement of demons, fear of the elements, and so on – is missing with us, it becomes unclear that we can even understand, let alone take seriously, the examinee's suggestion that it is the tree god, rather than Dutch elm disease, which is responsible for the deforestation. Beliefs, it is often and rightly remarked, require appropriate behaviour to be identified as the beliefs they are. In a society where it is impossible to exhibit certain behaviour – and remember that some behaviour logically requires the co-operation of others – it is unclear, therefore, whether members of that society can really hold the same beliefs as those in another.[33]

The final, and distinct, lesson to be drawn is against the hearing of false echoes across the valley which divides epistemology from education (even though there are some connecting paths). Hearing such echoes encourages people – especially philosophers of education[34] – to grossly exaggerate the impact that deep epistemological considerations can or should have upon educational practice. We must, in particular, be on guard against taking too seriously superficial analogies between an epistemological thesis and an educational proposal, lest we mistakenly see the one as supporting the other. As often as not, the resemblance goes no further than the occurrence of the same ambiguous or vague expressions in the descriptions of each. We saw this happening in the mathematics case. Mathematical entities, we were willing to suppose, are created rather than discovered – then, lo and behold, we found people concluding that maths must be a co-operative enterprise between teachers and pupils; that there are no 'experts' in maths, since each must do his own creative thing; that mathematical truth cannot be transmitted to individuals, but must be made up by them – and so on. But, of course, the sense in which, for the mathematical Constructivist, mathematical entities are 'created' is perfectly compatible with objective truth, expertise, and the most traditional teaching methods that any Victorian headmaster could dream of.

Let me give another example of a false echo. Some philosophers have held that some knowledge is innate, in which case there is certainly a sense in which such knowledge cannot be described as learned or taught. Some educationalists, fastening on to this, miraculously conclude that education in this field must, therefore, be 'child-centred', or must be a dialectical 'teasing-out' of what the child already knows. This is nonsense, for although, in a sense, the knowledge itself cannot be taught, what brings the knowledge to explicit consciousness certainly can. Leibniz thinks that all mathematical knowledge is innate – so the child knows, unconsciously, the value of Y, for any value of X, in the formula $2 \times X = Y$. Clearly that does not mean the child cannot learn the $2 \times$ table, or be told that 2×9 is 18, or be instructed in how to multiply – and so on. What has been instilled into him, if Leibniz were right, is not the knowledge – which is already there – but this expression and awareness of it.

In my discussion of the mathematics case, I offered a reason why the conflicting mathematical philosophies could not be expected to have different, radical effects on mathematical practice, including educative practice. An account of mathematical truth or knowledge, to be taken seriously, must be compatible with the bulk of our actual practice – with, for example, the massive agreement among us on how to continue series, or the utility of measuring instruments, or the ability to agree on assessing whether a child has got the right answer. (Wittgenstein's extreme Constructivism, far from offering a challenge to such ordinary practices, is largely motivated by the attempt to explain them.) If so, the serious conflicting philosophies cannot have any radical implications for this practice, with which they must all, by and large, be compatible. This point is surely generalizable. Innatism, for instance, could not be taken seriously were it incompatible with the obvious fact that we engage in the practice of teaching and instructing in mathematics or whatever.

I said there were connecting paths between epistemology and educational practice; and I certainly do not want to deny that some epistemological considerations can have some impact on some aspects of that practice. Nor do I wish to say that there are no conflicts between some plausible epistemological theses and our actual practice; nor that, when there are such conflicts, practice should always be left as it is. (In particular, I doubt, *pace* J. L. Austin *et al.*, that conflicts between philosophy and linguistic practice should generally be resolved in the latter's favour.) My guess is, however, that where a serious epistemological theory seems to have radical practical implications, either the theory or the practice has been misunderstood. Dr Johnson not only failed to refute Berkeley by stubbing his toe, he failed to understand him.

The official topic of this book, equality and education, has disappeared for several pages; an absence which needs explaining. At the beginning of this chapter, I called the Recker brand of egalitarianism the most fashionable of today's brands. Such is the impression I gain from students, at least. Purveyors of this brand, in fact, vent more spleen and scorn upon what they see as antediluvian brands than upon we non-egalitarians who are presumably beyond redemption (rather as Lenin reserved his most vitriolic polemics for fellow, but 'deviant', revolutionaries). To traditional demands for more equal shares in 'the system' – medical, legal, and so on, as well as educational – the retort has become: 'But it's "the system" which is responsible for the serious inequalities.' Like rancid butter, it is to be thrown out rather than spread more evenly. Although this is a new attitude, it is important to identify where the originality lies. It is not in the specific educational practices condemned by the Reckers. There have always been those who have objected to the apparatus of examination and assessment, to the subject-based curriculum, and to the 'transmission' of knowledge from teacher to taught. (Rousseau?) The sociological claims, too, are merely the working-out in the educational arena of main strands in twentieth-century sociology. And the epistemological theses – on my somewhat anodyne interpretations, at least – form a fairly well-established package of a pragmatist orientation which several philosophers have already bought. So, the originality lies in the way these various components have been united in an overall doctrine; in the way the educational critique is held to derive, *via* epistemological considerations, from sociological premises. If that doctrine had been persuasive, and if the educational changes urged had the imagined egalitarian consequences, then we would have been presented with a persuasive case for equality.

As the second 'if'-clause in the last sentence suggests, I might have speculated whether the changes advocated by the Reckers would in fact have the egalitarian consequences they suppose. It is not obvious, for example, that the effect of dismantling the present system of examination and assessment would not be arbitrariness and prejudice in job selection. And it is far from clear that the discarded 'experts' in the discarded subjects would be replaced by Illich's 'masters', 'true leaders', and 'great educators',[35] and not by an unappealing motley of cranks, gurus, and vociferous Trotskyites, unchecked by professional criteria, and characterized more by charisma or muscle than by wisdom. While such speculation is

131

interesting, I saw my main task to be that of discrediting the overall Recker doctrine. If that doctrine is a failure, then the educational critique – whatever the egalitarian result might or might not be – has been given no basis.

Although I have tried to be sympathetic, indeed charitable, in attempting to identify what the Reckers, their own worst enemies, may be getting at, my final estimate has been almost entirely negative. My final act of charity is to refer the reader to chapter 4 of Richard Pring's *Knowledge and Schooling* in which a somewhat more favourable verdict is reached.[36]

5 Culture, equality, and the curriculum

1 'Culture'

At first glance, the issue now tackled is the converse of the one discussed in the last chapter. There we were exploring the egalitarian implications of an epistemologically-based, radical attack on the standard curriculum. Here we shall be investigating the implications for the curriculum of a prior commitment to equality. In particular, we shall examine whether equality demands that all children should be taught a broadly similar curriculum or, rather, that different children should be taught very different curricula. For example, should some children receive a fairly traditional literary, 'liberal' education, while schooling for others is of a much more vocational, 'relevant' kind?

The issues of the two chapters, however, are intimately linked. I noted, for example, that one Recker complaint against the subject-based curriculum was the gap this allegedly creates between school knowledge and the knowledge children, especially working-class ones, encounter and require outside. Again, it was noted that, whatever the subsequent epistemological arguments, the Reckers' initial hostility to standard educational practice was a function of an egalitarian disappointment with the failure of such measures as comprehensivization to reduce differentials in the academic success of children from different social classes. But the real common factor is the appearance, in one guise or another, of relativism. In the last chapter, a radical kind of epistemological relativism was encountered. There can be no objective knowledge; one man's 'construction of reality' is as good as the next's; truth and validity are relative to social groups – and so on. I did not take such claims especially seriously, preferring to treat them as hysterical exaggeration of more sober ones that could have some feasible connection with the Reckers' sociological premises. Anyway, relativism of that brand needs to be distinguished from the one which will now interest us. This new brand is about the value of knowledge, not its nature or possibility. It is consistent, presumably, to hold that while there can be objective knowledge, there can be no objective criteria for judging that knowledge of one kind, or in one area, is superior to, of greater value than, some other.

This claim about the value of knowledge is, of course, but part of a wider relativistic attitude which I shall dub 'cultural relativism'. For it would be natural to proceed from the claim about knowledge to parallel claims about tastes, activities, interests, manners, and norms. Just as knowledge of physics and philosophy cannot be deemed superior in value to knowledge about football, so a taste for 'pop' music cannot be deemed inferior to a taste for the 'classics'. Pushpin and poetry; 'disco' dancing and ballet; politeness and 'hardness'; an interest in historical figures and an interest in the figures from *Coronation Street* – between such pairs, any evaluative preference can only be subjective or prejudiced. Since our schools clearly do prefer some knowledge, tastes, modes of behaviour, and so on, to others, and since they try to instil these preferences, they must be guilty of just such prejudice. In brief and exaggerated terms, this is the brand of relativism which many self-styled egalitarians today embrace, and the ramifications of which for the curriculum – especially the issue of diverse curricula – are to be examined.[1]

The chapter will take the following shape. In this section, I shall say a few words about culture, for it is about cultural values, in some sense, that the relativism just sketched is about. In section 2 I shall examine and reject the case for thinking that 'true' egalitarianism commits one to the existence of diverse curricula for diverse cultural groups. So I shall be defending what Mary Warnock calls 'the obvious view (namely that egalitarianism demands a common syllabus)'[2] – though not on the same grounds as various other writers have. In section 3, I go on to argue that there are, nevertheless, powerful arguments in favour of diverse curricula – albeit of a totally non-egalitarian kind. In fact, the interesting thing which will emerge in that section is that, given these arguments, it is *only* those of an egalitarian bent who can favour the common curriculum. This is interesting, because while it may be 'obvious' that this is an egalitarian commitment, it is far from obvious that this should be an egalitarian prerogative. Certainly the common curriculum has been favoured by any number of people who would not count themselves as egalitarians.

If cultural relativism – and such related notions as 'cultural deprivation', or 'cultural difference' – are to be understood, a few words are needed on the term 'culture'. At any rate, certain distinctions which get blurred by the catholic use of that term need to be made. It is arguable, indeed, that cultural relativism derives most

134

of its nourishment from a failure to make these distinctions. What follows is brief and fairly casual. It is not an 'analysis of culture', and I only say as much as is required, I hope, for certain confusions to be avoided.

The word 'culture' is very much up for grabs, since it is both vague and equivocal. That is: it has a number of senses, and these senses, as well as the distinctions between them, are none of them precise. Many people mistake words like this for ones which are both precise and univocal, but simply very hard to define satisfactorily ('gene' perhaps, or 'real' in the mathematical sense where it refers to a certain class of numbers). This fosters the unfortunate illusion among some writers who are merely stipulating a meaning for 'culture' that they are discovering its one 'true' meaning, and thereby the illusion of a victory against other writers who have simply made a different stipulation. Malinowski, for example, says it is 'radically wrong' to suggest that 'each culture only covers a small segment of its potential compass'. Certainly it is if, like Malinowski, you define 'culture' to mean a 'complete and self-sufficient' whole which 'satisfies the whole range of basic, instrumental, and integrative needs'.[3] But there is nothing 'radically right' in defining it that way, while outlawing any other way.

One sense of 'culture' is, to be sure, the one Malinowski was trying to capture. At least it has become a genuine sense as a result of Malinowski and other anthropologists creating it. In this sense, almost any aspect of life in a community – its utensils, cooking, factories, and laws as well as its music, architecture, and philosophy – belong to the culture of the community. This is not a sense that will be of much interest to us; it is too broad, covering as it does everything connected with men aside, perhaps, from their unadulterated natural environment.

The central, though vague, use of the term is, I should think, to refer to a certain limited range of society's products – including at least its literary, musical, dramatic, and architectural products. If someone tells me he is writing a book comparing New York and London cultural life, I will expect him to be comparing the respective worlds of books, plays, etc., but not the respective legal systems, factory methods, driving habits, or stock exchanges. There is little doubt that, left unqualified, the word 'culture' suggests to most of us whatever has to do with the arts – though just what that is remains very vague. Is ice-skating or dress-designing a sort of art?

Now culture, in this product-sense, is certainly going to concern us, but it will be useful for our purposes to extend this sense in a direction in which it is often and reasonably extended – so that it will embrace theoretical products as well as those of the arts. The following list will show the kind of thing I mean by 'theoretical products': Marx's theory of history, the DNA account of genes, the 'Big Bang' theory of the cosmos, Frege's account of mathematics as logic, Rawls's theory of justice, Freud's theory of the unconscious – and so on. I have in mind the 'big', important theories which, at a given time, dominate theoretical discussion within the various intellectual disciplines. This is a reasonable extension: if I pick up a book on ancient culture, I shall be disappointed if it tells me only about the pottery or music of the time, but nothing of the astronomy or metaphysics.

Next we have the sense which interested Matthew Arnold, and which we have in mind when we refer to 'men of culture', 'the cultured mind', 'uncultured Philistines', and so on. Such a sense is evaluative. The cultured man is not someone who is well-acquainted with just any old cultural products, but with the better of these. He is not a person with a taste for any old pictures, music, or knowledge, but one with a taste for Rembrandt rather than strip-cartoons, Brahms rather than the dirty songs Rugby XVs sing in the shower, philosophy rather than titbits of scandal. Notice the two terms 'acquaintance' and 'taste'; both are important. The cultured man must not only be well-acquainted with the better cultural products, but his tastes and preferences must be in this direction. To know all about Brahms's music, but to be regularly more satisfied with listening to 'Eskimo Nell' or 'The Good Ship Venus' is not the mark of a cultivated soul. Acquaintance and taste do not exhaust our conception of the man of culture. As Eliot stresses, we expect something in the way of manners. A man may sit through a concert knowledgeably enjoying his Brahms, but if he does so while eating fish and chips, crunching his knuckles, and swearing obscenely at the programme-sellers, we shall have our doubts concerning his cultural attainments. There is one ingredient which is not usually connoted by 'man of culture', but which it would be reasonable to add. There are self-styled 'men of culture' who pride themselves on not knowing the difference between a joule and an ampere, an electron and a molecule, an ego and an id. I can see no good reason to put the products of scientific thought outside the pale of a cultured man's acquaintance.

The final sense I shall note is also extremely vague. It is culture in the sense, roughly, of a style of life. This is the sense involved when it is said of a great city like New York that several cultures exist side by side – or when one refers to sub-cultures or to cultural 'clashes'. A culture in this sense is remarkably hard to identify and describe; for while there will be obvious, observable manifestations in the form of dress, say, or foods, there is also, in Raymond

Williams's useful phrase, the 'structure of feeling' one senses underlying these manifestations.[4] Encountering an alien community, it is
easier to experience than to describe this 'structure of feeling'. To
take an example of a kind which doubtless each reader could furnish
for himself, I can recall wandering about the area which lodged the
exiled Cuban community in Miami, and the vivid sense of being
in a community whose nature was thoroughly new to me. The facial
expressions, the smells from the shops, the rhythm of movement
on the sidewalks, the tone of the laughter, the excitability of the
women – these and myriad other signals created the impression of
people whose approach to, and consciousness of, life was very different from that of myself or those I had grown up with. In short, I had
touched, however superficially, another culture. A 'structure of
feeling' is certainly sufficiently real for one to find immense
difficulty – unless one is either very pliable or a consummate actor –
in entering, without embarrassment, into a new structure. Laughing
(or not laughing) at the wrong moment; too strong (or too weak) a
handshake; too much (or too little) display of emotion at some
circumstance – these and innumerable other 'gaffs' can quickly and
intensely bring home to the alien participant the remoteness of the
'structure of feeling' now being encountered from the one in which
he is comfortably at home.

There are interesting questions to raise about the relations
between the different senses of 'culture' – between cultural products,
cultured men, and styles of life (or 'structures of feeling'). For surely
it is not pure accident that the same word is employed. Certainly
it is possible to get the connections wrong. T. S. Eliot, for example,
speaks of men of culture as those who are 'more conscious' of culture
than those who unconsciously participate in it.[5] If this means that a
person who has an explicit understanding of a style of life is a man
of culture, then it cannot be right. To be a person of culture, one has
to have, oneself, appropriate tastes, interests, knowledge, and
manners; merely to know about the tastes, interests, knowledge,
and manners of others will not make one a cultured man. Again,
it is sometimes said that cultural products – books, paintings, and so
on – are the expression of culture in the style of life sense. But this
is not generally true in any serious sense of 'expression'. Apart from
the odd exception like D. H. Lawrence, those who write best about
working-class life are not themselves from that class, so they cannot
be expressing how it feels to live that life, however well they may
describe those feelings. Nor are the comfortable, middle-class men
who compose 'punk' music from their offices in Denmark Street
expressing their frustration with the monotony and squalor of life
in the slums. This point is of some importance for what follows later.

137

2 Cultural relativism

In this section I look at the argument for supposing that 'true' educational egalitarianism implies there should be radically different curricula, or syllabuses, for suitably different sorts of children.[6] I think the argument mistaken, but not for so simple a reason as is sometimes given. There are those who think that the common curriculum is a direct consequence of Rawls's 'difference principle' applied to education[7] – in terms of which principle, you will recall, I have usually been understanding egalitarianism. After all, they say, does not the principle require that everyone shall receive the same unless the worst-off are benefited by the differentials? So must not there be at least a very strong presumption in favour of all children being taught the same curriculum? Well, no, there must not, and to suppose otherwise is to misunderstand the 'difference principle', and in particular what is meant by 'sameness'. Rawls's own demand is that 'primary goods' be distributed equally, unless an unequal distribution benefits the worst-off. But it is quite possible for two people to receive the same amount of 'primary goods' whilst receiving them in very different forms. For example, one man may get his £100 in one hundred £1 notes, while the other gets his in ten £10 notes. In one sense they do not get the same, though in the important sense they do. Applied to education, the principle demands that all children should be educationally transformed to an equal degree, unless. . . . This means roughly, but not exactly, that each child should receive the same amount of educational goods, unless. . . . (See pp. 33f. for the explanation of 'educational transformation' and 'educational goods'.) But it in no way follows from this principle that children should be taught the same curriculum, unless. . . . It would only follow if it could be shown that just one curriculum can confer educational goods to the desired degree; or that there is only one general way in which they can be equally transformed. (Similarly, it would only follow from the demand for equality of income that each man should be paid one hundred £1 notes if £1 notes were the only currency.) Now perhaps these things can be shown, but the kind of egalitarian to be encountered in this chapter is just the kind who denies this.

There is, then, too quick a way of dismissing the idea that equality requires radically diverse curricula. But there is also much too quick a way some people use to convince us of this idea. Their reasoning goes as follows: an educational system in which children from one social class are regularly less successful than those from another is inegalitarian. So, if traditional remedies cannot put matters right, the remedy is to introduce a new curriculum in which children from the class in question will be just as successful as other children are in the original curriculum. But this reasoning is too hasty. From the existence of relative failure, it does not follow that the 'difference principle' is being broken; for perhaps the attempt to reduce the differential would result in the worst educated being worse educated still. Indeed there is nothing in the reasoning to make us think that this would not be the result of the proposed remedy. What disguises this is an error almost too glaring to require being pointed out. Equalizing success rates in different curricula does not mean equalizing educational success. I am just as good at jumping over three-foot poles as the Olympic champion is at jumping over eight-foot poles; that does not make me as successful a high-jumper as him. Nor would success in grasping the facile and the worthless be educational success.

Obviously there is a lacuna in the reasoning. What needs to be demonstrated is that the new curriculum at which those who had previously failed will now succeed is as valuable a one as the old. It is this lacuna which the cultural relativist tries to supply, and which only he could supply, for reasons which soon follow.

In recent years, cultural relativism has been intimately linked with the attack on the 'myth of cultural deprivation' (an attack we met with at the beginning of the previous chapter). Traditional egalitarian remedies, the attack goes, have assumed that children fail because they are deficient in culture and hence incapable of appreciating or benefiting from the cultural products which it is a large part of the curriculum's task to acquaint them with. But this assumption, the attack continues, is totally wrong. Such children – be they from identifiable ethnic groups or a particular social class – are not deficient in culture; it is merely that their culture is different from the one reflected and promoted in the standard curriculum. Such a claim is a generalization of the one which Wax and Wax, in an influential work, make about Sioux children:

> If the Indian child appears as 'culturally deprived', it is not
> because he is lacking in experience or in culture, but because
> the educational agencies are unwilling to recognize the
> alienness of his culture and the realities of his social world.[8]

The remedy, the attack concludes, is not to impose on the child a culture which is not his own, but first and foremost to 'learn his culture' and base his curriculum very largely upon it.

But no such remedy is called for unless one adds to Wax and Wax's point an evaluative element concerning the value of the child's own culture. If it is a perfectly awful one, it is difficult to see how its 'alienness' is a sufficient reason to respect it, however true it may be that this is the factor which explains the child's difficulties at school. (Was one to 'learn the culture' of little Nazi children in 1945 and base their curriculum on this culture?) Indeed, unless this evaluative element is added, I find it impossible to see a distinction between 'cultural deprivation' and 'cultural difference'. For to say that a child is culturally deprived cannot mean he has no culture, but rather that the culture he has is of a markedly inferior sort. There is no more incompatibility between saying of someone that he is culturally deprived and saying of him that he is culturally different than between having a deprived childhood and having a childhood. Cultural deprivation is only a myth if it is a myth that there is a superior culture, which the curriculum attempts to embody. Otherwise, acquaintance only with another culture will indeed be to be deprived, and it will be impossible to see how an egalitarian can avoid being committed to whatever common curriculum incorporates that superior culture. At least, it will be impossible to see this unless the egalitarian is obsessed with equality at the expense of any interest in the quality of the goods to be equally distributed. I do not know if such an obsession lies behind these words of one well-known opponent of cultural deprivationism: 'It is not a question of whether society's standards are worse or better than the school's values: the question is, should they be different?'[9] Certainly one cannot agree with these words, and neither can an egalitarian who is concerned with the quality of what is to be distributed. For surely if what the school provides is better in terms of educational goods then equality demands that all children should receive them, and not that some schools revert to providing some children with the inferior products of their own culture.

So the critic of cultural deprivationism is committed to a relativistic position concerning the values of different cultures. It is precisely because, for him, different curricula can reflect and promote equally valuable cultures that equality is compatible with diverse curricula. Indeed, equality would seem to demand this – for otherwise children will be failing who might have been succeeding in something no less valuable.

We need to take a closer look, then, at cultural relativism. Before that, however, I draw attention to a different educational policy relativists – and others, as well – sometimes support; what might be called the 'hotchpotch' curriculum. This has been ·particularly popular in the USA among those who refer to the 'equally valid' ethnic cultures coexisting in American society.[10] One way for curriculum design to reflect this multiplicity of 'equally valid' cultures is to have one big curriculum incorporating elements from the various cultures. 'The curriculum would in part be derived from the many cultures. . . . There is no reason why schools cannot foster the kind of learning suggested . . . by pursuing a great number of dialects, values, languages, historical accounts, interpretations of events, etc.'[11] To the extent that such a view derives from a relativistic attitude, its foundations will be examined. But, in this section, I shall devote no special attention to it – partly because, in its usual 'ethnic' form, it is a view that is more relevant in the American context; partly because considerations advanced in the following section (p. 155) form an implicit criticism.

What, exactly, are cultural relativists relativisitic about? I think it is clear what they need to be relativistic about, if their case for diverse curricula is to be made out – which is culture in the sense of cultural products. If their claim were to the effect that cultures, in either Malinowski's sense or the styles of life sense, are not to be deemed superior or inferior, then it is not clear what the impact of the claim – be it true or false, intelligible or otherwise – upon the curriculum debate could be. For it is not the task of schools – mainly because it is totally beyond their capacity – to create or impose styles of life. Some schools, no doubt, have the effect on some boys and girls of weaning them from one style of life into another. But this is not generally the case – and indeed, it is the basic premise on which the whole debate considered in this chapter rests, that the bulk of children coming from a certain style of life remain wedded to it despite the discrepancy between it and the culture typically enjoyed by, and perhaps advocated by, their teachers.

What schools can do – and what it is their pre-eminent task to do traditionally – is acquaint children with cultural products: with the knowledge, literature, art, and philosophy men have discovered or created. So if the cultural relativist wishes to press his case for diverse curricula, it must be upon cultural products – both those actually on offer in the curriculum, and those that might be instead – that he must focus. In many cases, unfortunately, this is just what he does not focus upon. In the course of an attack on cultural deprivationism, Nell Keddie proclaims that 'no group can be deprived of its own culture'.[12] This is a tautology if 'culture' refers to a style of life, but it is false if 'culture' refers to cultural products. Either the group may be deprived of 'its own culture' in the sense that it does not have one (its members are not culturally productive, or not distinctively so), or in the sense that most of the group fail to encounter or fail to appreciate whatever cultural products of any worth some of the members – or indeed, anyone at all – have produced.

I said it was 'unfortunate' that the focus is not typically on culture in the products sense, but it is easy to see the tactical advantage to the relativist of concentrating on styles of life. For it is much easier to be relativistic about styles of life – to hold that different styles are equally 'valid' – than to take the same attitude towards cultural products. The consequence is that an implausible relativism about cultural products feeds off a more plausible variety. (More plausible, yes; but not therefore true. As will emerge in a moment, there surely are criteria for judging whole styles of life.)

Let us, anyway, focus upon relativism about cultural products. Relativism, as I see it, must contain two ingredients: first, an analysis of the logical form of evaluative judgments about cultural products, and second, a claim about the permissible values (in the mathematician's sense) of a certain variable occurring in the analysis.

Let '$X > Y$' abbreviate such evaluative judgments as 'It is more rewarding to understand about the evolution of man than to know about digging gardens or wall-papering flats', 'The music of Brahms is superior to "punk" ', 'The great nineteenth-century novels are a more important literary achievement than post-war "kitchen-sink" writings'. The relativist's claim is that '$X > Y$' must always be expanded to '$X > Y$ for g', where g ranges over people or groups. That is, a judgment of cultural value only makes sense where there is explicit or implicit reference made to people or groups for whom something has cultural value. There is nothing odd in this idea of sentences being true or false only relative to a factor which is implicitly referred to. For example, 'John had a beard' is only true or false relative to a time implicitly referred to. Just as there can be no sense in asking, without such a reference to a time, whether 'John had a beard' is true, so, according to the relativist, there can be no sense in asking if a judgment about cultural value is true except with reference to certain people or groups. Just as 'John had a beard' can be true when one time is referred to but false when another time is referred to, so a cultural judgment can be true when some people or group is referred to but false when it is some other people or group.

This claim about logical form is a necessary component in relativism; but to actually reach relativism a further claim concerning the permissible values of g is required. It would scarcely be relativistic, in any usual sense, to take as the value of g, something like 'men of superior judgment'. For the idea that there are men of superior taste who can settle what is of cultural worth is just the kind of idea dismissal of which is associated with relativism. What sort of values for g do relativists entertain? We get an extreme form of relativism – usually called 'subjectivism' – if g is to be replaced by reference to any individual person. '$X > Y$' becomes '$X > Y$ for me (or for John, Mary, etc.)', with the effect that evaluative

142

judgments can only be true or false relative to some individual (the speaker usually). One gets an 'ethnic' version of relativism if the permissible values of *g* are ethnic communities. But the version which seems to be entertained by most of the relativists supporting diverse curricula – on this side of the Atlantic, at least – is the one in which the values of *g* are social classes, or something similar; communities of people identified in terms of some shared style of life, especially economic life. Thus 'X > Y' becomes 'X > Y for the middle class' or 'X > Y for the urban poor', and so on. (An uneasy amalgam of the two versions just mentioned occurs when the values of *g* are communities identified through a mixture of ethnic and socio-economic criteria – such as 'middle-class whites' or 'ghetto blacks'.)

It is not my aim to make a direct, frontal assault on relativism of this kind. I prefer, instead, to identify some of the more suspicious considerations which, I believe, serve to generate the doctrine. I prefer to do this, partly because one of the best ways of discrediting a highly counter-intuitive doctrine is to discredit its foundations, and partly because a direct assault would be a lengthy and involved task. It would be lengthy and involved not because relativism is a deep and subtle doctrine but because, on the contrary, it is packed with an enormous number of confusions. That the doctrine is highly counter-intuitive I take to be evident. It would have the consequence, for example, that the excellence of, *inter alia*, the *Bhagavad Gita*, *The Brothers Karamazov*, Beethoven's Late String Quartets, *The Critique of Pure Reason*, Nash's terraces, Diaghilev's productions, or the King James Version, is only excellence relative to certain communities. It would have the peculiar consequence that the reasons which can be given for the excellence of such products, and their superiority over other products in the areas, are only reasons for this or that community – in the way that the quality of the steaks served can be a reason for meat-eaters, but not vegetarians, to visit a certain restaurant. It may be, of course, that many or most people in certain communities are incapable of appreciating the excellence of such products, but that is irrelevant. Just as saying that a green patch is yellow for someone with jaundice is only a misleading way of saying he is unable to see its real colour, so to say that the products just mentioned are not excellent for certain people is only a misleading way of saying these people are incapable of recognizing their excellence. This is not to deny there can be extended and real debate over the cultural value of various products. Nor is it to deny that some products have the value they do, in part at least, because of their special relation with particular communities. The 'blues' songs of negro chain-gangs derive part of their value, certainly, from their being authentic expressions, by the men themselves, of their trials and tribulations.

This last example is pertinent to the first of the suspicious bases, on which cultural relativism rests, which I want to identify. The assumption seems to be made that the various social groups or classes, to which cultural value is allegedly relative, have their own distinctive and 'authentic' cultures. At any rate, one is always coming across references to the 'middle-class culture' that is 'imposed' upon those who should be enjoying their own 'black' or 'working-class culture'. If this assumption were true, it is easy to see how, through a muddle, one could reach a relativistic position. There is a sense in which the great works of Western literature, say, have a greater value for us than the corresponding works from the East. They are, after all, ours: they reflect and express our styles of life in ways that the great oriental books cannot. The Western consciousness, so to speak, lives in these works; whereas that which lives in the great books of the East is, to a degree, alien to us. But it should be clear from the way I am describing matters that nothing relativistic is implied. It is not that the *Bhagavad Gita* is great for Indians, but not for Frenchmen. It is as great as it is – whether for Indians, Frenchmen, or Martians. The sense in which our great works have greater value for us is not the relativist's sense. The point is, rather, that forced to make a choice, it is more important for us that we appreciate and enjoy the great works of our culture. Not only more important, but more feasible. To the extent that one learns about society and men from cultural products, the premium will be on those products from which we learn about our own society and ourselves. So, if it were true that the classes or groups our relativist refers to had their authentic cultural outputs, such an output would, in the sense just given, have a special value for the class or group from which it flowed. If, for example, there is an authentic working-class culture, some of the products in which are of value, then it will be especially apposite for members of that class to appreciate them, as part of their heritage, as an expression of their condition. This is not, to repeat, a relativistic claim, though it might be confused with one.

But there is no reason to accept the assumption. Indeed, it can only be made by someone who is confusing two senses of 'culture' – cultural products and styles of life – for there may well be a distinctive working-class style of life. No doubt, as Bantock points out, there was a time – 'Merrie Englande' perhaps – when working men produced a distinctive music, literature, and 'folk wisdom', but that time is long past.[13] Brass band music, or cockney rhymes, are hardly sufficient to constitute a discrete working-class cultural

144

output. Very little of what is read, listened to, or watched by working-class people is produced from within their ranks; nor is enjoyment of these things at all confined to this class. And what can be meant by 'middle-class culture'? It is true that most cultural products are the work of people from that class – but when it is stressed that these products range from the *War Requiem* to punk, from *The Times* to the *Sun*, from Marx and Engels's theory of capital to the National Front's theory of industrial unrest, it quickly becomes absurd to regard these products as a characteristic expression of a particular socio-economic condition. Nor is there sufficient uniformity in the tastes and interests of middle-class people – in what is enjoyed by them – for the reference to 'middle-class culture' to be anything but useless. It is true that most *aficionados* of 'high culture' come from this class, but it is only a small minority of the class who are such *aficionados*. Long gone are the Victorian days when the tastes of the emergent bourgeoisie exhibited some degree of homogeneity (though it is easy to exaggerate the extent of this uniformity). The question, says Nell Keddie, is 'not . . . whether middle class culture (whatever that vague term means) is desirable or not'.[14] Indeed it is not, for since that 'vague term' is devoid of meaning, so is the question.[15]

This is as good a point as any at which to mention the delicate balance a relativist must maintain if his doctrine is to have the curricular implication he desires. On the one hand, cultural value must be relative to a number of groups, otherwise we will not get diverse curricula. On the other hand, it must not be relative to too many groups, or to single individuals, otherwise there will be scarcely more justice in having a few curricula on offer than in having only one. The usual line, we have seen, is to take social classes – or ethnic communities – as the groups to which cultural value is supposed to be relative. But, apart from the problem previously discussed, this line seems remarkably arbitrary. Why would· not groups identified on geographical grounds, for example, be as good or bad a choice? Or why not make the two sexes the relevant groups? Some relativists, no doubt, have done just that: but this can only compound the feeling, which must anyway lurk, that the relativist – despite a disclaimer – does not first establish that cultural value is relative to certain groups and then infer that these groups require distinct educational treatment. Rather it is the other way round. He finds that children from certain groups are doing relatively badly in the standard system, and then dresses this up with a doctrine to the effect that, by no objective criteria, were they 'really' doing badly at all.

I now turn to the second dubious source of cultural relativism.

Relativism of any kind feeds off the assumption that there is massive disagreement among men – about what is true, right, beautiful, about what is of cultural worth. Unless the assumption is made, we shall not see the disagreements which doubtless do occur as ones which are unresolvable by rational, objective means, as ones which betoken an inevitable relativization of truth or value to the parties in the dispute. Rather, we shall prefer to see them as arising through the difficulties of applying principles and criteria that are generally agreed upon to complicated cases. Or, we shall see this disagreement as arising precisely because there *are* objective criteria – but ones which can, on occasion, conflict. Either way, the disagreements will be treated as local disturbances within an agreed framework which provides, in principle, the means for settling most disputes. In my view, the most effective way of scotching relativism is to demonstrate that there neither is, nor could be, the massive degree of disagreement the relativist assumes. Elsewhere, I have tried to demonstrate this in connection with moral relativism.[16] Whether I have succeeded or not, I hope I can get you to agree that our cultural relativists at least greatly exaggerate the extent of disagreement over cultural worth in the two ways to which I now draw attention.

First, they confuse judgments, between which there can be disagreement, with likes and dislikes, enjoyment and lack of enjoyment, between which there cannot. Clearly, there are any number of books, pieces of music, or titbits of information which I, like most people, can on occasion enjoy, without thereby judging them to be of any literary, musical or scientific merit. Equally, I am able to judge some things, which I cannot enjoy, to be of considerable merit – the oboe concerto I cannot listen to because the timbre of the instrument is offensive to me, or the war novel I am too squeamish to get through. It is not my experience that those who lack the capacity, or the willingness, to acquaint themselves with the best of men's cultural products express themselves by denying their value, or by claiming any great merit for the books, thoughts, music, or whatever, which they find engaging. This is a mode of expression foisted on them in relativists' descriptions. With or without regrets, such people are typically willing to concede that much of what is great and valuable is beyond the scope of their appreciation and enjoyment. So, one is certainly not entitled to infer from the myriad and totally different likes and dislikes which men exhibit that there is a correspondingly massive disagreement among them about merit and value.

The second way the relativist exaggerates disagreement in judgments is more subtle. Suppose Jack advises me I should steal money which will put me on my way to a fortune, while Jill tells me

I ought to do nothing of the sort. Are Jack and Jill in moral disagreement? Very likely not. Probably Jack would agree that, morally, it would be wrong to steal the money – but go on to add that morality is not everything in this rat-race of a life. What we probably have is not a disagreement within moral assessment, but a collision between moral assessment and something else. The anecdote illustrates a distinction the relativist typically fails to make – the distinction between disagreements within an area of assessment and collisions between different modes of assessment. Much that gets represented as disagreement over moral value, or aesthetic merit, or whatever, is nothing of the sort, but reflects rather the different weights people give to considerations of very different types. The distinction is particularly pertinent to the present discussion. There can, clearly, be great disagreement concerning what children ought to be reading, seeing, learning. It in no way follows that this is disagreement over the value of the cultural products *qua* cultural products. For example, *I* am going to suggest, following G. H. Bantock, that there are good reasons why a curriculum which transmits the best cultural products is not a suitable one for some children. In doing so, I am in no way challenging their title to be the best. Obviously one could have plenty of reasons for not favouring the transmission of what one admits to be superior cultural products. Dr Goebbels, for example, was well aware of the merit of the books (Thomas Mann's novels, for example) which he ordered to be burned, for political reasons. Nor was Plato unaware of Homer's greatness, though he thought him corrupting. It must not be pretended, then, that disagreement over what products are to be encouraged betokens an anarchy of cultural judgments of the sort to prompt a relativistic attitude.

The final murky source of cultural relativism is itself another sort of relativism – moral relativism. This comes in as many shapes and sizes as the cultural relativism which, if I am right, it helps foster. For some, Protagoras perhaps, moral judgments are only true or false relative to individuals (moral subjectivism); for others, Engels perhaps, they are true or false relative to social classes; for yet others, Hegel or Treitschke perhaps, they are true or false relative to nations – and so on. What the versions have in common is that there is no sense in supposing a moral principle has a validity that transcends its adoption by whatever individuals or groups are in question. I assert, without argument, that moral relativism is a peculiarly implausible form of relativism.[17] The importance of my assertion, if you accept it, is that since moral relativism helps underpin cultural relativism, the latter rests, in part, on a very shaky basis.

147

Between morality and culture (in both our main senses) there are deep and complicated connections. I shall only touch on what seems to me the more important of these. For a start, it is clear that we *do* assess styles of life, and that an important dimension of such assessment is the moral. I do not mean, of course, that sympathy or antipathy towards most of the things people living a certain style of life do is moral judgment on their behaviour. Most of the things people do are in a 'discretionary space', and morality neither forbids nor enjoins them. But, in at least two ways, moral thinking enters into the assessment. First, there is the obvious way. Styles of life differ in their proneness to encourage wrong-doing, or some particular kind of wrong-doing. It is surely a criticism of the chivalrous way of life led by a certain class in medieval Europe or Samurai Japan that its natural consequence was a lot of killing; and it is a moral criticism of our present, consumer-based society that it results in terrible brutality towards the animals we eat, wear, and test our cosmetics upon.[18] There is a less obvious way, too. It is surely part of the task of moral thinking to provide conceptions of 'the good life', of how it is that men, in ideal circumstances at least, should be living. For example, it is hard tò see what Marx's conception of a classless society of men freed from alienation is if not a moral one – for it is a conception of how human relations and work should be. This does not mean – and Marx did not take it to mean – that we are to condemn as immoral the behaviour of men who do not live in accordance with some such conception, for that would suggest, erroneously often, that the men, rather than circumstances, are to be blamed. Still, such conceptions are not without their implications for duties and obligations. If a style of life fails to match such a conception, then it becomes the duty of those – if there are any – who have the power to reduce the gap between the conception and reality to do so. If a life of perpetual toil and sweat is seen to be incompatible with any reasonable conception of 'the good life', then it is incumbent on governments, in so far as it is within their rightful power, to ensure that life does not become like this.

Now I have already mentioned a certain connection between styles of life and cultural products which, taken in conjunction with the point of the preceding paragraph, forges a certain link between morality and cultural products. Literature, music, myths, or whatever, can take on a value they would not otherwise have by being 'authentic' expressions of a style of life. It is not only architectural inferiority which renders neo-Gothic of less cultural value and interest than Gothic. To contemplate the great medieval cathedrals is to be put in touch with a civilization of whose beliefs and aspirations these buildings were an expression. Neo-Gothic does not similarly relate to the lives of men at the time the genre flourished. Now it is not always the case, of course, that the products we most admire, on this kind of basis, are expressions of styles of life we particularly admire. There is a powerful tendency, however, to find little or no value in the 'typical' products of a style of life that is particularly obnoxious. Probably the paintings of Ziegler and other artists of the Third Reich were no worse, in terms of craft or composition, than those of a century earlier – yet such paintings have become paradigms of the worthless.

Assessment of a moral kind enters, in a more direct way than via assessment of styles of life, into our judgments on cultural products. There are few who would want to equate literary worth, say, with moral worth: great novels might be corrupting and rotten ones may be uplifting. But it is arguable that the worth of great literature resides, in part at least, in the way it provides vital morally relevant knowledge – by, for example, offering coherent conceptions of 'the good life', or by making otherwise peculiar behaviour morally intelligible through depicting the 'saliences' that certain people might perceive in a situation.[19] Here is what the American philosopher, Hilary Putnam, says about Celine:

> if I read Celine's *Journey to the End of the Night* I do not *learn*
> that love does not exist, that all human beings are hateful and
> hating. . . . What I learn is to see the world as it looks to
> someone who is sure that hypothesis is correct. I see what
> plausibility that hypothesis has; what it would be like if it *were*
> true; how someone could possibly think that it *is* true . . . all
> this is still not empirical knowledge. Yet it is not correct to say
> that is not knowledge at all.[20]

He goes on to add that it is moral knowledge, for it is intimately to do with 'reasoning about how to live'. If the worth of fiction can partly reside in providing this moral knowledge so, argues Putnam, can the worth of scientific conceptions.

> I am not urging that science should be pursued only for
> practical ends or only for moral enlightenment. . . . But I
> contend that even the *philosophical* significance of science, let
> alone the practical significance, becomes hard to see without
> distortion when science and moral reflection are as sharply
> separated as they have become in our culture.[21]

He goes on to provide the telling example of how 'the overthrow of Euclidean geometry was not *just* the overthrow of a theory of space' but of a paradigm for those who had cleaved to 'the ideal of

149

certainty' – an ideal whose demise is pregnant with implications for 'moral (and social and religious) argument'.²²

The upshot of these rather vague reflections is this: to adopt the fashionable moral relativism which many profess these days (though few act out) is bound to encourage a wider relativism about culture. For to go relativistic about morals is to go relativistic about one of the main dimensions in which cultural assessment takes place. If moral relativism is a sin, then cultural relativism is born in sin.

I have not 'disproved' relativism by making a frontal attack on it. What I have done, I hope, is to confirm its intuitive implausibility by providing reminders of the obvious, and by discrediting the foundations on which it rests. With the demise of relativism, it must follow that the educational egalitarian is committed to the common curriculum – to as even a spread of the educational goods which that curriculum confers as possible. For once we concede the possibility of objectively determining which cultural products are of value, then equality in education, which is the provision of such goods, must be equality in acquaintance with them. The problem will remain for the egalitarian that some children are less able to appreciate and benefit from these goods – but his remedy must be either to expend greater effort on these children or to tackle the factors (home background, etc.) which account for their difficulties. The remedy cannot be to remove from such children the very possibility of benefiting from such products.

The egalitarian, or any one else, need not, of course, be satisfied with the present curriculum. Nor, given the very large number of worthwhile cultural products, is he committed to advocating that each child gets taught exactly the same. But, without relativism, the possibility must exist of devising at least the general structure of a curriculum which, if valuable at all, is valuable for everyone. For if the best cultural products are transmitted in such a structure, then there is no sense in saying that they are of value for these children but not for those.

Our conclusion, then, confirms what Mary Warnock called 'the obvious view'. Indeed, an argument to show that egalitarianism implies diverse curricula would have to have been very powerful to defeat a variety of presumptions against such an idea. For there are several considerations, not yet mentioned, which one would expect an egalitarian to appeal to in favour of a common curriculum. There is, for example, the 'life-chances' consideration. Unless there were a radical alteration in the present structure of examinations and qualifications, or in the selection criteria used by employers, then precluding some children from the dominant curriculum will be to outlaw certain kinds of employment for them. There is also the consideration, in one author's words, that 'a separate curriculum for children who live in the slums is only a subtle way of socializing them to accept their lot'.[23] Certainly an over-romantic picture of the poor and their culture – as if they were a threatened Mato Grosso tribe – could encourage a thoroughly inegalitarian phlegm towards improving their plight. Again there is the 'social mix' consideration, which was discussed earlier (pp. 87f.): this is a process that can hardly be encouraged by the geographical, physical, or intellectual distances required by diverse curricula.

It is perhaps worth adding that the main argument adduced in favour of the common curriculum does not look to be egalitarian in nature at all. It is simply this: if there is a curriculum better than others, then people should be taught this one. (As I pointed out in chapter 1, such an argument could be dressed up in the terminology of equality, but that would not make it an egalitarian argument. Clearly it does not meet the necessary condition of making essential reference to differentials. See pp. 5f.) Despite this, considerations will shortly be adduced to show that it is only someone of an egalitarian bent who could think such an argument clinches the case for a common curriculum.

3 Equality and the common curriculum

In this section I try to relate G. H. Bantock's incisive, and thoroughly depressing, diagnosis of contemporary culture to the issue of egalitarianism. In particular, I shall inquire into how it is that other writers, whose diagnosis is not so very different, arrive at totally opposed recommendations for education, and into the role that egalitarianism plays in this divergence. I shall not try to assess Bantock's diagnosis; I simply announce in advance that I find it highly persuasive.

Let me begin with something that, at first hearing, has a paradoxical ring – the claim that, in contemporary society, the main job of schooling, for many children, should not be to educate them. That this sounds paradoxical explains the apparent commitment that even non-egalitarians seem to have towards that common curriculum which is educationally richest. The paradox dissolves, however, once attention is paid to an equivocation in the word 'education'. If it is used to mean 'what schooling provides' then it is, of course, a tautology that the job of schools is to educate. But if it is used in the way that I, in keeping with many writers, have used it – to refer to the provision of a certain range of goods – then it will no longer follow that what all schools should be doing, or primarily doing, is to educate. In this sense of the term, for example, schools which see their main task as that of training for particular trades do not see their main job as that of education. And whatever one may think of the attitude of such schools, one cannot accuse it of being self-contradictory or paradoxical. So the 'paradox' reduces to the consistent, and I believe true, claim that in contemporary society it should not be the main job of certain schools to be introducing, acquainting, and imbuing their children into or with the educational goods, the cultural products, earlier described.

An inconsistency may seem to remain, however. For how can one stress, as I have been stressing, the genuine value of educatedness, yet now say that educatedness should not be the main goal for various schools to aim at? How can I square this with my defence of Scholesia's North school on the ground of its better education? There are two reasons why there is no inconsistency. First, the value of educating, like most values, is only prima facie, so that it can compete with and sometimes be overridden by others. Second, 'ought' implies 'can', so that 'cannot' cancels out the 'ought'. In other words, if it should be impossible in present circumstances – or possible only in conjunction with supplementary methods of an intolerable kind – for all schools to perform the job of educating, then the case for saying this is what they *should* all be doing evaporates. That the goal of educating should, for either of these reasons, sometimes be held in abeyance, ought to occasion no surprise. In wartime, for instance, some universities will largely suspend the task of educating in order to answer the more pressing demands for contributing to the war effort. And, however desirable it might be that everyone be acquainted with the latest advances in theoretical physics, no one seriously suggests that all children – especially sub-normal ones – *ought* to be taught about these advances. (One needs a distinction here between what is desirable, in the sense of being a state of affairs that would obtain in the best of all possible worlds, and what ought to be done. In circumstances where the desirable is totally unfeasible, there is no obligation even to try to bring it about.)

Bantock's case against the common curriculum – his case for saying that 'for the Newsom child, at least, the traditional curriculum should be scrapped'[24] – appeals to both the above considerations. And it does not rest on any relativistic rejection of the value of the goods provided in that curriculum; on the contrary, the culture so transmitted is 'one of the finest the world has seen'.[25] What he does is to provide a chilling portrait of contemporary social and cultural life, and an identification of the evils which press upon us in that life – especially upon the young, and the working-class young above all. The existence of these evils has two implications.

152

First, they are sufficiently great and pressing for the main job of schooling, with respect to 'the Newsom child, at least', to become that of helping people escape and resist them. And this is a job whose importance outweighs the importance of the job of education. It might be thought that it *is* education – the transmission of educational and cultural goods – which could best equip children in this fight. But here we must turn to the second of the implications. The evils are of a sort which make it difficult to the point of impossibility for some children to be educated – for them to appreciate, understand, 'make anything of', the better cultural products: 'we must accept that the environment itself contains profoundly *dis*-educative forces which must work against what the school is trying to do'.[26] Or, 'it is clear . . . that the school cannot compete in terms of genuine responsiveness and involvement';[27] or, 'the dilemma arises out of the fact that the schoolchild has not only much to learn – he has so much to unlearn: the emotional falseness of popular culture'.[28]

When we turn to another commentator on contemporary culture, Raymond Williams, the contrast is fascinating. For while the diagnosis is, in many respects, similar, the educational proposals are almost the reverse of Bantock's. Like Bantock, Williams stresses the evils of advertising, sensationalism in the mass media, the nauseating 'flattery' of the young by those whose products the young consume, the appalling level of vulgar taste, the cults of violence, or 'dropping out' which are eager to enmesh young novitiates – and so on. Like Bantock, he sees the struggle against these evils as a major imperative; and like him, again, he recognizes these evils as constituting a major educational problem – for the very evils which need curing make the cure so hard. Yet his remedy is very different. 'If children of moderate learning ability cannot acquire, in the time now given, the essentials of a contemporary general education, the only sensible answer is to give more time, not to dismiss some of the essentials with a resigned regret.'[29] In general, his remedy is *more* of the fairly familiar curriculum; for his 'essentials' include good literature, history, biological theory, and so on. This is a far cry from the curriculum Bantock recommends for 'the Newsom child, at least' – with its stress on the non-literary, the training of feelings and moral sense. From Williams's point of view, I imagine, Bantock is one of that dangerous group who would 'weaken belief in the practicability of further educational extension'.[30]

How from such similar bases are such divergent recommendations arrived at? I think there are three explanations: Bantock's more pessimistic diagnosis; his unwillingness to contemplate the measures which would be required (in conjunction with the

153

common curriculum) for schooling to have a chance of universal educational success; and his fear of the threat to the traditional curriculum which the attempt to make it the common one would pose. It is in connection with the second and third of these points especially that the debate becomes intertwined with the egalitarian issue. But let us take each of the three in turn.

Bantock's pessimism about educating 'the Newsom child' stems from a pessimistic element in his diagnosis of the root of the evils which abound. For he sees these as reflections, in industrialized, consumer societies, of deeply engrained features of human nature. They are not, in any simple sense, products of such societies, but the nearly inevitable shape which these ineradicable traits will assume in such societies. For example, the making of myths is taken as a fundamental human urge. In healthier times, this 'expressed in symbolic form permanent human conflicts', and resulted in the sagas, for example, or even the great religions. Nowadays 'our petty myths rest on nothing more substantial than dreams or fantasies, unanchored to any sort of reality other than the power aspirations of an ill-educated democracy'.[31] Orpheus has become the star of 'disco' films; Penelope the scandal-sheets' version of an ex-president's wife. For Williams, on the other hand, responsibility squarely attaches to a particular form of socio-economic organization – industrial capitalism. It is the profit motive, around which the system revolves, that is, directly or otherwise, but certainly above all, responsible for the cultural tawdriness which dominates. For, at some point, someone discovered that culture could be an industry like any other; and at some later point, someone discovered that the young could be treated as consumers of culture like any others.

This partially explains why Bantock cannot entertain a remedy which Williams sees as a necessary requirement if schooling is to succeed in educating. The latter writes: 'We should be much clearer about these cultural questions if we saw them as a consequence of a basically capitalist organization, and I at least know no better reason for capitalism to be ended.'[32] The remedy, in other words, is socialism – and socialism, presumably, of a very thorough-going kind which will incorporate considerable state control of the organs of culture. At any rate, the socialism would have to be of a massive, totalitarian sort if Bantock is right in diagnosing present evils as the reflection in industrial society of deep-rooted human traits. ('Totalitarian' in the genuine sense of having to control even the most 'inner' regions of men's lives.) Bantock, at least, shows no sympathy towards this remedy – perhaps because any dose of socialism sufficiently strong to poison the evils would kill off what is good in culture as well. No doubt neither he, nor anyone else, would want to base a case for or against socialism on purely, or usually even mainly, educational and cultural grounds. Clearly it is not within my brief to discuss these other grounds, though it is within that brief to make the fairly obvious connection of the preceding remarks with the issue of egalitarianism. In chapter 1 I rejected the idea that policies should only count as egalitarian if they derive from the paradigmatic egalitarian demand for equality of wealth – but there is no denying that this is the paradigmatic demand. Not all socialists, presumably, are egalitarians; but again there is no denying the egalitarian urge that is the basic driving force behind that doctrine. 'My socialism was above all the outcome of a sense of the injustice of things as they were', to repeat a comment of Harold Laski. So, given the dose of socialism that would be required, if Bantock is right (and Williams too), if universal sharing in a common curriculum is to be educationally effective, then we can see that those with a commitment to this curriculum must be those, first and foremost, with the egalitarian urge which generates, or excuses, socialism.

There is another way in which, given Bantock's premises, the demand for a common curriculum must imply a typically egalitarian outlook. Too many writers seem to assume that if it is possible to objectively determine that there is a curriculum of superior educational value, then all children ought to be taught it. But given that 'ought' implies 'can', this will only follow if, as Mary Warnock optimistically assumes, 'it is possible to devise a curriculum which is both common and middle-class, adaptable for all, and within which no one is doomed to failure or frustration', if it is feasible to have a 'curriculum which is genuinely suitable for all' [33] Now if Bantock is right, this is just what is not possible. What, perhaps, is feasible is a common curriculum that is amenable to all, in the sense that no children will totally fail to grasp what is taught, or find themselves totally unconcerned with it. But amenability is not suitability, if the latter notion is to retain its connotation of appropriateness and fittingness. For Bantock, any attempt to make the curriculum which is digestible by some digestible by all must necessarily dilute what is taught, and hence represent a betrayal of those who are able to enjoy a richer diet. Now this dilution of the curriculum into one amenable to all could be perfectly acceptable to the egalitarian. Indeed, just such a dilution would presumably have been required in Centre school, which our Scholesian egalitarian favoured. I do not now repeat my arguments against him; I merely stress that it is only the egalitarian, who is willing that the more able should not be educated as well as they might have been, who can favour the common, amenable-to-all, curriculum in the face of Bantock's premises.

155

I began this chapter by asking if an egalitarian committed to an even spread of educational goods is thereby committed to the common curriculum. I argued that he is, unless he adopts an implausible, though fashionable, relativism about culture. It did not follow in any immediate way from this that only egalitarians are so committed. But the import of the final section has been that, given a certain diagnosis of the cultural evils which make education for all so difficult, then in at least two ways a commitment to the common curriculum will be an egalitarian prerogative. For anyone with such a commitment must either be bent in favour of a certain social system, totalitarian socialism, or must be willing to see the curriculum diluted at the expense of the more able. I have already argued against the latter, and I have already excused myself from considering the former, draconian policy – though I imagine few would, by now, fail to discern a lack of sympathy with it. I must then, and albeit with Williams's 'resigned regret', favour Bantock's diversity of curricula.

6 Conclusion – inegalitarianism

Am I an inegalitarian? Must someone who rejects egalitarian principles, and policies as well (except when, *per accidens*, they coincide with what he would independently advocate on other grounds), thereby be 'for' inequality? Or can his position be analogous to that of a man who, while critical of religious belief, is not necessarily 'for' atheism? I am, of course, whatever someone taking the line I have taken in this book is; and that will not be altered by affixing or detaching the label 'inegalitarian'. I do not raise the question for purely autobiographical reasons – but partly because it seemed to interest several participants at the 1973 conference when I gave my paper 'Quality and equality', and because it is a convenient peg on which to hang some final reflections.

My co-symposiast in 1973, Tim O'Hagan, accused me of being 'bashful' in not readily accepting the 'inegalitarian' label. I received more than a little help from my friends – R. F. Atkinson in his chairman's remarks, and Antony Flew in a review of the conference proceedings for *The Times Higher Education Supplement* – who agreed that it would be misleading to attach this label. It is with a slight sense of betrayal, therefore, that I now confess to being less shy about accepting it. I think it would be more misleading to reject it. This is partly because I am now fully emancipated from that tradition which has managed to make 'equality' a term of praise, but mainly for the reasons which will emerge in this brief chapter.

O'Hagan distinguishes 'negative' from 'positive' inegalitarianism – the latter taking various forms, such as 'aesthetic' and 'market' inegalitarianism. A 'negative' inegalitarian is one who tolerates present inequalities, but only 'in order to attain a situation in which both quality and equality can be promoted together'.[1] The Third World leaders, on whose existence I speculated on p. 79, would be 'negative' inegalitarians since, although they have equality as an aim, present circumstances require that educational resources be concentrated on producing an 'élite' of doctors, engineers, or teachers, if that and other aims are to be achieved. Rawls, as we saw, would also advocate 'negative' inegalitarianism under certain

157

conditions – those, namely, where the total of 'primary goods' is so small that implementation of the 'difference principle' is to be postponed until there are more goods to be distributed.

Obviously I am not an inegalitarian in this sense – not because I am something less (a 'non-egalitarian', or whatever), but because I am something more. My defence of educational inequality was definitely not in terms of a future equality it could be expected to yield. Certainly that was not the *point* of educational inequality; nor would I be the least tempted to condemn present inequality because it has little chance of achieving equality in the longer term. (The two parts of that sentence do not say the same thing. It is possible to think that X should be condemned if it does not produce Y without thinking that the point of X was to produce Y. I do not tell you the truth about yourself in order to cheer you up, but if it made you depressed, I might decide to be less frank.)

Am I, then, one of O'Hagan's 'positive' inegalitarians – someone, that is, who thinks that 'inequality in education . . . is a value to be pursued for its own sake'?[2] It is difficult to say, since I am not sure what it would be to value inequality 'for its own sake'. By parity with the egalitarian advocacy of equality for its own sake, one might expect the 'positive' inegalitarian to be adopting something like the following principle: some people ought to get more simply because others are getting less than, or the same as, them. Or, perhaps: only those inequalities are unjustified which do not benefit the best-off. Clearly, I do not subscribe to such inversions of the 'difference principle'. They have a ring of madness about them,[3] and share with egalitarian principles the basic defect of making differentials the determinants of what people should be getting.

Leaving behind him the misleading expression 'for its own sake', O'Hagan goes on to explain why, for him, I am a 'positive' inegalitarian. It is because I am a 'positive qualitarian' – that is, I advocate favouring the pursuit of educational excellence (in the sense explained in chapter 2) – and take it that this pursuit is incompatible with the pursuit of equality. This, he says, 'amounts to a thesis of positive inegalitarianism'.[4] But this is a bit too quick. Certainly it is possible to be pro-X without being anti-Y, even though X and Y are incompatible. After all, one may be unaware of the incompatibility. And it is possible even when one is not unaware of the incompatibility. At any rate, it could be highly misleading to describe the person's position as being that of an anti-Yist. I may believe that controlling inflation is incompatible with full employment: but because I advocate the control of inflation does not mean I am *against* full employment. After all, if an economist of genius comes up with a plan by which we can have both – a possibility I do not entirely rule out – then, of course, I will welcome the plan. Moreover, I may foresee a day – and think it a happier day – when, in changed circumstances, full employment without inflation is possible.

Still, the claim to be pro-X without being anti-Y begins to look strained the more convinced one is that X and Y must, and always will, be incompatible. Since O'Hagan is right in saying that, for me, excellence and equality are for ever incompatible, then surely my resistance to the label 'inegalitarian' would begin to look strained. The denial that one is anti-Y is, moreover, strained beyond breaking-point if one thinks the incompatibility between X and Y is of a logical sort. (What would we make of someone who claimed to be for husbands dominating marriages but not against wives being dominated?) Since there are a number of senses in which I find logical tension between the pursuits of excellence and equality, then again I think it wisest to accept the charge of being inegalitarian. Let me take these points – about eternal incompatibility, and logical incompatibility – in turn.

'For ever', as a song reminds us, 'is a long, long time.' The 'for ever' I have in mind is the foreseeable future which astrologers, but not planners, may be forgiven for looking beyond. It is a 'for ever' which does not include the day when someone invents 'knowledge capsules' with which to swallow the wisdom of the ages, or the day when some nuclear alchemist transmutes sewage into petroleum. During this 'for ever' it is impossible that everyone should be educated to the level of excellence attained by some. O'Hagan, it seems, wants to deny this – partly because he envisages a 'rationalized system of production inaugurated by socialism [in which] scarcity will be overcome',[5] and partly because he thinks educational investment is subject to such diminishing returns that 'it is simply not the case that e.g. the continual improvement of the student/staff ratio ... will continue to improve educational quality'.[6] The reply to the first point is that it smacks of fantasy. The day when resources, and public willingness, are so great that we invest in the education of even dull children not only the same that is expended on the education of the brightest, but the much greater amount that would be required to close the gap caused by their dullness, is not one that any responsible planner can look forward to. The reply to the second point is that while there might be a point where further investment of resources would not significantly improve educatedness, there is not the least reason to suppose that reaching this point would coincide with equality. And this is because, of course, there are any number of factors, other than resources in any normal sense, which make for or against a person's

159

educatedness. We have encountered many of these already. Parental behaviour, the child's peer group, the child's desires and interests, Bantock's 'counter-educational' social forces – and so on. There is only one way in which one can conceive of equality at a high level of educational quality – and that is by conceiving the kind of draconian socialism which reared its head at the end of the preceding chapter: a brand of socialism in which, *inter alia*, parental treatment, cultural environment, children's pleasures and ambitions, would be thoroughly dragooned. Socialism, to do the egalitarian trick, would have to be much more than O'Hagan's 'rationalized system of production'. Fortunately, I do not foresee these draconian days – partly because I do not envisage the emergence of the Dracos, but mainly because I cannot imagine they either could, or would want to, pitch their egalitarian aims in education at anything approximating to a level of excellence.

If some of the things I said in the book are correct, it is not for empirical reasons alone that excellence and equality are not attainable together. There is logical tension as well – or, better, a number of tensions which, with more or less accuracy, I dub 'logical'. Some philosophers, attuned to contrasting 'logical' and 'empirical', will complain, 'Look, the incompatibility cannot be both empirical and logical. If it's the latter, then all the empirical stuff you have just mentioned is redundant, beside the point.' The reply is that what the empirical incompatibility is between is importantly different from what the logical tension is between – though both can be expressed by the (therefore) ambiguous sentence, 'It is impossible to have excellence and equality.' When, for empirical reasons, two situations cannot coexist, there is an empirical incompatibility between the situations. When for reasons of logic (and semantics) two descriptions of a situation cannot both be true, there is logical (semantical) inconsistency between the descriptions. Someone says, 'Those bachelors cannot be married.' Is he making a statement of empirical fact or of logic? He might mean that those people over there, who are bachelors, are physically or legally prevented from being married (they are not of the racial purity the authorities demand, say). That is an empirical claim. Or he might mean that, since the description 'bachelor' applies to the men, the description 'married' cannot also apply to them. This is a statement of logic (semantics). When I said that there are empirical reasons why we shall never have excellence and equality, I meant that we shall never have a situation in which everyone reaches a level attained by some – a level which, by the criteria I employ in making the claim, is one of excellence. When I say that there is logical incompatibility, I mean – to begin with, anyway – that in any situation where there is equality it would be improper, on semantical grounds, for persons in that situation to describe the level attained as one of excellence. The reason, of course, is that 'excellent' is, as some philosophers used to say, a 'grading' word. Where there are no gradations, there is nothing to refer to as 'excellent' — or 'rotten' either. This will be so whether the level in question is one that Einstein reached or one that Simple Simon reached.

I do not consider the point of logic, or the semantical point on which it is based, to be especially thrilling in itself. What is interesting, and what I tried to describe in chapter 2, is the fundamental human trait which, I believe, underlies it — which explains why it would be so peculiar to describe as 'excellent' a level generally attained, why it is that 'excellent' requires there to be gradations in order to have an application. I mean, of course, the fundamental concern with transcending present limits, with seeking out and trying to conquer new peaks — with, in short, excellence. Were it possible for everyone to reach a level which, previously, only a few had reached, this concern would take the form of envisaging changes, improvements, raising the sights to a new target which, by its very nature, only a few can foreseeably approach. One day, conceivably, this new target will in turn become feasible for the many — but then the process will merely repeat itself.

Another tension which, for want of a better term, I dub 'logical', also emerged in chapter 2. Sane egalitarians do not demand equality at any old level, but at the highest level generally attainable. But we must first identify what can be attained — and it is arguable that this can only be done, with any confidence, by seeing some people actually attain it. And this requires inequality. If so, equality could, at best, be a momentarily acceptable state — one which is put up with during those moments of rest before, so to speak, the vanguard is sent off to explore new regions and scout out the dangers that lurk there.

Finally: a number of broad, empirical assumptions have been made throughout this book, and my case for selective, mixed quality education, in which the pursuit of excellence is favoured, is based upon these. Such assumptions as: educational resources are scarce; unstreamed classes are detrimental to the most able; most parents cannot be got to do as much for their children educationally as a few do for theirs. These and other assumptions — or most of them — are true; but the main reason I make them is for the debate about egalitarianism to get off the ground. Let me explain (though the point has emerged quite frequently before).

Suppose these assumptions were wildly wrong — that, for example, it was an easy matter to devote unlimited resources to

161

educating the duller without taking anything away from the best educated, or that unstreamed classes benefited everybody. In such Utopian conditions, there would be no difficulty in achieving equality at a level of excellence. Does it follow that the demand for excellence is now reconcilable with egalitarianism – with the principles embraced by egalitarians? No – for in such conditions, egalitarian principles can get no purchase.

In chapter 1, I stressed the distinction between the substance and the rhetoric of egalitarianism. Not every demand of the form 'There should be equality of X' is, or can be, an egalitarian one. Often the insertion of 'equality', or its cognates, is completely redundant. For example, 'The innocent should be equal in their immunity from punishment' merely says the innocent should not be punished – which is a principle of legal justice, about which there is nothing egalitarian. The egalitarian shows his stripes by grounding his demands that people should be treated a certain way on considerations of how others are being treated. The typical egalitarian demand is that some should receive less because others are receiving less. (Rational egalitarians would also add that such a demand is only appropriate when the worse-off would benefit by the better-off receiving less.) Now, under the imagined Utopian conditions, there is simply no scope for producing this sort of reason or ground in favour of policies such as destreaming, devoting more resources to the worse-off, etc. Of course classes should be unstreamed if everyone would benefit. This is nothing but a simple consequence of the fact that education is a value. Of course all parents should be got to do as much for their children educationally as a few do for theirs, if this is something they can quite easily and painlessly be got to do. Again, this is a consequence of education being valuable. That some children are doing better than others could not figure as any extra reason for implementing the policies. To suppose it could would be like supposing people should nurse their colds not only to get better but to be more like people who do not have colds.

It follows that there are no conditions under which a proponent of excellence and a proponent of egalitarianism can join hands. Under conditions where the broad empirical assumptions hold, the proposals run counter to one another. Under the Utopian conditions just imagined there is nothing for the egalitarian *qua* egalitarian to demand – for the conditions are not such that he can ground his demands on the considerations which identify him as an egalitarian. It is analogous to the point Kant makes about duty and pleasure. While it is conceivable that people should always be naturally inclined to do what it is, in fact, their duty to do, the principles of duty-for-its-own-sake and hedonism are not thereby reconciled.

162

In the kingdom of men, advocacy of conscientiousness runs counter to advocacy of pleasure; while in the kingdom of angels, appealing to conscientiousness is entirely *de trop*.

In a number of different ways, then, the pursuits of excellence and of equality are logically at odds. Given the empirical incompatibilities earlier described, it must be misleading for me to announce a commitment to excellence whilst denying that I am against equality. So I accept, without bashfulness, the 'inegalitarian' label.

Notes and references

1 Egalitarianism

1 A. H. Halsey, 'Sociology and the equality debate', *Oxford Review of Education*, 1, 1975, p. 10.
2 Brian Simon, reported in *The Times*, 27 September 1965.
3 See the passages quoted by Mary Warnock, *Schools of Thought*, Faber & Faber, 1977, pp. 42 ff.
4 C. Rosenberg, *Education and Society*, a 'Rank and File' pamphlet, p. 24.
5 Ivan Illich, *Deschooling Society*, Penguin, 1976.
6 Both reports are quoted in J. Stuart Maclure, *Educational Documents*, Methuen, 1971.
7 A factor mentioned by A. G. N. Flew in a number of places, e.g. 'Equality *or* justice', in P. French (ed.), *Studies in Ethical Theory*, University of Minnesota, 1978.
8 Quoted by Halsey, op. cit., p. 9, who himself seems to take the attitude in question.
9 Quoted in G. P. Gooch, *Political Thought from Bacon to Halifax*, Williams & Norgate, 1914, p. 130.
10 Thomas More, *Utopia*, Dent, 1957, p. 50.
11 This needs some qualification. It is not obvious that it would be reasonable to educate just one or two cave children in a society of totally uneducated primitives. The desirability of education, and of much else, is *ceteris paribus*; and facts about its possible availability can be among those which affect the reasonableness of pursuing it. This should not make us think that the desirability of educating some people is, after all, grounded on what others are getting. It is one thing to use the mere fact that some people are getting or not getting something as a ground for giving or not giving it to others; quite another to think that such a fact has contributed to a state of affairs in which the *ceteris paribus* clause of some principle is not fulfilled, so that it becomes unreasonable to act upon it. Suppose no one except Johnny has eaten: egalitarian and non-egalitarian reasons, both of which mention this fact, could be given for not letting Johnny eat. The egalitarian uses the fact that no one else has eaten as a sufficient reason, by itself. That is very different from the non-egalitarian reason that, due to their hunger, the ones who have not eaten will tear Johnny to pieces when they see him given a meal. The

164

egalitarian reason makes essential reference to the others' not having eaten; whereas the other reason mentions this fact only because it is contingently related to the people's disposition to tear Johnny to pieces.

12 See R. Wollheim, 'Equality', *Proceedings of the Aristotelian Society*, 1956. Also Warnock, op. cit., p. 27.

13 This point is made in a good article by T. Raz, 'Principles of equality', *Mind*, LXXXVII, 1978. He seems in agreement with much that I say in this chapter which, although written before his paper appeared, has been adjusted in a number of respects to take account of some of his points.

14 C. Jencks, *Inequality*, Penguin, 1975, p. 11.

15 Such doubts are expressed, *inter alia*, in the findings of the Jencks research team (see *Inequality*), and D. Thompson's paper, *Forum*, 16, 2, 1972, which challenges the standard assumption about the relative advantage to duller children of non-streaming.

16 Tyrrell Burgess, 'Foreword' to Jencks, op. cit., p. 2.

17 This real nature of debates gets disguised by the fact that context often makes it clear which equality is at issue, thereby obviating the need to refer to it specifically. Compare the way in which we often get by, when discussing the similarity between two things, without having to make explicit the respect in which they are being compared – context making it clear what this is.

18 For example, Sir Isaiah Berlin, 'Equality', *Proceedings of the Aristotelian Society*, 1956.

19 Jencks and his team base their qualified egalitarianism on the Principle of Utility plus premise (b). For some reason they forget premise (a). Clearly, though, it is crucial. If there were 'pleasure devourers', maximum total utility would require concentrating goods on them.

20 The conclusion here is but a reflection of the general objection to utilitarianism which complains of the principle's insensitivity to the kinds of utility to be maximized.

21 Jencks *et al.* agree that the premise is totally false when applied to educational goods. Indeed it is this which prompts them to be 'much less concerned' with the distribution of these goods.

22 R. S. Peters, *Ethics and Education*, Allen & Unwin, 1970, p. 121.

23 Ibid., p. 126.

24 The idea that there is a presumption in favour of treating people similarly runs, of course, into the same logical problem as the closely related idea, discussed on p. 15, to the effect that inequalities always require justification. For since treating people similarly necessarily implies treating them dissimilarly in some other respect, it is impossible to see how the presumption can be for similar, rather than dissimilar, treatment.

25 See Bernard Williams, 'The idea of equality', in P. Laslett and W. Runciman (eds), *Philosophy, Politics, and Society*, Blackwell, 1962.

26 Harold Laski in *I Believe, The Personal Philosophies of Twenty-Three Eminent Men and Women of our Time*, Allen & Unwin, 1940, p. 167.

27 Robert Nozick, *Anarchy, State, and Utopia*, Basic Books, 1975.
28 This is what A. G. N. Flew, in 'Equality *or* justice', rightly urges the egalitarian to do.
29 Quoted in T. Sowell, 'Affirmative action reconsidered', *The Public Interest*, 1975, p. 51.
30 John Rawls, *A Theory of Justice*, Clarendon Press, 1972.
31 Ibid., p. 83.
32 Ibid., p. 153.
33 Rawls's 'first principle of justice' – 'each person is to have an equal right to the most extensive basic liberty compatible with a similar liberty for others' – is not, on the other hand, egalitarian. At least it is not on its most favourable reading. That some people do not have certain basic liberties is never a reason, in itself, for others not having them. The only reason for restricting the liberties of some is that they use these to prevent others having them.
34 Nozick, op. cit., lists a number of principles stronger than Rawls's.

2 Equality in education

1 J. S. Coleman, 'Rawls, Nozick, and educational equality', *The Public Interest*, 44, 1976, p. 122.
2 Ibid., p. 101.
3 Ibid.
4 Ibid.
5 Scholesians, you will notice, are not uninfluenced by some of our recent writers on education – by Peters, Oakeshott, and Mary Warnock, for instance.
6 Actually these definitions are too crude. For example, it is not required that X be the one who has done something reprehensible, etc.; it would be enough if someone had done it on his behalf.
7 John Rawls, *A Theory of Justice*, Clarendon Press, 1972, p. 104.
8 Ibid.
9 For a stress on this criterion, see S. Kripke, 'Naming and necessity', in D. Davidson and G. Harman (eds), *Semantics of Natural Language*, Dordrecht, 1971.
10 The point I am making is also made by A. G. N. Flew, 'Three ideals of equality' (unpublished lecture).
11 Well, I suppose it is denied by Hindus who think that one's innate abilities in one life are karmic deserts from an earlier one; but then they would not deny the non-deserved nature of one's innate abilities in one's very first life.
12 As Nozick (*Anarchy, State, and Utopia*, Basic Books, 1975) has pointed out, the desert versus entitlement distinction is most important, especially in connection with arguments over private property. To get a case against private property, it is not enough to show – which might not be too hard – that most people do not deserve their property; you have to show – which is much harder – that they are not entitled to it. It is worth noting that Rawls is committed to the

idea of there being undeserved entitlements, since the people in his
'original position' have a collective entitlement to available primary
goods, and to those that will be obtained.

13 'Egalitarianism and an academic "élite" ', in C. B. Cox and A. E.
Dyson (eds), *Fight for Education: A Black Paper*, Critical Quarterly
Society, 1969, p. 64.

14 Ibid., p. 66.

15 Thus it would be peculiar to regard the diverse residents of
'Millionaires' Row' as constituting a particular élite, even though
each resident – the general, the judge, the minister, the bishop –
might be a member of some élite.

16 By such a test, I imagine, it would be reasonable to label Oxford
dons, but not university teachers in general, an élite. I leave it to the
reader to apply the test.

17 R. Grunberger, *A Social History of the Third Reich*, Penguin, 1971,
pp. 379 f.

18 See R. P. Wolff, *Understanding Rawls*, Princeton, 1977, for these and
other criticisms.

19 Actually it is very unclear on what grounds Rawls does restrict the
application of the 'difference principle' so that it applies neither to
trivia like cakes at a party, nor to the distribution of things even
more important than 'primary goods' – e.g. to the distribution of eyes
or kidneys.

20 These presuppositions of Rawls's position are brought out in the
excellent review by Thomas Nagel, *Philosophical Review*, 82, 1973.

21 Herman Hesse, *Magister Ludi*, Bantam, 1970, pp. 213 f.

22 Nietzsche, *Thus Spoke Zarathustra*, in W. Kaufmann (ed.), *The Portable
Nietzsche*, Viking Press, 1954, p. 213.

23 Some people would argue that, just as the criteria for excellence are
relative to the general level, so are the criteria for what is an
adequate minimum. This might be seen as an objection to an
apparent implication of an earlier remark of mine, to the effect that
it is possible to achieve an adequate minimum. This rather difficult
issue is taken up in the following chapter when I talk about 'relative
deprivation'.

24 M. Oakeshott, 'Education: the engagement and its frustrations', in
R. F. Dearden, P. H. Hirst, and R. S. Peters (eds), *Education and the
Development of Reason*, Routledge & Kegan Paul, 1972.

25 T. S. Eliot, *Notes Towards the Definition of Culture*, Faber & Faber,
1948, p. 99.

26 See the papers by H. A. Lewis and myself in the forthcoming
proceedings of the 1979 Joint Session of the Aristotelian Society and
the Mind Association.

27 G. E. Moore, *Principia Ethica*, Cambridge, 1960, p. 197.

28 Rawls, op. cit., p. 325.

29 Ibid., p. 332.

30 Ibid., p. 329.

31 Ibid., p. 328.

32 The point made in this paragraph is made at greater length in my paper, 'Quality and Equality', in S. Brown (ed.), *Philosophers Discuss Education*, Macmillan, 1975 (Proceedings of 1973 conference).

3 Education, equality, and society

1 T. S. Eliot, *Notes Towards the Definition of Culture*, Faber & Faber, 1948.
2 B. Williams, 'The idea of equality', in P. Laslett and W. Runciman (eds), *Philosophy, Politics and Society*, Blackwell, 1962, describes this tendency well.
3 J. E. Floud, A. H. Halsey, and F. M. Martin, *Social Class and Educational Opportunity*, Heinemann, 1957, p. XVI.
4 Harvard Educational Review Board (eds), *Equal Educational Opportunity*, Harvard University Press, 1969.
5 In my original draft I parodied the idea that all would be well if only there was equality across social classes by saying that one could as well argue that what is wrong with the figures for infant mortality is not that they show children dying, but that they show more deaths among one class than among another. I am no longer clear this would be accepted by everyone as a *reductio ad absurdum*, for in *Unequal Britain* (Arrow, 1973), Frank Field manages to give the impression, on p. 9, that it *is* the distribution of death across classes, rather than death itself, which is the real problem. Despite a reduction in infant mortality, he complains, 'the occupational and class differences remained stubbornly the same'. One hopes that Mr Field would be shocked to find his words create this impression – but that they do is a sign of how second-nature the idea has become that it is class differentials which are the 'real' problem.
6 'The concept of equality of educational opportunity', in *Equal Educational Opportunity*, op. cit., pp. 18–19.
7 Ibid., p. 17.
8 D. P. Moynihan, 'Sources of resistance to the Coleman Report', in *Equal Educational Opportunity*, op. cit., p. 28.
9 C. Rosenberg, *Education and Society*, a 'Rank and File' pamphlet, pp. 14–15.
10 Field, op. cit., p. 17.
11 Rosenberg, op. cit., p. 14.
12 J. R. Lucas, 'Equality in education', in B. Wilson (ed.), *Education, Equality, and Society*, Allen & Unwin, 1975, p. 52.
13 I assume, for argument's sake, that admission based on such a ground would be an evil – but this is an oversimplification. One can surely think of jobs where a person's social class is, in itself, both a relevant and rational consideration. It is difficult to see how someone could succeed as the queen's equerry who did not hail from a certain class – or how someone could function as a miners' shop-steward who was not of working-class stock. Egalitarians, incidentally, are usually quite happy with admissions in some areas being based on class

criteria. I have not heard them complain about the policy of some
Oxford colleges to reserve a number of places for working-class
students from comprehensives.

14 See Williams, op. cit., for a discussion of the second alternative,
when he speaks of 'sham' equality.
15 Floud, Halsey, and Martin, op. cit., p. 143.
16 Field, op. cit., p. 28.
17 P. Robinson, *Education and Poverty*, Methuen, 1976, p. 15.
18 For example, Anthony Crosland, *The Conservative Enemy*, Cape, 1962,
and Floud, Halsey, and Martin, op. cit.
19 Lucas, op. cit.
20 R. F. Atkinson, 'Chairman's remarks', in *Philosophers Discuss Education*,
op. cit., p. 151.
21 This consideration is made much of – though little evidence is
adduced in support – by R. Wasserstrom, 'The university and the
case for preferential treatment', *American Philosophical Quarterly*, 13,
1976.
22 John Dewey, *Democracy and Education*, Free Press, 1946, p. 86.
23 Ibid., p. 83.
24 Ibid., p. 20.
25 Ibid., p. 99.
26 Ibid., p. 29.
27 Ibid., p. 16.
28 W. V. Quine is justified, in his John Dewey lectures, *Ontological
Relativity*, Columbia University, 1969, in attributing to Dewey the
attack on 'private languages' which Wittgenstein developed twenty
years later. Like Quine, I think Dewey was roughly right in his
account of meanings; hence I shall not, in my subsequent criticisms,
make use of G. H. Bantock's (in B. Wilson (ed.) op. cit.) main point
against Dewey – which relies on a somewhat romantic idea of
'private', 'individual' meanings.
29 One story of how it happens is persuasively told by Quine in *The
Roots of Reference*, Illinois, 1974.
30 Dewey, op. cit., p. 84.
31 'Equality and education', in B. Wilson (ed.), op. cit., p. 141.
32 Lucas, op. cit., p. 59.
33 Ibid.

Appendix: Private schooling

1 See my 'Responsibility and "The System"', in P. French (ed.),
Individual and Collective Responsibility, Schenkman, 1972.
2 For a detailed discussion of this matter, see B. Cohen, 'Equality,
freedom, and independent schools', *Journal of Philosophy of Education*,
12, 1978.
3 G. Grigson, review of J. Gathorne-Hardy's *The Public School
Phenomenon* (Hodder and Stoughton, 1977), in *Country Life*, 1977.

4 Epistemological egalitarianism

1 M. Young and G. Whitty (eds), *Society, State, and Schooling*, Falmer Press, 1977, pp. 7–8 and 16.
2 Ibid., p. 6.
3 N. Keddie, 'Classroom knowledge', in M. Young (ed.), *Knowledge and Control: New Directions for the Sociology of Education*, Collier-Macmillan, 1971, p. 156.
4 Ibid.
5 In attempting to distinguish, say, between sociology and philosophy, I do not regard myself as begging any questions against the Reckers who, as we shall see, are hostile to divisions. My attempt does not presuppose that there are two deeply distinct kinds of knowledge involved. Wittgenstein and Quine have both thought of their claims as distinguished from those of the natural historian and scientist only by their extreme generality. Even if this is the 'only' difference, it is a very important one.
6 Ivan Illich, *Deschooling Society*, Penguin, 1976, p. 37.
7 M. Young, 'Curriculum change: limits and possibilities', in Young and Whitty, op. cit., p. 241.
8 Alfred Schutz, 'Concept and theory formation in the social sciences', in D. Emmet and A. MacIntyre (eds), *Sociological Theory and Philosophical Analysis*, Macmillan, 1970, p. 15.
9 D. Gorbutt, 'The new sociology of education', *Education for Teaching*, autumn 1972, p. 7.
10 G. Esland, 'Teaching and learning as the organization of knowledge', in M. Young (ed.), *Knowledge and Control*, pp. 75, 77, 78.
11 M. Young, 'Curriculum change: limits and possibilities', p. 238.
12 M. Young, 'An approach to the study of curricula as socially organized knowledge', in M. Young (ed.), *Knowledge and Control*, p. 23.
13 Gorbutt, op. cit., p. 7.
14 Quoted by Esland, op. cit., from Mills's 'Language, logic, and culture', 1939.
15 Esland, op. cit., p. 78.
16 Something like the above account is accepted by Quine and Popper (for rather different reasons).
17 I have used the term to highlight the active, theory-constructing nature of men. It is certainly not meant to carry any connotation that acceptance of a theory is a matter of personal whim or prejudice.
18 'The problem of rationality in the social world', in Emmet and MacIntyre, op. cit., p. 113.
19 Among recent philosophers, normally dubbed 'analytic', who are, or have been, of a Monist turn of mind are Nelson Goodman, Morton White, Hilary Putnam, and W. V. Quine.
20 H. Putnam, 'Is logic empirical?', *Boston Studies in the Philosophy of Science*, vol. 197. Interestingly, Quine, who would subscribe to something like the first two theses, does not favour the policy of allowing standard logic to face revision. See especially his *Philosophy of Logic*, Prentice-Hall, 1970.

21 'The Sociology of Knowledge: A dialogue between John White and Michael Young', *Education for Teaching*, 98, 1975, p. 5.

22 J. Habermas, 'Selbstreflexion leistet keine Begründung', *Theorie und Praxis*, 1971.

23 Richard Pring, 'Knowledge out of control', *Education for Teaching*, autumn 1972, p. 27.

24 See my 'The law of non-contradiction', *Proceedings of the 16th World Congress of Philosophy*, 1978.

25 M. Young, 'Introduction' to *Knowledge and Control*, p. 6.

26 See my 'Alternative logic in primitive thought', *Man: The Journal of the Royal Anthropological Society*, vol. 10, 1975.

27 M. Young, 'Curriculum change: limits and possibilities', p. 239.

28 Dummett has argued, ingeniously, that statements about the inaccessible historical past should not be counted as either true or false. But this argument should not be used to justify a general historical scepticism or 'free-for-all' among people as to the nature of the past; for Dummett's point only applies to statements which *anyway* no one could have grounds for accepting or rejecting. Here, as elsewhere, the philosophical point is supposed to reflect practice, not give birth to a new one. 'The Reality of the Past', *Proceedings of the Aristotelian Society*, LXIX, 1968–9.

29 Dummett, it is worth noting, thinks that considerable light is thrown on the nature of mathematical entities by an analogy with fictional creatures. 'Wittgenstein's philosophy of mathematics', in G. Pitcher (ed.), *Wittgenstein: The Philosophical Investigations*, Macmillan, 1964.

30 J. H. Newman, *The Idea of a University*, Clarendon Press, 1976, pp. 52–4.

31 G. Whitty, 'Sociology and the problem of radical educational change', in Young and Whitty, op. cit., p. 40.

32 See Bernard Williams, 'The truth in relativism', *Proceedings of the Aristotelian Society*, LXXV, 1974–5.

33 See Peter Winch, *The Idea of a Social Science*, Routledge & Kegan Paul, 1970, and other writings of his.

34 Such exaggeration is by no means the prerogative of the Reckers. In a recent book by A. Brent, *Philosophical Foundations for the Curriculum*, Allen & Unwin, 1978, extraordinary connections between specific educational practices and deep epistemological theses are, without much argument, taken to hold. See my review of this book in *The Times Higher Education Supplement*, 1978.

35 Illich, op. cit., chapter 6.

36 Richard Pring, *Knowledge and Schooling*, Open Books, 1976.

5 Culture, equality, and the curriculum

1 It should not be thought that the sort of view described in this paragraph is either especially new or a prerogative of the 'enlightened left'. Consider this remark: 'the lowliest apprentice at his lathe who whistles a gay song in essence does the same as the artist. In the work of a composer, man's greatest gifts are expressed in the same

way as in a neatly trimmed garden or a freshly painted fence'. The writer is Hadamovsky, head of Nazi radio. Quoted in R. Grunberger, *A Social History of the Third Reich*, Penguin, 1971, p. 516.

2 Mary Warnock, *Schools of Thought*, Faber & Faber, 1977, p. 84.

3 B. Malinowski, *A Scientific Theory of Culture*, OUP, 1944, p. 46.

4 Raymond Williams, *The Long Revolution*, Penguin, 1961, p. 64.

5 T. S. Eliot, *Notes Towards the Definition of Culture*, Faber & Faber, 1948, p. 48.

6 Among those who take this view are E. Midwinter, *Projections. An Educational Priority*, Ward Lock, 1972, and N. Keddie, in her editorial introduction to *Tinker, Tailor. The Myth of Cultural Deprivation*, Penguin, 1973, as well as several of the contributors to that volume.

7 For example, Denis Lawton, *Class, Culture, and the Curriculum*, Routledge & Kegan Paul, 1975.

8 Quoted in P. Robinson, *Education and Poverty*, Methuen, 1976, p. 44.

9 Midwinter, op. cit., p. 101.

10 See, for example, the numerous works of Michael Novak, such as *The Rise of the Unmeltable Ethnics*, New York, 1971, or N. Glazer, according to whom 'by their very nature ethnic claims do not allow of a universal scale against which they can be measured', 'Ethnicity and the schools', *Commentary*, 1974, p. 58.

11 R. Pratte, 'Cultural diversity and education', in K. Strike and K. Egan (eds), *Ethics and Educational Policy*, Routledge & Kegan Paul, 1978, p. 164.

12 Keddie, op. cit., p. 8.

13 'Equality and Education', in B. Wilson (ed.), *Education, Equality, and Society*, Allen & Unwin, 1975, p. 153.

14 Keddie, op. cit., p. 8.

15 'Black culture', as referred to in the USA, fares a bit better than 'working-class culture', though it is very easy to exaggerate the extent to which the cultural enjoyment of contemporary American blacks is enjoyment of their own distinctive products, or of a type significantly concentrated among blacks. Thus one hears the strange demand for 'black philosophy': if this means philosophy produced by blacks, then there is none to speak of; if it means philosophical study of issues that concern blacks – such as justice, inherited intelligence, and the like – then it is not a study of issues that are at all uniquely associated with blacks.

16 David E. Cooper, 'Moral relativism', *Mid-West Studies in Philosophy*, vol. III, 1978.

17 Though see my 'Moral relativism' for some argument. The only really interesting defence of moral relativism I know of is Gilbert Harman's, in 'Moral relativism defended', *Philosophical Review*, vol. 84, 1975.

18 For a totally damning indictment of our treatment of animals, see P. Singer, *Animal Liberation*, Cape, 1976.

19 The terminology, and the point, are John McDowell's in an as yet unpublished paper 'Reason and virtue'.

20 Hilary Putnam, *Meaning and the Moral Sciences*, Routledge & Kegan Paul, 1978, pp. 89–90.
21 Ibid., p. 90.
22 Ibid., p. 91.
23 Robinson, op. cit., p. 80.
24 G. H. Bantock, *Culture, Industrialization, and Education*, Routledge & Kegan Paul, 1968, p. 87.
25 Ibid.
26 Ibid., p. 43.
27 Ibid., p. 68.
28 Ibid., p. 83.
29 Williams, op. cit., p. 174.
30 Ibid., p. 378.
31 Bantock, op. cit., p. 55.
32 Williams, op. cit., p. 367.
33 Warnock, op. cit., p. 80.

6 Conclusion – inegalitarianism

1 Tim O'Hagan, 'Quality and equality in education: a critique of David Cooper', in S. Brown (ed.), *Philosophers Discuss Education*, Macmillan, 1975, p. 137.
2 Ibid., p. 138.
3 Are they more mad than egalitarian principles? I have the feeling they are, but do not know how to justify that feeling. Perhaps I am not yet fully emancipated from the favourable connotations of 'equality'.
4 O'Hagan, op. cit., p. 136.
5 Ibid., p. 139.
6 Ibid., p. 140.

Index

175